# THE NEW ORGANIC FOOD GUIDE

## Alan Gear

**J. M. Dent & Sons Ltd**
London and Melbourne

First published 1987
© Henry Doubleday Research Association, 1987

This book is set in 10½/11½ pt Baskerville by
Input Typesetting Ltd, London SW19 8DR
Made in Great Britain by
The Guernsey Press Co. Ltd.,
Guernsey C.I. for
J. M. Dent & Sons Ltd
Aldine House, 33 Welbeck Street, London W1M 8LX

British Library Cataloguing in Publication Data

Gear, Alan
  The new organic food guide.—(Healthright)
  1. Natural foods industry—Great Britain
  —Directories
  I. Title   II. Series
  381'.456646     HD9011.3

ISBN 0–460–02454–X

# THE NEW ORGANIC FOOD GUIDE

# CONTENTS

CONTENTS

# ACKNOWLEDGMENTS

A book such as this is not possible without the help of a great many people.

Firstly I would like to thank everyone who so freely volunteered the information which makes up the Guide. I would also like to acknowledge the help of Mrs May Field who had the unenviable task of sending out and collating all of the questionnaires. Her work would not have been possible without the help of the back-up team at the Henry Doubleday Research Association which supplied all the paperwork and handled the correspondence.

I should also like to thank the various organic farmers who allowed me to wander at will over their farms and who courteously responded to my prying questions. The results of my interrogations can be found in Chapter 6.

Clare Marriage of Doves Farm is also to be thanked for supplying me with, and writing, most of Chapter 8. As a founder-member of the Federation of Organic Food Manufacturers, her knowledge of the organic dried food industry is far greater than mine and the book is immeasurably strengthened by her contribution.

Thanks are also due to my secretary, Chris Bailey, who has unerringly managed to translate and type my oft-illegible script. This is no mean feat, as anyone who knows my handwriting is aware. Also to Jocelyn Burton, my editor, who made valuable suggestions and provided information as to the finer points of English grammar.

I should also like to thank everyone who has provided me with inspiration. The organic movement is singularly well blessed with thoughtful people who put the welfare of their land, livestock and the environment before themselves. It has been my great joy in life to have been associated with many of them and I trust that through this book I will be able, however humbly, to speak for them.

Last and not least I would like to thank Jackie, my wife, who has suffered and continues to suffer numerous disruptions to our social life for the sake of this book and the cause in which we both passionately believe. I do hope you will find it of value.

The information given in *The New Organic Food Guide* was believed to be correct at the time of publication, but the author regrets that he cannot be held responsible for any mistakes, or change in circumstances, that may have occurred.

Furthermore, although all of the individuals and shops who have supplied information have indicated that their produce is grown according to organic principles, the author and publishers cannot offer any further guarantee.

If any supplier of organic produce is known to you, and is not listed here, please contact us so that we can include them in the next edition.

# PREFACE TO THE NEW EDITION

For anyone looking back over the four years since the appearance of the first edition of *The Organic Food Guide*, it is astonishing to view the amount of progress that has been made in the acceptance and availability of organic food.

Then there were very few shops selling fresh organic produce. These were usually wholefood stores which stocked only a few lines. Quality was indifferent and supply infrequent. With few exceptions it would have been quite impossible to buy organically grown vegetables with any consistency. Supplies of organic fruit were virtually non-existent.

Indeed, when the various organizations concerned with organic growing decided to put out the first Guide there was a good deal of debate as to whether or not this would be a good thing. Growers were few and widely scattered. No distribution network for fresh produce existed. Farmers had no option but to sell from home. The only way for the consumer to get organic vegetables was simply to trek out into the country. Growers were unwilling to expand because they were unsure of demand. Yet there was a real worry that by writing the book we might create a demand that could not be met. It was a gamble, but it paid off.

The entries that go to make up this edition are by contrast mostly based in towns. Farmers and growers have to a large extent disappeared from its pages. This does not mean that they have gone out of business; quite the reverse, in fact. They are working flat out to meet demand. All of their produce is sold direct to shops, supermarkets or the wholesalers who are springing up. Although most do not have either the produce or time to cater for farm gate sales, a number still like to keep in direct touch with their customers.

Coverage of the country is getting better all the time. Almost all the major cities and most of the main towns now have places where you can buy organic dried goods and organically grown fresh produce all the year round. In response to the demand, especially from the multiple stores, for better quality you will find organic vegetables produced and packaged every bit as well as their chemically grown counterparts. Organic fruit, including citrus fruit, is now widely available, though almost all of it is grown abroad. Vast quantities of fresh organic produce are currently imported and it is to be hoped that many more home producers will step in to fill the gap.

This, then, could even be the last *Organic Food Guide* I write, for the strength of public demand for wholesome products suggests that stores selling organic food may soon be as commonplace as post offices. Without a doubt, the way forward is organic.

January 1987

Alan Gear
Executive Director
Henry Doubleday Research Association

# INTRODUCTION

Farming in Britain today is an industry under siege. Battered by accusations that it is simultaneously destroying the country-side whilst milking the taxpayer, it reels from crisis to crisis. What has happened to the image of what has consistently been heralded as our most successful enterprise? The ever-increasing output, achieved with a declining workforce – a miracle of productivity – has foundered on a sea of surpluses. Like a suspect modern drug, all that we ever hear about nowadays are the undesirable side-effects. This week nitrates in drinking water or pesticide poisoning of wildlife. Next week grubbing of hedgerows or draining of wetlands. Animal rights campaigners draw attention to the miserable existence of factory-farmed livestock. High summer sees the opening of the straw-burning season, hardly guaranteed to increase goodwill towards the farming fraternity. The list is endless. Indeed, apart from the nuclear industry it is hard to think of any other economic activity that has a worse public image – this despite the best efforts of the National Farmers' Union, often described as the most effective political lobby in the country.

During a consumer survey carried out in 1985 amongst 500 high-street shoppers in three Berkshire towns, the following somewhat perjorative statement was put: 'The countryside and the environment are being *destroyed* by today's farming methods.' Over 60 per cent of those interviewed agreed, and almost 25 per cent strongly agreed, that this was indeed the case. A further 28 per cent had no opinion on the subject whilst a mere 10 per cent disagreed, with an additional 0.9 per cent strongly disagreeing. The important word to note here is the highly emotive term destroying. We are not talking about changing, or even damaging, the countryside. As far as a representative majority of the inhabitants of these Berkshire towns are concerned, their environment is being destroyed by farmers. One wonders at the response had the question been put in Cambridgeshire, or some of the other eastern counties which have borne the brunt of 'prairie-ization'.

Even the much-heralded productivity and efficiency of our farmers has been questioned of late. Spurred on by a system of grants, subsidies and Government exhortations, the farmers have responded magnificently. There is no place for market forces here, no limits or market saturation. Just keep on producing and pile up the surpluses in Europe. When the mountains become embarrassingly visible they can be sold off cheap to the Eastern Bloc, or some politically acceptable scheme devised for giving them away. Alternatively, the food can simply be destroyed.

It is quite remarkable that this 'Alice in Wonderland' situation has persisted for as long as it has. The reason can only be put down to public ignorance. However, in 1982 Tory MP Richard Body turned the spotlight on the grant and subsidy structure. Using official statistics, Body calculated that during 1983 for every £100 net earned by the farmer a further £200 was spent by Government or EEC agencies on agricultural support of one sort or another. The figure has almost certainly risen in the intervening period, and this at a time when public expenditure in every other direction is under attack. Is it any wonder that the public is becoming increasingly vocal in its condemnation of a system which on the one hand encourages massive surpluses at the taxpayer's expense whilst at the same time it assaults the countryside? This is without even mentioning the stockpiling and wasting of food whilst millions around the globe go hungry.

However, times are changing, as the dairy farmers now know to their cost. For the last three years there has been a quota on milk production. Farmers are being forced to cut back – often with disastrous financial consequences. Next it will be the turn of cereal producers, though at the time of writing it is not certain exactly what form the restrictions will take. Everywhere among farmers there is gloom and despondency – a feeling that they are trapped on a treadmill of ever-rising input costs set against declining returns for their products. Squeezed at both ends, many farmers who borrowed heavily during the heady days of agricultural expansion in the 1970s are now staring bankruptcy in the face. The only option open is to sell their farms, yet with plummeting land prices what can they get for them, and more importantly who would want to buy?

Various solutions to these problems are currently being peddled but in most cases it is symptoms rather than root causes that are being addressed. Countryside campaigners want to see a re-orientation of grants, so that they favour conservation rather than intensive husbandry methods. There is talk of taking land out of cultivation altogether, as currently happens in the USA, or adopting 'low input' methods of agriculture in which less fertilizer and pesticides are used, resulting in lower yields and consequently smaller surpluses.

A top official in the Ministry of Agriculture has even speculated on the likely emergence of a divided Britain: 'You could get two distinct parts of the country. In one part, mainly in the eastern half of the country, mainly on the better land, there would be very intensive agriculture, high input, high output, as much being grown on one acre as used to be grown on two acres; and in much of the rest of the country – particularly much of the western and northern part of the country – there would really be little economic basis for agriculture and, therefore, those parts would possibly have to become a pleasure park.' This is a prospect which is likely to alienate everyone save the prosperous large cereal producers in the east.

Whilst the conservationists are leading the consumer movement against the effects of modern farming methods on the countryside, there is an even larger lobby at work on the quality of food. No longer is it only the 'crank' and 'health food freak' who stops to think about the food he or she is eating. The message that 'we are what we eat' and that the food we consume has a great deal to do with whether or not we stay healthy has at last been taken up by the population at large. You only have to walk around any supermarket to notice the intense interest being taken in the small print on the labels. Does it contain E this or that? If it does, indeed if it contains any artificial colouring or preservatives at all, then for many people out it goes. It matters not that the food processors insist there is no possible danger to health. Alternatives exist which don't contain additives so why take the risk? This consumer backlash against adulterated food is now so great that food manufacturers are falling over backwards in their keenness to eliminate additives from their products.

It would be naive to assume that this awakened consumer awareness is going to stop once the question of additives has been settled. The next focus of concern will be that of contaminants. Regrettably, the products of our countryside fail to live up to the twin promises of purity and goodness so lovingly presented in television commercials. Crops subjected to a high pesticide regime in the fields leave the farm gate complete with residues of these substances. Livestock dosed with antibiotics, hormones and other substances pass on traces in the meat and dairy produce. If such chemicals are to be used then contamination is unavoidable.

As with food additives, the chemical industry insists that such low levels of pesticides, or antibiotics or other substances that persist in food are harmless. Given that until recently there was little alternative the public just had to put up with these assurances. Not any longer. Organically grown food, that is food which has been produced without recourse to artificial fertilizers and poisonous sprays, is becoming increasingly available. As with food containing additives, you are not obliged simply to trust the experts – you can buy organically grown instead.

It is my view that a major shift in agricultural practices towards organic methods would not only result in produce which satisfied the consumer demand for 'safe' and nutritious food but would also alleviate many of the environmental concerns expressed by conservationists. There would be a return to more traditional mixed farming with animals reared outdoors. This would reverse the trend of ever-larger featureless fields, for hedges would be required to keep the stock in. Agricultural pollution from fertilizers and animal slurry would be significantly reduced. Persistent pesticides would not be needed. Aerial crop-spraying and straw-burning would disappear. Furthermore, organic farming with its higher labour input would not only help stem the flow of labour from the countryside but would create new jobs.

Such a solution to our agricultural dilemma may seem extreme and impossibly utopian. Yet I believe the attempt has to be made. Tinkering at the fringes is not sufficient. We have created, out of plentiful supplies of cheap energy, a polluting, dangerous and resource-wasting system of farming. As the twenty-first century approaches, we are moving into a world where resource and energy scarcity will assume a much more critical importance. Only those farming methods which take account of these constraints will survive. As conventional farming continues to dither, unable to offer any way forward, the time is ripe to turn to the now unorthodox, yet environmentally sound, biological methods of producing food.

This book then has two functions. The first is to supply a list of addresses where organic fresh food can be obtained. The other and perhaps main purpose is to address many of the questions sketched out here. Part I looks at the overall problems inherent in modern farming. Chapter 1 covers environmental issues such as pesticide and fertilizer abuse, straw and slurry disposal, soil erosion and genetic loss. In Chapter 2, I draw attention to the additives which are routinely fed to farm animals, from antibiotics to tranquillizing drugs. The final chapter in this section looks at the end-result of modern farming – the food we eat. Containing traces of pesticides, residues of this and that, nitrates from over-fertilization and so on – how safe is it?

The purpose of the second part of the book is to try and answer some of the questions that are asked about organic farming and organic food. Does it mean going back to the Dark Ages? Would we all starve if fertilizers and pesticides weren't used? Is organic food any better for us, indeed is there any difference at all? A chapter on practical examples highlights some of the successes and problems encountered by a number of British farmers and growers.

In both Parts I and II, I have tried not to make statements which cannot be backed up by scientific facts that can be checked. The numbers which appear throughout the text refer to the list of references to be found in Appendix 4.

Finally, Part III gives a region-by-region gazetteer of suppliers of organic fresh food, a chapter on the typical types and brand names of dried organic produce and a list of the wholesalers dealing in organic food. From this it should be possible for almost everyone to find a suitable supplier not too far from their own home.

# PART I

## MODERN FARMING – AN INDICTMENT

## 1 ASSAULT ON THE LAND

## What Price Modern Agriculture?

The twentieth century has seen the total ascendancy of industrial technology in all walks of life and in all corners of the globe. By its standards 'progress' is measured. Anyone or anything which does not conform to this outlook is labelled 'Luddite'. Modern farming is yet one more example of this industrialization of society. Our countryside has become a huge outdoor food factory. Each farm, each region has its own speciality. In the warm and dry eastern side of the country monster machines range over huge featureless fields of wheat or barley. Over in the west where the climate is wetter and grass grows well, the dairy industry is based. As for pigs and chickens – it doesn't really matter where they are located, for being permanently confined indoors they are quite independent of geography.

This specialization and economy of scale has brought great benefits in terms of the amount of food produced from our land. Yields have rocketed and continue to rise, year by year. There is no shortage of food to be found in the shops, indeed surplus food is something of an embarrassment. Gradually the collective memory of food insecurity, so vivid during the war years, has faded. We now take for granted an adequate provision of a rich and varied range of foods.

For years people have marvelled at the application of industrial technology in our fields and the ever-increasing output from our farms. Agriculture is the most efficient industry in Britain, according to the National Farmers' Union. So why is there growing public unease at the direction in which farming is heading? Is there another darker side to the story that has remained hidden behind all the talk of record yields and efficiency?

The removal of hedges and the enlargement of fields is, perhaps, the most visible change that has taken place in the countryside. Travelling by train through southern and eastern counties today can be a depressingly tedious business. It can sometimes take minutes just to pass one field. Features of local interest that used to distinguish one area from another have been ruthlessly erased so that counties merge imperceptibly one with the other. Hedgerow trees have been a major casualty of this process, quite apart from the additional depredations of Dutch Elm Disease. Less visible, but equally dramatic, changes in terms of their effects on wildlife have been taking place in the countryside. In the quest for more land for agriculture we have been busily destroying much of the land previously untouched. Woodland has been cleared, ponds filled in, wetlands drained, old pasture ploughed up, moorland reclaimed and so on. Wild creatures and plants, denied a place to live out their lives, have been forced into ever smaller sanctuaries. For many, all that is left are the narrow strips along motorways, roadside verges and in nature reserves. Many have died out altogether.

Those that do remain in the farmers' fields have to run the gauntlet of the agrochemicals that make up the armoury of the 'progressive' modern agrobusinessman. This means regular dosing with insecticides, fungicides, herbicides and all of the other 'icides' which are routinely used to kill all unwanted life. In the summer months it may mean fleeing from the flames as the wasted straw and stubble is put to the torch and black acrid smoke fills the air.

Nor is it just wildlife that is in danger. Modern farming has other harmful environmental side-effects which directly put our own life-support systems at risk. Much of the chemical fertilizer applied to crops ultimately finds its way into watercourses where it encourages abundant weed growth which chokes out other aquatic organisms. Animal slurry leaks away from factory farms and into our rivers. Our drinking water supplies are contaminated by nitrate pollution to such an extent that many Water Authorities now supply water that, according to EEC and World Health Organisation standards, is unfit to drink.

In the even longer term there is the, largely unseen, threat to our soils. We are dosing our plants with artificial fertilizers whilst systematically starving the life in the soil. No attempt is made to put anything back, and in consequence soil fertility is declining. We are literally mining our soils – farming has become an extractive industry. Not surprisingly, soil organic matter levels are falling and the agents of soil erosion are taking their toll. This is made worse by the use of large heavy machinery and the absence of hedges and windbreaks. All the ingredients are in place for wind and water to blow and wash soil away. This is what is happening, at an increasing pace, on British soils today.

Here then, are the major minuses which have to be set against the rhetoric of wonder yields, 'green revolutions' and 'cheap' food. For how cheap is food which is bought at the cost of poisoned water supplies, the destruction of wildlife and steadily deteriorating soils? These are some of the questions which will be looked at in more depth in this chapter.

## The Changing Countryside

It is difficult to imagine that horses were still an important source of motive power on post-World War II farms. Then, the mixed family farm was the predominant unit of agriculture. Animal-rearing enterprises ran side by side with those of cereal growing. The manure from the former was used to fertilize the latter. Wheat or barley straw was used either as animal bedding, for feed, or else was composted and returned to the

3

land. Crop rotations were employed as a means of controlling pests and diseases. Although the farmer was to an extent dependent on outside inputs, there was a large degree of self-sufficiency.

In order to support this way of farming, the land would have been divided up between pasture and arable – grass and crops. Hedges and other field boundaries, often laid down several hundred years ago, prevented livestock from straying.

Then came the post-war drive for increased production using artificial fertilizers and the new wonder sprays invented during the war as part of the research drive to produce nerve gases. Although artificial fertilizers were first produced towards the end of the nineteenth century they had not been taken up on any great scale. But with the introduction of Government subsidies in 1951 and 1952 the expenditure on fertilizers, which had grown gradually from £27 million in 1941 to £54 million in 1951, shot up to £70 million in 1952/3.[1]

With animal manure rendered redundant by the use of artificial fertilizers the next logical step was to do away with animals altogether. Thus began the development of the stockless arable farms which are such a feature of our landscape today. As ever larger, and more powerful, machinery came to be developed the network of hedgerows and small fields, no longer needed to contain livestock, came to be viewed as an anachronistic irrelevance hindering agricultural progress. It was much more efficient to plough a large uniform area where time wouldn't be wasted in negotiating awkward corners or in opening and closing farm gates. There was the problem of annual hedge maintenance, of trimming and training. Hedges can act as a reservoir for farm pests such as aphids and rabbits. Much easier to just bulldoze them out of the way.

Between 1946 and 1973, it has been estimated, some 140,000 miles of hedgerow were destroyed. Of this 20,000 miles were lost to motorways, industrial development and quarrying. The remaining 120,000 miles were grubbed up by farmers.[1] In Cambridgeshire the *average* field size is now 34 acres compared with 14 acres in 1945. Fields in what was Huntingdonshire are larger still, averaging 54 acres. Many fields must therefore run to several hundred acres apiece in order to give this average figure, which means a single field can be larger than an entire typical British post-war farm, or indeed a European farm today.

Nor is this a phenomenon confined entirely to stockless farms. Increasingly, dairy farmers are keeping their cows indoors, growing high-yielding grasses in fields which are harvested by machine and then taken to the animals. The same imperatives which drive cereal farmers to destroy hedges also apply to these dairy farmers, with similar consequences. In the traditional dairying county of Somerset, for instance, the average field size has almost doubled during the last forty years from under 9 acres in 1945 to 16 acres in 1983.[2]

Woodland, too, has fallen to the axe, or rather the chainsaw. Between a third and a half of all of our lowland ancient woodland, that is woods which pre-date 1600, has gone since 1947.[3] This does not include the estimated loss of some 24 million hedgerow trees since 1951.[4]

These are but the most dramatic manifestations of the expansion of agricultural output and the changes from traditional farming practices. Marion Shoard in her polemic, *The Theft of the Countryside*, paints a dramatic picture of the impact of modern agriculture on the landscape, but perhaps the most sobering statistics come from Dr Derek Ratcliffe, Chief Scientist of the Government-backed Nature Conservancy Council. In the following league table the catastrophic loss of specific types of habitat, very largely due to agriculture, is starkly laid out:

　　95 per cent of lowland herb-rich meadows destroyed.
　　80 per cent of lowland grasslands or sheep walks on chalk
　　　　and limestone destroyed.
　　50–60 per cent of lowland heaths destroyed.
　　Many lakes significantly changed by farm battery slurry,
　　　　fertilizer run-off and sewage pollution. Further
　　　　pollution from pesticides and drainage operations.
　　50 per cent of lowland fens destroyed or significantly
　　　　damaged.
　　60 per cent of lowland raised mires destroyed.
　　50 per cent of upland grasslands, heaths and mires
　　　　destroyed.

To this should be added the damage done to archaeological sites where grassland has been ploughed up, the filling-in of farm ponds (perhaps half of all those in southern and eastern England have gone since 1945) and the destruction of footpaths and other public rights of way.

Faced with such a loss of habitat, it is hardly surprising that many animal and plant species have suffered dramatic population declines. Dr Ratcliffe goes on to list some of the damage done to wildlife:

> 10 species of butterfly seriously endangered. The Large Blue became extinct in 1979.
> 4 species of dragonfly have become extinct since 1953. 6 more species are seriously endangered.
> 36 species of resident bird have gone into long-term decline over the last 35 years.
> Several of the 15 species of bats are at risk of extinction.
> 10 species of plant have become extinct since 1930. 317 species are regarded as rare. 117 have shown at least 33 per cent decline since 1970.

To give a single graphic example of how the loss of habitat can profoundly affect a species, in 1940 the frog population of what was then Huntingdonshire was around 500 frogs for every 100 acres. By 1974, as a result of the filling-in of most of the ponds, this figure had dropped to just one per 100 acres.[1] This amounts to little less than an act of genocide on the natural kingdom.

Since Marion Shoard wrote her brave book, much has been written on the threat facing Britain's countryside and wildlife from modern agriculture. Rather than dwell further on this here, therefore, I would refer the reader to more appropriate sources listed in the references. As will be seen later, though, most of the problems I have outlined could be avoided entirely, or significantly ameliorated, if organic farming methods were adopted.

## Pesticides

Ever since the dawn of agriculture, farmers have had to contend with the problems of pests and diseases afflicting their crops. From earliest times until as recently as the mid-1940s the range of chemical options were few. These consisted of natural plant extracts such as derris, pyrethrum and nicotine for use against insects; copper and sulphur compounds used against fungal diseases, plus an assortment of rather more deadly substances based on mercury and arsenic. Chemical weed control – or herbicides as they are known today – to all intents and purposes did not exist at all. Weeds were kept in check by mechanical means such as hoeing and by the use of crop rotations. None of the traditional substances exerted a wider influence on the environment because, firstly, they were not used in any significant quantity; secondly, in the case of insecticides, they broke down and became harmless within a matter of hours, or days at the most; and thirdly, in the case of sulphur and copper, they were naturally derived soil constituents.

Although one synthetic chemical, dinitro-ortho-cresol (DNOC), had been invented and introduced as a weedkiller in 1932, the real chemical revolution did not begin in earnest until the late forties. The first synthetic insecticides (pesticide is used in this book as a term which embraces all the 'icides') were invented during World War II. DDT was initially manufactured in 1940 for use against lice, fleas, flies and mosquitoes and rapidly became general issue throughout the Allied Forces. It was the first of a range of insecticides known by their chemical composition as organochlorine or chlorinated hydrocarbon insecticides. Meanwhile, in Germany, the search for an effective nerve gas had led to the development of the organophosphorous group of insecticidal compounds. Herbicides such as MCPA and 2, 4-D were also invented during the war period.

The scene was set for a rapid expansion of pesticide use. Chemicals such as DDT were taken up and used enthusiastically throughout the immediate post-war period. New compounds began to appear on the market. In 1950 there were only 15 insecticides and fungicides in common use in agriculture. By 1975 this had mushroomed to over 200 active ingredients contained within more than 800 commercial formulations.[5] Last year there were over 400 chemicals in well over 1,000 commercial applications cleared for use in the UK under the Pesticides Safety Precaution Scheme.

The British Agrochemical Association, which is the organization representing pesticide manufacturers, reported home sales in 1984 of 29.6 million kilograms of active ingredient, worth £346 million.[6] Worldwide some 2,300 million kilograms of pesticides were used during 1985 representing approximately a pound weight for every man, woman and child on the planet.[7]

## Effects of Pesticides on Wildlife

With such colossal quantities of chemicals being loaded into the environment it is not surprising that effects other than those desired began to be noticed. Rachel Carson in her classic book *Silent Spring*,[8] published in 1962, first drew public attention to the way in which DDT and other organochlorine insecticides behaved in the environment; in particular to their potentially disastrous effect on wildlife. Insects which were the target of sprays retained the DDT in their bodies. This was then passed on to higher organisms which ate them, and so on up the food chain, with the amounts of DDT in the body getting higher all the time.

The most graphic illustration of biomagnification, the name given to this phenomenon, was that of Clear Lake in California. It was treated with DDD, a relative of DDT, in 1949 at 0.014 to 0.02 p.p.m. (parts per million) to control gnats which were troubling anglers. The DDD accumulated through the food chain from plankton to plankton-eating fish, to carnivorous fish to Western grebes at the top of the food chain, by which time their body fat contained 1,600 p.p.m. of DDD, a biomagnification factor of 100,000.

During the 1960s, we in Britain began to experience the first of these environmental side-effects. From 1955 to 1962 peregrine falcons suffered a dramatic decline. Their numbers only began to pick up again with the restrictions imposed in 1962 on the use of persistent organochlorine pesticides such as Dieldrin on seed dressings. Pigeons poisoned with treated seed were eaten by foxes, which in turn led to a national outbreak of 'fox death' in 1961. Badgers, too, suffered a similar fate. For many years the pesticide industry, denying that their products could be responsible for the poisonings, engaged in a long and sterile debate on the levels of pesticides required to kill individual species. If, for example, under laboratory conditions, a test bird such as a young pheasant died at a typical concentration of a pesticide of x p.p.m., whereas dead pheasants in the wild were being discovered with body levels of less than x p.p.m., then according to the manufacturers the pesticide could not be held to blame.

Eventually, in experiments involving kestrels, it was learned that pesticides given to a bird sitting on a perch in a cage would be stored harmlessly in the body fat, whereas for a wild bird flying freely the chemical went straight into the blood stream. Consequently a much lower dose could be fatal. This problem of pesticides' being released into the body when fat is mobilized has special implications for creatures such as hedgehogs and bats which hibernate during the winter and which rely on fat reserves to sustain them during this period. It also affects our own health if we are suffering from a chronic illness associated with weight loss or if fat is lost in other ways, as in human breast milk, for example (see Chapter 3).

In 1965 another alarming fact was discovered about DDT and other organochlorine compounds. Traces were detected in the body fat of creatures living in Antarctica. Not only are such chemicals extremely persistent (gamma BHC can remain for an estimated 14 years) but they also have the capacity to be transported by wind and water to all corners of the globe.

(Although DDT was finally banned for all uses in 1984, Friends of the Earth campaigners experienced no difficulty in buying two five-gallon drums from a chemical dealer in June 1985. Dieldrin, voluntarily withdrawn since 1975, was, according to the Royal Society for the Protection of Birds, responsible for the poisoning of at least 14 herons on the Worcestershire Avon ten years later.)

Since there is virtually no monitoring of wildlife it is extremely difficult to know how many creatures die each year as a direct result of pesticide poisoning. However, secondary effects such as the elimination of weeds which harbour insects will lead to an equally dramatic decline in animal numbers through a loss of food supply. Partridge chicks, for example, are particularly dependent on insects during the first few months of their lives. Intensive spraying of cereal crops has successfully eliminated these sources of food, and consequently young chicks starve to death. The sharp decline in numbers of birds of prey during the 1950s and 1960s is another example of indirect mortality. Birds were not killed outright but instead laid eggs with thin shells which frequently broke before hatching. Although the worst of the persistent offenders have at least in theory been banned or severely restricted, who can say how many other such sub-level effects, as yet unidentified, are still at work today?

## Are Pesticides Necessary?

The first question to ask, in view of the enormous chemical effort that has been waged against insects in the last forty years, is 'Why haven't we killed them all?' Insect damage ought to be getting less and less, whereas the truth of the matter is that the problem is getting worse year by year. David Pimental and his co-workers in the USA have estimated that crop losses to insects have *increased* from 7 per cent in the 1940s to 13 per cent at present, despite a ten-fold increase in annual use of insecticides.[9] 'Pesticides often *cause* actual pest increases rather than controlling them, and more and more frequently are creating new pests of species that formerly were harmless rarities.' So says Professor Paul Debach of the University of California.[10]

This astounding statement needs to be explored in more detail if we are to understand why it is that pesticides, far from being the answer to pest control, help in fact to make the situation worse.

All pests have their natural enemies which help to keep their numbers in check. When pesticides are sprayed on pests they will inevitably kill these beneficial creatures as well. This means that when the next pest invasion occurs there are fewer, if any, natural controls left. An equally serious tendency is that of pesticides to speed up natural selection. Almost without exception, wherever sprays are used there will be some pests that, for one reason or another, are unaffected. With an absence of natural enemies and reduced competition these so-called 'resistant' individuals are able to breed unchecked. The next spraying further eliminates the weak, so strengthening the resistant strain. Eventually the entire pest population becomes completely unaffected by the chemical which then has to be abandoned in favour of another, and the whole process repeats itself.

This problem of resistance is now extremely serious. Whereas in 1954 there were only 25 insects worldwide which showed resistance to insecticides, this figure had shot up to 185 by 1965 and in 1980 stood at 432.[7] Even weeds and fungi are now showing resistance to sprays. Indeed, the life of a new chemical in terms of its usefulness against its target organisms is getting shorter all the time. So much so that manufacturers now urge caution on the part of the farmer and warn not to 'overuse' their product but instead to alternate it with another chemical in order to prolong its useful life.

A practical example of the negative effects of pesticides, with cotton growing in Mexico, is taken from Debach. He describes how, in the Rio Grande Valley, cotton pests, mainly the boll weevil, were adequately controlled with chlorinated hydrocarbon insecticides for nearly 15 years until the boll weevil became resistant to them in the late 1950s. The organophosphorous compounds, especially methyl parathion, were then used for boll weevil control – to great effect – and as a result DDT became necessary to control the previously insignificant pests, the bollworm and tobacco budworm. 'By 1962, the latter two became resistant to DDT, other chlorinated hydrocarbons and to carbamate insecticides, but could still be killed by heavy dosages of methyl parathion. This control began to become unsatisfactory by 1968 when some growers treated 15–18 times and failed to obtain satisfactory results. Now the pest control situation was suddenly reversed as the bollworm and tobacco budworm, two pests formerly of minor importance, became more serious than the boll weevil which faded to insignificance.' Cotton production in the Rio Grande Valley has today almost entirely disappeared; 700,000 acres were abandoned in 1970.

David Bull gives an illustration of the same problem taken from the Sudan. Cotton is now sprayed on average 9 times a year compared with only once in 1946. Yields have fallen from 170 kgs per acre in the early 1970s to 100 kgs per acre by 1980 – about the same as the yields obtained before World War II and the widespread introduction of pesticides.[7]

This story has been repeated the world over on crops such as rice, citrus fruits, olives, sugar cane, coconuts and a host of other lesser crops. Numerous further examples are to be found in Debach and Bull.

In Britain the most spectacular creation of a 'man-made' pest is that of the red spider mite – a pest of orchards. Prior to the 1920s it presented few problems, living amongst the lichens and mosses to be found on the trunk and branches of apple trees and held in check by a variety of predators. Then, with the adoption of winter tar oil washes to clean the bark, the destruction of overwintering predators enabled newly hatched red spider eggs in the spring to thrive. However, it was not until the introduction of DDT and BHC that the problem became acute. Red spider mites were shown to be resistant to the sprays which otherwise eliminated most insect life in orchards. An inevitable population explosion followed which to this day has not been properly contained.[11]

At the British Crop Protection Conference in November 1983, a scientist pointed out that fungicides used on cereal crops were responsible for the rapid disappearance of the insect predators which controlled pests such as aphids. Apparently most of the fungicide went straight into the soil, where it killed soil fungi which were the first link in the insect food chain. Fungicide use had led to a 50 per cent drop in the diversity of life forms found under cereal crops.[12] An absence of aphid predators thus led to the need for an insecticidal spray against these pests.

It is the view of Francis Chaboussou, former Director of the French National Institute for Agronomic Research, that pesticides not only poison insect and other animal life, they also poison the plants as well. Such plants, whilst not being directly killed, are much less able to withstand attack from pests and diseases and so succumb to these secondary forces. Only this explanation, according to Chaboussou in an interesting article in The Ecologist (Vol. 16. No. 1, 1986), could account for certain huge increases in diseases of cereal and other crops, which could not be explained directly by a reduction in predators. He considers that pesticides and fertilizers, both singly and acting together, alter the internal chemistry of the plant in favour of pathogens.

# The Pesticide Treadmill

You may by now be asking, if pesticides are so ineffective, why farmers keep on using them. Why don't they just stop? Unfortunately it is not as easy as all that. Use of pesticides has to be seen in the entire context of industrialized farming. A major problem is that because of the continuous use of sprays over a long period our farmland has become severely depleted of natural enemies. Not using anything at all would therefore lead to devastating attacks on crops.

Plant breeders over the years have developed varieties which respond to fertilizers in order to produce large yields (more about this later). These plants invariably pay the biological cost of such abundance in terms of greater susceptibility to pests and diseases. Crops grown with artificial fertilizers are also more likely to be attacked by pests. It is easier, for instance, for aphids such as greenfly physically to penetrate the cell walls of chemically fertilized plants than to attack more naturally grown plants.

Cabbage white caterpillars, if given a choice between cabbages grown with or without artificial fertilizers, will tend to lay their eggs on the former. It appears that the insects are attracted by the greener colour of the nitrogen-rich artificially fed plants.[13]

Attempts to extract ever more from the soil using increasing amounts of artificial fertilizers lead inevitably to declining soil fertility and increasing pest and disease attack. This in turn leads to the use of pesticides which, as pests develop resistance and natural enemies are obliterated, must forever be stepped up. The farmer is trapped on a treadmill of his own making.

Our own attitudes to food, though, are equally to blame. We have come to expect completely blemish-free produce presented in shiny plastic-wrapped pre-packs. We recoil from food showing the slightest surface marking. Do we really want to eat food which may have been sprayed numerous times during its life from the field to our table? For to ensure the level of cosmetic purity that is demanded today of some crops, chemicals have to be applied almost continuously. For example, no less than 46 sprayings were recorded on a single crop of lettuce in 1982, involving the use of four different chemicals.[14]

The major problem with pesticides is that they are non-specific. That is, they exert effects both direct and indirect far beyond that of the primary objective of killing the pest, disease, weed or whatever. Use of pesticides indicates a simplistic and crude approach to natural systems which ultimately is self-defeating. Nature is a complicated balance of individual relationships between organisms. Disruption of this balance, whether it be through spraying, growing large areas of single crops, neglecting soil organisms or in fact most of the other routine practices of conventional agriculture, is inviting trouble. The way forward lies in recognizing these natural processes and seeking to work with, rather than against them.

## Problems with Fertilizers

Whilst it is easy to see why people get upset at the use of pesticides, it is not quite so obvious why there should be an objection to fertilizers. Surpluses notwithstanding, their sole purpose is to enable more food to be grown – where can the harm be in this? The answer once again, in a theme that runs right through this book, is that things are not quite that simple. Once again there are the inevitable side-effects.

The first thing to be aware of is the amount of fertilizer which is now being used. Those record harvests, which were trumpeted year after year, though rather underplayed these days, were gained at the cost of massive increases in fertilizer applications. In 1939 the UK used 50,000 tonnes of nitrogen fertilizers.[15] By 1982 this had gone up to 1.4 million tonnes,[1] a 28-fold increase. Although much of this would have been employed on arable land, a significant proportion is assigned to pasture land where it has the effect of producing more grass for livestock.

Unfortunately, at least half of all nitrogen fertilizer applied to the soil is wasted.[16] Nitrate nitrogen dissolves easily in water and once in the soil most of that part which is not taken up by the crop instead finds its way into the field-drainage system. The rest is bound up with soil particles or alternatively lost to the atmosphere where it helps contribute to the phenomenon known as acid rain.[1]

However, it is the nitrate in water which is most damaging

and which has led to some observers' referring to the nitrate time bomb.

## The Nitrate Time Bomb

Although nitrate can be quickly leached from fields in surface water run-off, it moves downwards through the soil at a much slower pace. A rate of about a metre a year is not untypical, which means that if a well for drinking water is 25 metres deep, it could take 25 years before nitrate begins to show up in the water. River water will, of course, display the effects of nitrate pollution very much sooner.

What are the health hazards from nitrate pollution of drinking water? An uncontestable effect is the condition known as methaemoglobinaemia, which gives rise to the potentially fatal 'blue baby syndrome' in infants. Although this disease is rare in Britain, the risks have been considered sufficiently serious by a number of UK water authorities for them to have issued bottled water to nursing mothers. A more disputed hazard is that of stomach cancer (see Chapter 3).

The World Health Organisation has recommended a maximum limit of 100 mg nitrate per litre, with a suggested upper level of 50 mg per litre. This latter figure has been taken on board by the EEC as the maximum admissible concentration in its Directive 80/778, issued in July 1985. The WHO's limit for nitrate in drinking water, above which health problems may possibly occur, is 11.3 mg per litre. This has also been adopted by the EEC as the recommended maximum level.

In the UK, nitrate nitrogen levels of 15–20 mg per litre below arable fields are entirely typical.[17] This is posing quite a problem for the Water Authorities, since in some areas the EEC mandatory limits are being exceeded. The response of the British Government has been to give a 'derogation' (i.e. they ignore it) of 80 mg per litre to those areas involved. At the time of writing this includes more than 50 districts in Lincolnshire, Cambridgeshire, Norfolk, Staffordshire and Yorkshire.[1]

The Royal Society, in a 250-page report on the nitrate problem,[18] has estimated the cost of taking nitrates out of Britain's water supplies to be up to £1,600 million over the next twenty years, a sum which a number of experts feel to be on the conservative side. Nor have we yet witnessed the full extent of the problem. Levels of nitrate currently showing up in our deep groundwater drinking supplies are due to the fertilizers applied twenty or more years ago. How much higher will they be twenty or thirty years from now? This is the true and sinister nature of the nitrate time bomb.

An article in *Farming News* (29.11.85), headlined 'Time Bomb Ticking in That Water', began: 'Political pressure for curbs on nitrogen fertilizer use is mounting as nitrates seeping into groundwater threaten to make many supplies undrinkable. Anglian Water Authority chiefs predict that in the worst affected areas nitrate levels could go up to 200 mg a litre, or *four times the EEC limit* [my emphasis].'

The article went on to suggest that the only way of making any real impact on the situation would be to turn over East Anglia and other predominantly all-cereal areas from intensive arable to moderate/low grassland systems. Apparently the National Farmers' Union is now looking at the possibility of a tax on nitrogen such as already exists in Sweden.

Not all of the responsibility for the nitrate contamination of water supplies can be attributed to use of fertilizers. Ploughing up grassland to grow cereals releases large amounts of nitrogen as the grass rots in the soil. Untreated sewage flushed into rivers also adds its share. However, unrestrained fertilizer use together with battery animal slurry are by far the greatest contributory factors.

## Farm Slurry

Serious pollution problems also arise from modern intensive methods of keeping livestock. Animals, instead of being allowed to roam the fields, are kept cooped up in sheds. Consequently, all of the manure and urine is concentrated in one spot where it is usually diluted with water to make for easier handling. The question then arises of what to do with this slurry. More often than not it is just pumped into settlement ponds otherwise known as slurry lagoons. These might be constructed with concrete walls, earth banks or cobbled together from corrugated iron or other farm scrap. Inevitably they leak.

According to the Ministry of Agriculture, Fisheries and Food, almost 3,000 pollution incidents occurred during 1984.[1] This greatly understates the problem. Many cases go unreported and much depends on the zeal of the local Water Authority in tracking down offenders. The North West Water Authority, for instance, logged three times as many cases of pollution caused by farm effluent in 1983 as in a typical year.[19]

Another pollution problem has been brought about by the move to making silage. Fewer farmers are making hay these days. Instead, grass is cut whilst still green, then fermented in huge silage clamps. Leakage from these can also cause tremendous problems. A 200-tonne clamp of unwilted silage is equivalent in pollution terms to one day's untreated sewage from a town of 75,000 people.[1]

Apart from expressions of regret and exhortations to farmers to try harder in future the Ministry offers little in the way of advice. However, the Government-appointed Royal Commission on Environmental Pollution did come up with one idea: ' . . . the use of poultry manure as a cattle feed ingredient could make a significant contribution to the disposal problem and should be encouraged'.[20] But there is a drawback: ' . . . there may be a carry-over into the cattle feed of residues of *veterinary* [my emphasis] products which are present in waste from broiler production'.

## Other Effects of Fertilizers

I have deliberately concentrated on the nitrate pollution aspect of fertilizer use because to my mind it is the most damaging and in the long run most potentially catastrophic. Nevertheless, nutrient-rich pollutants emanating from farms, such as slurry, silage, or fertilizers other than nitrogen fertilizers, can also play havoc with streams, rivers and lakes. Algae and aquatic plants stimulated by the enriched water grow profusely, often to the point where waterways can be choked with vegetation. When they die the extra oxygen required in decomposition can so deplete the water of this essential element that fish and other animal life simply suffocate.

These, then, are the inevitable results of the adoption by farmers of artificial fertilizer regimes. This is not to say that organic farms are entirely free from pollution risks. Untreated animal slurry if spread directly on to the land could be equally damaging. However, organic farmers usually keep fewer animals on a given area of land and they try to treat any slurry, by aeration, before applying it. It has also been shown that a tremendous reduction in the downward movement of nitrates in the soil occurs when composted material is used as compared to artificial fertilizers.[22]

There are a number of other harmful environmental effects arising from the use of artificial fertilizers on which I shall dwell briefly. For instance, there is the question of the disruption to soil organisms. Naturally occurring bacteria that are able to fix atmospheric nitrogen and can be responsible for producing as much as 80 kg of nitrate nitrogen in an acre of soil no longer operate when nitrogen is supplied artificially from a bag. Worms will move out of soils that have been dressed with artificial fertilizers. Given the insignificant research effort that has gone into understanding the relationships between the many different soil organisms, or the functions they exercise individually and collectively, we can only begin to guess at what other effects fertilizers might have.

Use of fertilizers also disturbs the balance of nutrients in the soil. Nitrogen fertilizers, for instance, reduce available copper. Phosphorus reduces zinc, calcium reduces manganese, whilst potassium reduces available sodium, calcium, magnesium and boron.[21] Since fertilizers containing nitrogen, phosphorus and potassium (NPK) are universal in agriculture it is easy to see the potential for soil mineral deficiencies. The implications of this for the food we eat are discussed in Chapter 5. (I shall also consign fertilizer-implicated issues such as the misuse of finite resources, the ascendancy of modern seed monocultures, and the decline in soil fertility to more appropriate sections.)

Fertilizers, however, are but one, though perhaps the major, part of the post-World War II chemical revolution that has freed the farmer from his traditional dependence on animal manure. This revolution has enabled a specialization to take place which in turn has led to many of the problems outlined in this and other chapters. Cereal producers by and large keep no livestock and so rely on fertilizers out of the bag. Soil fertility declines, thus necessitating more and more applications of fertilizer, much of which gets washed into waterways, poisoning drinking-water supplies and killing fish. Intensive livestock producers, on the other hand, have more manure than they know what to do with. Slurry is stored in lagoons from which it frequently escapes into watercourses giving rise to the same effects as those caused by artificial fertilizers.

Sooner or later we are going to have to bring all parties together again – plant, animal and farmer in harmony – which is what organic growers have been doing all along.

## Straw-Burning

Blackened fields in August are now a traditional feature of the British pastoral scene, the warm summer sky dark with smoke and laden with smuts as the unwanted straw from the always expanding cereal acreage is reduced to ashes.

It is true that things have improved slightly since the nadir of 1983. The NFU's straw- and stubble-burning code is now much tougher. Wider ploughed strips around fields prevent the worst of the damage to hedgerows and trees, but it is plain to see for anyone travelling about the countryside in summer that the code is frequently ignored.

It is estimated that at least half of the 13 or so million tonnes of straw produced each year is destroyed in this way.[23] Quite apart from the appalling atmospheric pollution involved, this is equivalent to the wanton burning of over 3.5 million tons of coal. It may be argued that at a time of global low energy costs this is something of an irrelevance. Once again, though, modern economic forces are totally out of touch with ecological realities. Within a decade or two at most supplies of oil, the most versatile of our fossil fuels, will be running down. We may even be putting down significant areas of cropland to fuel crops such as fast-growing willow species. Then the mindless energy profligacy of these present decades will be seen in true perspective.

Yet we have not always burned. Little if any straw was destroyed by farmers before the 1950s, so what has accounted for the change? The answer lies in the specialization of farming referred to in the last section. On mixed farms in the past straw was used both for livestock feed and for bedding. Surplus straw was composted with animal manure and spread back onto the land. None was wasted – it was recognized for the precious asset it is. Nowadays most cereal producers do not keep live-stock, whilst intensive livestock producers do not use straw. You even have the ludicrous situation whereby straw from the east of England is transported by lorry halfway across the country to serve those livestock farmers in the west who still use it.

Indignant public pressure has forced farmers to look again at the wastefulness of their present practices. Despite stalling tactics, a total ban on straw-burning will doubtless eventually be introduced. This, though, brings the question of what to do with it. Soil fertility on many farms is so low that there are insufficient soil organisms to properly decompose the waste, so making incorporation of the straw into the soil a risky business. If it is to be burnt, better that it be used in farm boilers for heating the farmhouse where at least it will do some good. There are also various novel suggestions for alternative uses put forward from time to time, usually involving the paper and board industries.

But none of this really addresses the main problem. Do we wish to continue propping up a basically unsustainable farming system of which straw-burning is yet another sickly manifes-tation? Or do we move on to progressive organic systems in which straw has an important role to play?

## Soil Erosion

You may be forgiven for wondering what a section on soil erosion is doing in an assessment of British agriculture. Surely there can be no problem here – soil erosion is something that happens far away in the Third World, not in our temperate climate? That is indeed the view of many in the agricultural establishment, reflected in such comments as those of P. Needham, head of Soil Science at the Agricultural Develop-ment and Advisory Service.[24] ' . . . ill-founded and sweeping statements about the health of the nation's soils are still being made. Despite these expressed fears, yields of most crops have continued to increase leading to embarrassing surpluses of some.'

Yet of late a few notes of warning have begun to be heard.

In 1983 the Government-backed Soil Survey of England and Wales reported that, 'On average about twice as many fields within the sample localities were eroded in 1983 as in 1982; in Norfolk the factor was 8, in Nottinghamshire 6 and in Hampshire, Dorset, Somerset and Staffordshire 3.' Dr R. Evans, one of the staff involved in the survey, went on to say, 'Results from the two years' work confirm that erosion is far more widespread and serious now than in the past.'[25]

The naturalist Ted Ellis, writing in the *Guardian*,[26] noted: ' . . . when rainfall is exceptionally heavy, as has happened over Christmas, its effects have been spectacular on many of Norfolk's farmlands. Erosion of the soil has been greatest on fields from which sugar beet has been lifted recently. I saw a demonstration of this on 26 December when I walked through a valley woodland bordering the lower edge of an 80-acre beet field which had been enlarged through the removal of hedges formerly enclosing several smaller fields. Following the descent of almost two inches of rain, red, clayey silt was gushing from the furrows and converging to form temporary streams which cut ever more deeply into the soil and eventually found egress through a major woodland track and thence to a fen and broad beyond. The force of this effluent was such that even some of the sliced beet tops were carried away from the field. The nearby river, with its tributaries, has a watershed of approximately 2,000 square miles, much of which consists of arable land whose drainage has been improved greatly in recent years. The run-off of topsoil during rainy periods in late autumn and winter must be appreciable and undoubtedly all the greater since so many hedges have been removed. The intrusion of silt not only places an additional burden on watercourses. The residues of agricultural fertilizers, pesticides and clay particles spreading over peat tend to affect communities of plants and animals in the wetlands and their waterways.'

On a global scale the situation is serious indeed. An estimated 25.4 billion tons of topsoil are lost from croplands each year.[27] Although the formation of soil from the disintegrating of rocks and its subsequent erosion by wind and water are entirely natural processes, what we should be concerned about is the rate of excessive topsoil loss as a result of human activity.

Although I am focusing here only on agricultural practices,

a major worldwide factor in soil loss is the removal of tree cover for firewood or commercial reasons. The large-scale deforestation of the Himalayas, for example, has led to such loss of soil from the mountainous slopes of Nepal that a new island, which could justifiably be claimed as Nepalese territory, is growing up in the Bay of Bengal. An associated effect is the now traditional annual flooding of Northern India as the silt-laden waters rush down to the sea.

Lester Brown of the UN-backed Worldwatch Institute has assembled figures which show excessive topsoil loss in the USA of some 1.7 billion tons per year affecting 44 per cent of all cropland. Half the topsoil in the state of Iowa has been lost during the last twenty-five years. Every year in the USSR over a million acres of cropland are abandoned because they are so severely eroded they are no longer worth farming. Prophetically, a US aid mission to Addis Ababa reported in 1978: ' . . . there is an environmental nightmare unfolding before our eyes . . . over 1 billion tons of topsoil flow from Ethiopia's highlands each year'.[27] With such colossal losses of such a precious asset what will be the consequences for feeding future generations?

## What Happens When Topsoil Is Removed?

Environmental considerations such as those described by Ellis apart, what are the implications of topsoil loss to the farmer? Obviously nutrients are washed or blown away and there is degradation of the physical structure of the soil. The inherent productivity of the land is diminished. But this can be offset by increasing the amount of fertilizer used and installing irrigation equipment to counter the reduced water-carrying capacity of the soil. To an extent, therefore, the symptoms of soil rundown and erosion can be masked by increasing agricultural inputs. This would help to explain the complacent statement of Mr Needham, quoted earlier.

A study carried out in Southern Iowa, USA, illustrates the problem in more detail.[28] Researchers set up three soil erosion categories: slightly eroded, moderately eroded and severely eroded. In 1974, out of a total of 3.5 million acres of cropland under investigation, 2.1 million acres fell into one of the three groups, with the largest acreage in the moderately eroded category. It was estimated that by the year 2020, if current agricultural practices continue, the largest share would be in the severely eroded category. In making this transition an additional 38 pounds more NPK fertilizer per acre, and 38 per cent more energy, would be needed to grow the crop. Yields of maize would correspondingly drop by 16 bushels an acre in the progression from slightly to moderately eroded soils and a further 7 bushels in the regression to the worst category.

The following quotation illustrates the stark choice facing Iowa's farmers today: ' . . . if farmers were to invest in appropriate conservation measures their profit margins would disappear entirely, forcing them into bankruptcy. Alternatively they could follow existing agricultural practices and avoid near-term bankruptcy but face the problem of declining productivity over the long term and eventual abandonment of the land, if not by this generation then by the next. In the absence of a governmental cost-sharing programme a farmer's only choice is whether to go out of business sooner or later.'[27]

## What Are the Reasons for Soil Erosion?

Once again the source of the problem lies in modern intensive farming methods, especially in the virtually total neglect of the soil. Continuous arable cropping, with one cereal crop following another with monotonous regularity, successively depletes the soil of nutrients so that the farmer becomes entirely dependent on artificial fertilizers for the growth of the crop. Failure to return organic matter to the soil, in the form of animal manure, composted straw, ploughed-in temporary grass crops grown as part of a traditional crop rotation, and other farm wastes, ensures a progressive reduction in the organic content of the soil. When this happens the soil loses its 'spongy' quality – it is less able to hold water and it becomes compact – so that access by air and water, both essential for plant growth, is severely impaired. In addition, organic matter is the vital binding ingredient in soils, holding particularly the lighter sands and loams together.

Under the punishing compaction of extremely heavy farm machinery, much of which has axle-weights heavier than are permitted on public tarmac highways, the soil then begins to break down. And removal of soil is made even easier by the grubbing-out of hedges and other natural obstacles, together with the policy of routing tractor operations such as spraying and drilling along fixed 'tramlines' up and down fields. These make almost perfect gullies in which water-bearing topsoil can rush away.

As early as the 1930s it was shown that soil erosion is far worse where the land is left bare or under row crops such as cereals, when compared with land growing cover crops such as hay or pasture. Research in Missouri, USA,[29] showed an increase in soil erosion from 2.7 tons per acre annually when land was in a crop rotation involving maize, wheat and clover to 19.7 tons per acre when the same land was planted continuously with maize. The message is unmistakable.

Perhaps even more so than the nitrate time bomb, soil erosion is a potential eco-catastrophe ticking away at the foundations of our food security. As UK expert Harrison Reed states,[30] ' . . . soil erosion is one of the big threats looming on the horizon for British agriculture'. Or as agricultural economist L. K. Fischer of the University of Nebraska put it, ' . . . we must cease to behave as if there were no tomorrow, or tomorrow will be bleak indeed for those who must spend their lives there'.[31] Meanwhile, the reaction of the British Government has been to halve the Scientific Staff of the Soil Survey of England and Wales from 60 to 30, to slash its grant and to fail to guarantee support from 1987 onwards.[32]

## Genetic Erosion

I shall end this chapter by looking at another tendency of modern agriculture which has not yet properly penetrated public consciousness yet has implications every bit as dramatic as those already mentioned. The issue concerns what is known as genetic erosion, which put more simply means a reduction in the number of varieties or breeds of different plants or animals used in agriculture.

This is most apparent in the case of farm animals. Farmers have bred livestock over the centuries, specially suited to their own local conditions. This has given us a wealth of different breeds, yet how many of these breeds are in evidence today?

How often do you see anything other than the ubiquitous black-and-white Friesian cow grazing the fields? It is the same with pigs; the large white either on its own, or crossed with the Welsh or Landrace, reigns supreme. Breeds that can thrive outdoors such as the Tamworth, the Gloucester Old Spot, or the Wessex Saddleback are to all intents and purposes commercially extinct. As for chickens, everything has been abandoned in favour of a few high-yielding hybrid strains that behave like egg factories for a year and then, worn out with it all, are sent to the meat-paste manufacturers.

Similar things have been happening to our food plants. Three-quarters of all Canadian wheat comes from just four varieties. A similar percentage of potatoes grown in America relies on only four types, whilst the entire American pea acreage is grown from two varieties. Almost all the coffee plants in Brazil derive from a single shrub.[33] In the UK during the last decade, over a thousand vegetable varieties have been lost from cultivation.[34]

## Why Has This Happened?

This specialization of agriculture has come about almost entirely as a result of the new industrialized farming methods that have displaced traditional agriculture. When animals are kept in environmentally controlled sheds, only high-yielding breeds are needed and there is no necessity to take account of local conditions. In the case of crops, the situation has been exacerbated by the various plant patent laws that have been introduced into many countries and the consequent involvement of multi-national companies in the seed business.

There is, unfortunately, not the space here to go into all of the ramifications of the seed patenting laws. More details can be found in such books as Pat Mooney's *Seeds of the Earth*.[35] In essence, though, it is no longer possible for seeds to be traded freely. Only those maintained on a Government register may be sold. If unlisted seeds are sold the seedsman risks a fine. The financial implications of negotiating the regulations and maintaining traditional varieties are such that only the larger companies can afford to get involved. Consequently, during the

1970s many hundreds of seed companies throughout the world either went out of business or were taken over.

Furthermore, the kinds of companies which became involved in such takeovers were usually connected with the chemical industry. By 1983 the oil giant Shell had become the largest corporate owner of seed companies in the world. Is it any surprise, therefore, that as seed companies passed into the hands of pesticide and fertilizer manufacturers the content of their seed catalogues began to reflect those varieties which responded best to such products?

## Why Should Specialization Cause Concern?

It is high time that we became concerned at the monopolistic patterns whereby a handful of companies control, via the sale and development of only those seed varieties which suit their products, the world food supply. But this is not the only important consequence of genetic erosion.

It is extraordinarily dangerous to rely on just a few varieties, especially when this involves major food sources such as cereals. What if a new uncontrollable disease should appear and devastate the crop? The average life-span of the type of grain grown in Europe is only a few years. Insects and diseases change and adapt, as indeed do other factors such as the climate or atmospheric pollution. Where do we turn if disaster strikes? We have eliminated most of our traditional varieties.

Most of our food plants originally came from overseas, usually from the developing countries, where there was a great deal of genetic diversity. However, the same trends which have occurred in the West are already manifesting themselves in these countries, as traditional peasant varieties are being ousted by newly bred 'Green Revolution seeds'. These are much higher yielding but the price is paid in costs of imported fertilizers and irrigation equipment. Furthermore, they are usually much more susceptible to diseases. Use of pesticides increases dramatically wherever Green Revolution strains are introduced.

The social implications of this have been disastrous. Only the richer landowners are able to afford the new seeds, technology and other inputs that are required, whilst the higher yields have meant that traditional producers have been unable to compete. As a result, peasants are driven from the land and peasant seed varieties become extinct. In India, if the present rate of destruction continues, there will be only 50 varieties of rice by the end of the century compared with the 30,000 that existed in 1900. Egypt, the original home of the onion, now produces only one variety.[33]

So the source-material for new varieties is disappearing at an alarming rate. At a time when our monoculture methods of growing food encourage attack by pests and diseases we are simultaneously destroying our ability to obtain new genetic material to combat these.

There are, fortunately, some initiatives under way which try to act as a holding operation until sense prevails. The Rare Breeds Survival Trust, set up to maintain traditional breeds of livestock, has progressed from being treated, at its inception, as a somewhat whimsical body by the farming establishment to being viewed as an important conserver of genetic diversity.

The Henry Doubleday Research Association, through its ex-director Lawrence Hills, campaigned in favour of traditional varieties and for the establishment of a vegetable gene bank. This was finally established in 1980 at the National Vegetable Research Station at Wellesbourne, Warwickshire. There are a number of other such seed banks around the globe, but this 'ark' approach is an insufficient answer to the problem. The banks, themselves, will always remain vulnerable to accidental damage, as happened recently with the fire at the potato institute in Peru, whilst the question of who has access to the genetic source material thus stored is currently the subject of acute political controversy.

Ultimately, genetic erosion cannot be differentiated from any of the various other environmental problems inherent in our system of agriculture. Each is inextricably bound up with the other, and efforts to tackle one problem without addressing the root cause of all are doomed to failure. It is the way in which we cultivate our land, our whole attitude to Nature and to farming, that must change – nothing less will do.

## 2   FOOD FIT FOR ANIMALS?

## Animal Factories

Nowhere has the revolution which has occurred in British agriculture since World War II been more keenly felt than in the area of animal husbandry. It has been transformed out of all recognition. The mixed family farm with its 'Old Macdonald' range of livestock, if not entirely extinct, is most definitely an endangered species. As with cereals and field crops, it is the specialist who reigns supreme today.

In 1964 Ruth Harrison wrote a book called *Animal Machines*.[36] It described the appalling conditions under which most livestock spent their lives. Chickens kept in cages so small they could barely turn around. Pigs forced to exist in darkened sheds on concrete floors never seeing the light of day and so completely unused to exercise that they were incapable of making the final journey up the ramp and into the lorry that would take them to the abattoir. Veal calves kept in tiny cramped crates on slatted floors. Only sheep, which are notoriously difficult to keep confined, escaped this remorseless drive towards intensification.

Despite the outcry the book provoked, these methods continue more or less unchanged to the present day. Perhaps we have been persuaded by the farming apologists who maintain that all is well, for the chickens lay eggs and the pigs put on weight. Surely, unhappy animals would not thrive? Perhaps we have been taken in by the advertising industry which woos us with nostalgic images of a tranquil rural idyll. Cattle and sheep grazing contentedly in lush and verdant pastures, hens clucking contentedly around the farmyard – all viewed through the warm glow of a soft-focus lens. Food from Britain, the marketing organization set up a few years ago to try and dispose of some of our embarrassing surpluses, employs just such a scene for its logo. Or perhaps, we have been persuaded that there is no real alternative so we just shut our eyes to the suffering.

Of course, the majority of us never get to see the sort of conditions that prevail inside the innocuous groupings of long sheds that are dotted about the countryside. Perhaps our only direct encounter with the factory farming process is when we come across one of those lorries carrying chickens to the slaughterhouse. Crates stuffed full of birds piled suffocatingly one on top of another, thousands to a lorry. It is not surprising that you rarely see such lorries in broad daylight.

For my own part I have seen inside factory farms at first hand. Quite frankly I find them disgusting. That this is an emotional response I do not dispute, but you do not have to be a vegetarian to believe strongly that all creatures have the right not only to as natural an existence as possible but also to a dignified death. This they patently do not get at present. I sense that the current meteoric rise in popularity of vegetarianism and veganism has much to do with popular repugnance at factory farming methods.

It is not my intention, however, to go into lurid detail over the conditions prevailing in intensive animal houses. Organizations such as The Farm and Food Society (page 207) wage a constant battle on behalf of farm animal welfare. Instead I shall focus attention on a subject which has received relatively little publicity – namely the food that is routinely fed to livestock.

## What Goes into Livestock Feed?

It is sometimes jokingly said that if you ask a child where milk comes from the answer is 'from a bottle of course'. Whether or not this level of ignorance is widespread, it is probably true that most people, if asked what cows eat, would answer unhesitatingly, 'grass'. But in fact more and more livestock, particularly pigs and poultry, and to a lesser extent cattle and sheep, are spending their entire lives without seeing a single blade.

Traditionally livestock were kept in the fields during the spring and summer months, feeding not only on grasses and other green forage, but also on whatever else could be found by scratching or grubbing about. This diet would be supplemented to a greater or lesser degree by other feeds, usually in the form of cereal concentrates such as wheat or barley. In winter, when the grass stopped growing and conditions underfoot became wet and unsuitable, livestock, especially cattle, would be brought 'indoors' to strawed yards. Here they would have all their food brought to them, which usually meant either roots and tubers, hay (from grasses, cereals and legumes), straw (from cereals, peas and beans), concentrates or a combination of all three.

With the move towards intensive livestock systems, where the animals were denied access to pasture for grazing and foraging, the composition of the diet assumed even greater importance. It no longer became a question of just feeding the animal, but of doing so in the most economical and cost-effective way. Furthermore, the discovery that certain antibiotics and hormones could increase the rate at which young animals put on weight led to the widespread inclusion of these substances in the diet. Diseases, often caused by the close confinement of the animals, could be reduced by routine application of drugs, so these were added. In addition, there is a whole range of other substances – minerals, vitamins, enzymes, colourings and flavourings, antioxidants – which are now routinely added to the diet by the feed manufacturers.

The purpose of this chapter is to chart a way for the consumer through the maze of varied constituents which make up modern livestock concentrate rations.

## Major Ingredients

Animal concentrates are foods which have a high food-value in relation to their volume, with a low fibre content. This contrasts with grass and other fodder which provides roughage and bulk. Concentrates can be selected for their high protein content or for their carbohydrate or fat. Cereal grains are the traditional concentrate feeding-stuff but use is now made of oil seeds and cakes, leguminous seeds, by-products of human food manufacture and various other more esoteric substances, as shown in the table below.

## Major ingredients of animal feeds

| Cereals | Fats and oils |
|---|---|
| Barley | Tallow |
| Wheat | Blended fats |
| Oats | Maize oil |
| Maize (whole and flaked) | Soya oil |
| Sorghum | Sunflower oil |
| **Cereal by-products** | **Miscellaneous** |
| Barley grain screenings | Biscuit meal |
| Maize gluten feed | Grass/lucerne |
| Wheat feed | Beet pulp |
| Oat feed | Malt wastes |
| Rice bran | Molasses |
| **Animal proteins** | Tapioca |
| Fish meal | Dried poultry manure |
| Hydrolized feather meal | Treated straw |
| Meat and bone meal | Crisp waste |
| Blood meal | Wood flour |
| Delactosed whey | Mushroom compost |
| Skim milk powder | Grape waste |
| Fat-filled milk | Urea |
| Poultry offal | Apple pomace |
| **Vegetable proteins** | |
| Linseed rapeseed extract | |
| Soya bean meal | |
| Sunflower exract | |
| Olive extract | |
| Beans | |

Note the number of ingredients that come from impoverished Third World countries.

The amounts, usually expressed as a percentage, of protein, oil, crude fibre and ash (mineral content) in the feed, have by law to be printed on each bag but, of course, this gives no indication of what actually is inside. It would probably be impossible to do so, for the formulations change daily in response to worldwide changes in prices. Given the range of ingredients available and the sophisticated composition of modern rations it is becoming next to impossible to make the calculations manually, and the whole operation is increasingly being done by computer. (If tapioca today is a few pence cheaper than yesterday and if this information, when fed into the computer, gives an overall cost reduction over an alternative substance, then the tapioca gets preference.)

## Growth Promoters

*Antibiotics.* Most people probably think of antibiotics as being used in medicine, both human and veterinary, in the fight against disease. They are derived from moulds and other micro-organisms which are able either to destroy or seriously impair the activity of harmful parasitic micro-organisms. However, it has been discovered that antibiotics, added to feed, can increase the growth-rate of most young animals. What probably happens is that the antibiotics kill any harmful bacteria that might otherwise produce mild infections which the stockman wouldn't notice. Alternatively, they might destroy organisms in the gut which compete with the animal for the food.

Throughout the 1950s and early 1960s antibiotics such as penicillin, chlortetracycline, oxytetracycline and tylosin were routinely added to the diet of chickens and calves, especially veal calves. After a while, though, the effect appeared to wear off and it became apparent that the disease bacteria were becoming resistant. As a result a Royal Commission was set up to investigate the use of antibiotics in animal husbandry and the Swann Report, published in 1969, banned the use of all the antibiotics mentioned previously, together with any that might have a use in human medicine.

That the concern was justified is demonstrated by a survey

showing that more than 70 per cent of all strains of staphylo-cocci in hospital patients are now resistant to penicillin. The problem is that resistance can be carried over from one bacterial species to another, a phenomenon known as 'Trans-ferred Drug Resistance', and resistance can be developed extremely rapidly. For instance, a bacterial strain can become 1,000 times more resistant to streptomycin (the primary drug used in treating tuberculosis) in as short a time as twenty-four hours. This resistance is permanent.

Nevertheless, certain antibiotics are still allowed to be added routinely to animal foods. Examples include zinc bacitracin, virginiamycin, flavomycin, and moenomycin. (It should be stated that this applies only to the feeding of young animals. If antibiotics are fed to adult beasts, particularly ruminants, which rely on a complex interaction between micro-organisms in the gut, it is tantamount to giving them a disease and in some cases can be extremely serious. Consequently, antibiotics are not put into feed which is destined for mature and breeding animals.)

*Hormones and anabolic steroids.* In the same way that scientific discoveries about the ability of antibiotics to increase liveweight gain led to their use in feeding stuffs, so further understanding of the role of hormones in the animal, together with the ability to synthesize some of them, led to a similar use, or perhaps one should say misuse.

Natural hormones are secreted by various glands and travel via the bloodstream to different parts of the body, where they affect, amongst other things, developing muscle tissue. Other hormones which have specific effects, such as the thryoid hormone, thyroxine, or those hormones which affect sexual development, such as oestrogen and progesterone, also encourage the animal to put on weight. Thyroxine is given to promote milk yields of dairy cows and to get more wool from sheep; progesterones are given to control the oestrus cycle in sheep, pigs and cattle (in other words they are 'put on the Pill'), and the egg-laying cycle in poultry.

Again, as for antibiotics, after a period of generally accepted use those in authority began to have second thoughts, as resi-dues started to show up in the flesh and the implications for

human health began to take preference over financial considerations. A ban on certain substances followed, together with
recommended withdrawal periods covering the time
approaching slaughter, in an attempt to reduce residue levels.
The problem is that although synthetic substances may be
identified in the flesh it is not so easy to prove that regulations
have been infringed when naturally occurring hormones are
involved.

Anabolic steroids, which are also added to feed, are similar
in their action to hormones, and in fact both possess the useful
characteristic, as far as the farmer is concerned, of encouraging
the growth of muscle tissue at the expense of fatty tissue. In
other words they promote lean rather than fatty meat.

Hormones need not be given purely in the feed – many are
injected into the animal or implanted as pellets under the
skin, the favourite place being just behind the ear. The more
commonly used products in the UK are Finaplix (trenbolone
acetate), Ralgro (zeranol) and Compudose (oestradiol).

However, in February 1986, the EEC, in response to
consumer pressure throughout Europe, decided to prohibit the
use of growth promoting hormones in livestock. Michael
Jopling, the British Minister of Agriculture, initially opposed
the measure which will nevertheless come into force in January
1988.

A number of commentators have also drawn attention to the
black market in hormones and antibiotics which is likely to
get larger still when the ban takes effect. The Pharmaceutical
Society, in a recent report,[37] claims that contraband farm drug
trafficking is a multi-million pound business. Its spokesman is
quoted as saying: ' . . . we are concerned about cases where an
unsuspecting farmer could be using products banned in the
UK. In one case we found a beef producer using illegal
promoters with no knowledge of withdrawal periods. Another
case revealed the use of antibiotics banned in the UK, but on
free sale in America.' With virtually no policing of farm drugs
it is difficult to know how the Government intends to enforce
the ban, if at all.

*Other substances.* Various other substances are used to promote
growth and of these perhaps the best known is copper, as fed

to pigs. This is added as copper sulphate, at the rate of about one kg in every tonne of feed (approximately 250 mg of copper per kg) and at this dose gives a significant improvement in food conversion, of the order of 9 per cent.

Copper is only fed to growing pigs intended for slaughter because surplus copper is stored in the liver and could poison adult stock if fed continuously. This much is already known, but it is now being discovered from research carried out in Germany that adding copper to the diet at normal doses results in the increased resistance to antibiotics of bacteria in the animal's gut. A similar phenomenon has also been observed in chickens fed with growth promoters, where salmonella bacteria artificially introduced into the birds persisted for a significantly longer period than in those not receiving growth promoters. Those farmers who keep sheep, or calves, as well as pigs face the additional hazard of copper intoxication if they graze pasture contaminated with pig droppings. Indeed in the Benelux countries there are cases of sheep having died after grazing pastures treated with copper-contaminated pig droppings.

In the USA, where much of the cattle production is of an intensive nature, the growth promoter 'Romensin', or monensin sodium, is widely used. This works by modifying the digestive system of the animal, resulting primarily in a reduction in the amount of methane produced. The energy saved can be utilized in putting on weight. Romensin is now widely incorporated into concentrated feeds in the UK, where it is often combined with other growth promoters.

This is by no means the whole story on growth promoters, since new substances are being tried all the time. Tranquillizers are sometimes given, as it appears that these aid growth. The Ministry of Agriculture, in its Bulletin No. 174 entitled 'Poultry Nutrition', lists among 'other growth promoting substances': 'organic arsenical compounds, nitrovin, quindoxin and surface active agents such as detergents including quaternary ammonium compounds (QAC). . . . These substances have no known nutritive value but possess an anti-bacterial activity. Their mode of action is probably similar to that of the antibiotics.'

## Prophylactic Additives

Antibiotics are given not only as growth promoters but also to counter potential, as well as actual, diseases. Some of these are only available on veterinary prescription but a good number may be freely administered by the farmer. Then there are anti-fungal and anti-protozoal compounds such as nitrofurans, sulphonamides, arsenicals and quinolines. Anthelmintics control infection brought about by the presence of parasitic worms, particularly in the stomach and intestines of cattle. Turkeys are routinely given 'Emtryl', 'Salfuride' or other anti-blackhead drugs, whilst coccidiosis of chickens is guarded against by feeding the birds 'Amprolium', 'Coyden' or any of the many alternative coccidiostats.

## Mineral Additives

Minerals are usually added to the diet to counter any deficiencies which might otherwise occur if the animal were given the feed alone, and so reduce the risk of actual deficiency diseases.

Calcium is often present at high levels in compound feeds, as limestone, bone flour, or di-calcium phosphate. Problems can arise, though, if the animals are put out on to heavily limed or alkaline soils, since the extra calcium in the feed can make trace elements such as zinc, manganese, iodine and cobalt unavailable. Zinc is added to pig diets high in maize and soya bean to prevent parakeratosis. Magnesium is added to cattle feeds to guard against deficiency. The recommended daily intake is 56 grams of calcined magnesite.

Sodium carbonate is used to counter excess acidity in the rumen of cattle. It perhaps ought to be added that under natural conditions acidosis is a complaint which rarely occurs. The same could be said for a good number of other diseases and disorders which arise under intensive conditions.

## Antioxidants

To prevent the destruction of vitamins A and E and the formation of unpalatable, rancid-tasting substances during storage, antioxidants are often added to feeds rich in fats. High fat (high-energy) feeds are given to certain classes of pigs and poultry. The antioxidants used include butylated hydroxy-toluene, butylated hydroxy-anisole and ethoxyquin.

## Binders

Various additives whose purpose is to change the physical properties of the feed may be put into compounded feeds. They are required, for instance, if pellets or 'nuts' are being manufactured, primarily to hold the food in the desired shape. Lignosulphates are the chemicals which most effectively do this, 'Durabond' and 'Wafolin' being the brand leaders. Dried clay may also be used.

## Colourings, Flavourings and Spices

Strong-smelling, or sweet-tasting, substances such as fenugreek, aniseed, honey or caramel are often added to animal feeding stuffs. The theory is that the food is made more palatable. Although the flavours no doubt disguise differences between old and new batches, in all probability the major effect is on the farmer who as often as not will choose between different feeds, all other things being equal, on the evidence of his 'nose'.

Putting additives in the feed for the benefit of the customer, rather than the animal, is the reasoning behind the inclusion of xanthophyll, caraphyll, beta-apo-8-carotenal and even Tartrazine (E102) in poultry diets. These are all yellow dyes which deepen the colour of battery egg yolks, which would otherwise be an insipid pale yellow.

## Contaminants

All raw materials used in animal feeds vary widely in physical and nutritional quality. Imported raw materials are often, in the words of the trade, 'liable to admixture with siliceous material' which means that sand is put in to make up the weight. There is also the problem of pesticide contamination particularly with feedstuff coming from the Third World. Since 24 per cent of the world use of insecticides is on cotton crops, cotton-seed cake could be expected to carry residues. Products which have been in store, or transported by ship, may well have been treated with pesticides against deterioration.

## Other Additives

In addition to everything already mentioned, there are doubtless many other substances that could be added to the list. Vitamins and amino acids, especially methionine and lysine, are routinely included in compound feeds. Insecticides and fungicides may be added. Just as substances such as fenugreek are included to stimulate appetite, so appetite depressants have been formulated for reducing the ad-lib consumption of laying hens and bacon pigs. The situation is changing all the time.

## Some permitted additives in animal feed, for which no veterinary prescription is required

**Coccidiostats** (against the poultry disease coccidiosis)
Amprolium
Arpocox
Coyden
DNOT
Elancoban
Pancoxin
Stenerol

**Growth promoters**
Romensin (cattle)
Tylamix (pigs)
Fedan (pigs)
Avotan (pigs, poultry)
Eskalin (cows, pigs, poultry)
Flavomycin (cows, pigs, poultry)

Payzone (cows, pigs, poultry)
Virginiamycin (cows, pigs, poultry)
Zinc bacitracin (cows, pigs, poultry)

**Anti-blackhead drugs** (turkeys)
Emtryl
Salfuride

**Pig-disease drugs**
Dynamutilin (swine dysentery)
Nemafax (pig wormer)

## Typical Diets

The following is a summary of the typical concentrate diets which are fed to livestock. It is included to enable you to ask the right questions when tackling a farmer who offers meat and dairy products which, whilst not carrying an organic symbol, are sold as 'additive free' or 'naturally raised'. Ask to see some of the bags of feed he uses and check the labels. Remember, information is the key to consumer strength.

## Cattle

*Cattle feed* (adults and breeding animals) – will usually contain mineral additives such as calcined magnesite or di-calcium phosphate. No antibiotic or other growth promoters are likely to be included but in the case of beef cattle feed the non-hormone substance Romensin could well have been used.

*Calf powders* – are fed after the first four or five days as replacements for milk. They will usually contain vitamins and minerals, trace elements and a growth promoter such as Eskalin.

*Calf feeds* – follow on from powders. They will almost certainly contain a growth promoter such as Payzone.

## Pigs

*Sow feeds* – will contain vitamins and minerals but not growth promoters.

*Piglet feeds* – so-called 'creep' pellets are fed after weaning from two to three weeks old onwards. They will usually contain growth promoters in the form of copper sulphate and an antibiotic such as flavomycin. At about eight weeks piglets move on to 'finisher' rations which will also contain copper plus another growth-promoting substance.

## Sheep

*Ewes* – the diet will have been fortified with calcined magnesite, plus minerals and vitamins.

*Lamb feeds* – creep pellets are fed to week-old lambs until they are put on to a coarser mix. Feeds will in all probability contain growth promoters.

## Poultry

*Layers' feeds* – laying hens will be given feed supplemented with vitamins and minerals. The feed will also have a carotene derivative added to give the egg yolk a yellow, wholesome colour, and limestone to strengthen the shell.

*Chick feeds* – will have coccidiostats added as routine. In the case of young turkeys, anti-blackhead drugs will complement the anti-coccidiosis medications. Birds ultimately destined for slaughter will receive a growth promoter such as Payzone.

# 3   CONTAMINATED FOOD?

The last few years have seen something of a revolution in the attitudes of the public at large towards the relationship between food and health. The belief that 'you are what you eat' is no longer confined to the health-obsessed few but has been taken on board by, if not the majority, certainly a large proportion of the population. No longer is health something that can be left to the doctor as someone to turn to who will patch things up. Increasingly the emphasis is being put on prevention, on taking a personal responsibility for positive health rather than being a passive recipient of disease treatment. In this, food is but part of a move toward healthier lifestyles involving more exercise, reduction in stress, eliminating smoking and so on. But whilst fitness gimmicks such as jogging, aerobics and so on may rise or fall in popularity, awareness of the links between food and disease just keeps on growing.

It seems that we might now be ready to accept the findings of Sir Robert McCarrison,[38] whose pioneering work in India during the early part of this century graphically illustrated the importance of diet in the prevention of disease. As part of his duties as Director of Nutrition Research in India he was obliged to travel extensively throughout the entire sub-continent. He noticed that the overall health of the population differed markedly from region to region. Peoples in the north such as the Hunzas and Sikhs were considerably healthier than those such as the Madrassis in the south. They lived longer, more infants survived at birth, and the number of diseases requiring surgery was much less.

Geographical and other factors apart, the key difference between these communities was the food they consumed. The Hunzas ate a diet of chapattis made from wholemeal flour, uncooked green vegetables, pulses, fresh fruit, sprouted grains, butter, fresh whole milk and, occasionally, fresh meat. On the contrary the southern races survived on a diet of largely refined foods such as white rice, little milk and dairy produce plus a few generally overcooked vegetables. Could these dietary differences be responsible for the difference in health? In a complete reversal of standard scientific practice McCarrison took these observations of life and translated them into experiments with laboratory rats.

Of the very many experiments which he undertook, all of which reinforced his hypothesis that diet is a vital, if not the most vital, factor in maintaining health, perhaps the following example is most startling.

. . . two groups of young rats, of the same age, were confined in two large cages of the same size. Everything was the same for each group except food. One group was fed on a good diet, similar to that of a Northern Indian race whose physique and health were good . . . The other was fed on a diet in common use by many people in this country; a diet consisting of white bread and margarine, tinned meat, vegetables boiled with soda, cheap tinned jam, tea, sugar and a little milk, a diet which does not contain enough milk, milk products, green leaf vegetables and whole-meal bread for proper nutrition. This is what happened. The rats fed on the good diet grew well, there was little disease amongst them and they lived happily together. Those fed on the bad diet did not grow well, many became ill and they lived unhappily together; so much so that by the sixtieth day of the experiment the stronger ones amongst them began to kill and eat the weaker, so that I had to separate them. The diseases from which they suffered were of three chief kinds – diseases of the lungs, diseases of the stomach and intestines, and diseases of the nerves; diseases from which one in every three sick persons, among the insured classes, in England and Wales, suffer.

In subsequent experiments the rats were linked to other Indian peoples by their diet. In every case the average standard of health of a given human group was faithfully mirrored in the rats.

The three factors which Sir Robert McCarrison considered essential to the production of what he called perfectly constituted food were: (1) Food should be grown on a healthy soil. (2) Food should be eaten whole. (3) Food should be eaten fresh. Only by adopting organic farming methods, therefore, is it possible to follow McCarrison's advice.

Trying to steer a sensible route through the maze of often conflicting dietary advice can be a daunting task. Should we eat sugar? Is margarine better for us than butter? Should we cut down on salt? Is meat bad for us, or ought we to eat white flesh rather than red meat? What about fish taken from waters polluted by chemical wastes or radioactivity? The list is endless. For every authority calling for a curb on this or that there is a counter voice, usually from the industry concerned, assuring us that all is well and that the fears are groundless.

The problem is that more often than not we just don't have the scientific information on which to make a reasoned judgment. Either the work has not been done, or else there is conflicting evidence. It is notoriously difficult to set up clinical trials where food is involved. Furthermore, it is very expensive and often can only be afforded by government agencies, or else by companies who have a vested interest in the end result. As a general rule a check on who is behind a particular pronouncer of dietary views will help to put them into perspective.

Regrettably there has been very little serious nutritional study done to date. Until recently nutrition barely figured in the medical syllabus for the training of GPs. As far as the Government is concerned, all is well provided we all have enough calories and eat enough protein each day to ensure a rising average height and weight. It is hardly surprising that ambitious doctors and scientists turn to more glamorous fields of study. This is slowly beginning to change but for the time being one can do no better than apply one's own common sense to the practical interpretation of advice such as McCarrison's.

Take, for instance, the controversy over whether or not to eat animal fat. Of the many millions of words that have been expended on the subject the overwhelming view expressed favours a reduction in hard saturated animal fats which are said to be harmful. We should not eat butter; instead we should eat margarine made from soft unsaturated vegetable oils. This flies in the face of McCarrison, for surely a natural product such as meat or butter must be preferable to manufactured substitutes such as TVP or margarine. Certainly, the bulk of the evidence would appear to support the argument for greatly reducing consumption of animal products. Yet what exactly are we referring to?

As has been mentioned earlier, the vast majority of livestock is kept under intensive conditions. A typical modern carcase may contain 25–30 per cent fat and only 50–55 per cent lean. This fat runs throughout the meat. On the other hand, a cow free to select its own food and range over the land has been shown to have only 3.9 per cent of carcase fat and a lean tissue mass of 79 per cent.[39] Furthermore, the tendency is for the fat to be concentrated in an outer layer which can be cut off. This enormous difference in the proportion of fat to lean inevitably invites speculation as to whether it is not modern farming methods which are causing the problems, rather than there being anything intrinsically unhealthy about meat itself.

## Food: Additives and Contaminants

At last, it would seem, food additives are on the retreat. The steady advance throughout the sixties and seventies of a food industry which had been progressively adulterating our food has been forced to a halt. That a food giant such as Birds Eye has to announce that it will no longer be using artificial colourings and preservatives in its products, indicates the depth of consumer resistance. We have suddenly woken up to what is going on. As things stand, a manufacturer is free to choose from any of several thousand chemicals to put into the food we eat, usually for no better reason than that it suits the manufacturing and distribution process.

I do not intend to get involved here in the argument against the use of food additives – the colourings, flavourings, antioxidants, emulsifiers and other substances that are routinely added to food by the processors once it arrives at the factory. Much has been written elsewhere, indeed there has been such a volume of literature on the subject as to make it nearly a full-time job just to keep abreast of all that has been published.

Instead, let us look at what might be termed contaminants. These are the undesirable by-products of farming methods which leave the farm either within or on the food. Examples include bacterial and hormone residues in meat, nitrates in vegetables and pesticide residues in crops. For anyone who has, say, gone to the trouble of buying a loaf made from 100 per cent wholemeal flour it is rather disquieting to realize that the fungicide and insecticide dressings used to prevent attack from moulds and insects in store are still there in the bread, whereas with a white loaf the outer husk would have been milled away. The next stage in consumer awareness is recognition of undesirable inputs into the farming process, and with it a move towards organic farming methods every bit as strong as the campaign against food additives.

## Pesticides

Early in 1986 The London Food Commission published a report[40] in which it claimed that at least 92 pesticides which have been cleared for use in Britain are capable of causing cancer, birth defects or genetic damage in humans. A whole series of measures designed to tighten up the approval system and use of pesticides in the field were proposed.

Hot on its heels came the official Government report of the Working Party on Pesticide Residues (1982–85).[41] It concluded that there is nothing to worry about: 'The surveillance of groups of staple foods and other components of the diet has provided a reassuring picture. The levels of organochlorine compounds in the average UK diet have declined over the past two decades.

Consistent with this, the residue concentrations of many organochlorine compounds in fat and milk from consumers have continued to decline. Residues of other pesticides were found infrequently in the average UK diet.'

Who are we to trust? Is there really nothing to worry about as the Ministry would have us believe? Is the report from The London Food Commission yet another example of scurrilous scaremongering?

The claims made by the Commission were based on a preliminary trawl through published toxicity data and some 52 references are cited. Much of this work would have been based on animal testing with all the inherent problems of extrapolating the results of such trials in order to estimate the effect on human health. It is clearly not in the interests of pesticide manufacturers to release information that might be damaging to their products, and what limited published research is available usually comes from often underfunded, independent sources. The major body of toxicological data is in fact supplied to the Ministry by manufacturers as part of the Pesticide Safety Precautions Scheme but this is covered by the Official Secrets Act. Even access by serious researchers to the toxicity studies alone, with formulation details remaining secret, has been denied. In any event, one has to question whether short-term laboratory testing could ever accurately reflect the impact of a compound when released into the environment.

Just occasionally a major scandal occurs which casts a cloud over the whole issue of the safety testing of pesticides. In the late 1970s it was discovered that scientists working for International Bio Test of Illinois, a major independent company, had rigged the data from animal tests. More than 100 pesticides and drugs had received clearance for use based on faulty evidence. Animals which had died during the tests were simply thrown away and fresh animals substituted. Although three of the top administrators were finally jailed, all of the suspect chemicals continued to be marketed during the safety review which followed the fraud.

The main plank of the Government Working Party's pesticide study was a Total Diet Survey which involved sampling a range of typical foods which constitute the average UK diet as defined by the National Food Survey. All nine organochlorine pesticides (for example DDT and dieldrin) showed a decline since the last survey in 1975–77. There was little evidence of contamination by organophosphorous pesticides (for example malathion). The main fault with this study would appear to be in the small number of samples. Only 24 Total Diet Samples of each food group were taken throughout the three-year period, and there were a large number of approved pesticides for which no analysis at all was made. Such a survey would also fail to identify localized serious contamination, as in the case of the acute poisoning of over 1,350 people in America in the summer of 1985 from eating watermelons contaminated with Aldicarb. There is also the problem of those whose diet does not conform to the average, such as vegetarians who would inevitably consume a higher proportion of vegetables and fruit – a major target for insecticide use – than most.

Another part of the Government report looks at the levels of organochlorine residues in body fat. These were taken from 187 dead people aged five and upwards. All had residues of all compounds tested, although again the figures were lower than in the previous survey. Apart from pp'DDE (a breakdown product of DDT), all values were less than 1 milligram of residue per kilogram of body fat. However, the levels of pesticide in four samples from infants aged from 5 days to 3 months were almost the same as for those of the adults, suggesting that their body load could have been derived from their mother's milk.

A small survey of pesticide residues in breast milk drawn from one region of Scotland, confirmed that organochlorine compounds were being passed on to infants via this channel. Indeed, tucked away in Appendix 1 of the Report is the admission, not even mentioned in the Conclusions, that ' . . . the levels of organochlorines in the milk sampled were such that intakes by breast-fed infants would exceed adult intakes from average diets, and would exceed the World Health Organisation (WHO) recommended acceptable daily intakes (ADIs) which have been set for pp'DDE, pp'DDT and Dieldrin'. Whether or not the Scottish sample is typical of Britain as a whole is not known for the analysis has not been carried out elsewhere.

# How Safe Is Safe?

The whole question of what constitutes an 'acceptable daily intake' is extremely difficult to assess. The definition employed by the Government is, 'the amount of a chemical which can be consumed every day for an individual's entire lifetime in the practical certainty, *on the basis of all known facts* [my emphasis], that no harm will result'! Generally speaking the WHO figures are arrived at from animal studies taking an arbitrary safety factor of 100. Almost invariably safety figures have been revised downwards in the light of new experience, suggesting that original figures were set too high.

An illuminating example in this respect is afforded by the PBB disaster in Michigan in the mid-seventies. In 1973 a consignment of cattle feed was accidentally contaminated with polybrominated biphenyl, PBB, a chemical used as a fire retardant. Some cattle received enormous doses and suffered immediate and acute poisoning. As a result of this contamination a maximum residue level of PBB of 1 p.p.m. (part per million) was set by the US Food and Drugs Administration. As more evidence accumulated it was realized that this level had been set too high for safety and it was reduced to 0.3 p.p.m. in November 1974. It must be said that this figure was influenced to an extent by the analytical limits of the measuring apparatus, and the amount of compensation to be paid to farmers. By 1977 the level was reduced still further by a factor of 15 to 0.02 p.p.m., overruling the recommendations of a technical panel which had proposed zero limit, or in the absence of this, a level of 0.001 p.p.m. Joyce Egginton, in her book *Bitter Harvest*,[42] traces the course of the disaster in which over 35,000 cattle were ultimately slaughtered and nine million people contaminated. How many of the conditions reported to doctors such as dizziness, nausea, bronchitis, aching joints, etc., were in fact due to low-level PBB poisoning will never be known.

The whole question of the impact on our long-term health of the sort of levels of pesticides which the Government finds so reassuring has not even begun to be adequately researched. In Britain a few doctors such as Dr Jean Monro of Sunbury Hill Clinic have started to draw attention to food intolerance and hypersensitivity as a result of exposure to pesticide contamination, but Dr Monro's is very much a lone voice at present.

In the USA Dr John Laseter and Dr William Rea[43] at the Environmental Health Centre, Dallas, Texas tested 200 patients for the presence of pesticides in their blood. Only two patients were entirely free and most had between three and four pesticide compounds in their bloodstream. In the view of Laseter and Rea there is a link between pesticides in the blood and the patient's condition, be it a behavioural disorder or a disorder of the immune system. The pesticides most frequently found were Hexachlorobenzene (HCB), DDT, Heptachlor epoxide, Endosulfan, Dieldrin and Chlordane. The most frequent, or typical, symptoms that they found to be associated with these substances were headaches, tremor, malaise, lassitude, low energy, muscle weakness, depression, anxiety, poor memory, loss of co-ordination, eating disturbances, dermatitis, convulsions and gastrointestinal disturbances.

Of 3,000 patients who attended Dr Monro's allergy clinic almost one-sixth complained that crop sprays or pesticides adversely affect them.[44] These patients are now being routinely tested for pesticide levels in their blood. One patient, for instance, who was found to have an extremely high level of DDE, had recently given birth to a severely congenitally handicapped and mentally retarded child.[44]

The Government Working Party's survey of food bought in shops revealed 184 out of the 648 samples of home-grown produce and over half of the 1,001 samples of imported produce to contain detectable levels of pesticide. It is true that these levels were low, being measured in millionths of a gram. Yet we expect modern chemical drugs to be effective at these same concentrations, so who is to say that pesticides at these levels do not also have an effect? Hypersensitive patients may be the modern-day equivalent of canaries down the mines, warning us of the dangers we face from eating pesticide-contaminated food.

## Do Pesticides Make You Fat?

In Chapter 1 we looked at some of the effects of biocides on wildlife. A group of animals particularly at risk are those which are exposed to pesticides during hibernation when fat containing these chemicals is broken down. It has long been recognized that pesticides taken in by humans are also stored in body fat. Indeed there can be few of us who do not register at least one or two pesticides in our body fat.

As fat is broken down, for whatever reason, these pesticides will be released into our bloodstream and will be dealt with by the usual processes for eliminating waste products. The problem arises where excessive amounts of fat are mobilized. This happens if a person is suffering from a wasting disease, or alternatively if a crash diet is embarked upon. The subsequent liberation of pesticides into the blood could then prove to be dangerous.

Now two authors have suggested that one of the reasons why crash diets so often fail to work may have something to do with a defence reaction by the body. Arabella Melville and Colin Johnson in their book *Persistent Fat and How to Lose It*[45] address the problem, common in dieting, whereby some people are unable to lose weight no matter how hard they try. In an intriguing theory they suggest that the body protects itself from what could be a dangerous dose of pesticides by steadfastly refusing to break down fat. The authors maintain that only by gradually changing to a wholefood organic diet and by eliminating other potentially harmful substances from their environment will dieters lose weight.

## Direct Health Hazards from Pesticides

So far we have considered only pesticides which get into our bodies via our food. The other route is via the air we breathe. You don't have to live in the country in order to come into contact with pesticide-laden air. The fine droplets which come out of a sprayer, whether it be from the air or the ground, can be carried on the wind far from the point of application. Of course the problem is far worse for those whose employment brings them into direct contact with pesticides.

According to the Agriculture Select Committee of the House of Commons[46] at least 4,000 people in Britain suffer acute poisoning from pesticides every year. Even this may be an underestimate according to Dr Virginia Murray of the National

Poisons Unit of the NHS, who believes that the true figure is very much higher because many poisonings go unreported.

In 1986, three unions representing workers in agriculture, forestry, local government and pest control sent out questionnaires to thousands of their members seeking detailed evidence to support complaints about skin disorders, headaches, dizziness and fear of cancer. Their replies, when collated, are likely to bring into sharp focus the true extent of pesticide poisoning.

Within agriculture as a whole there are relatively high death rates from leukaemia and diabetes. Wives in particular seem prone to diseases of the circulatory and respiratory systems, to diabetes and cancer of the cervix. In a report published by the Centre for Agricultural Strategy[47] some doctors are quoted as suggesting that herbicides may be involved in certain cancers, particularly when the operators are exposed to traces of many chemicals over a long period of time. A major investigation of death records for the years 1957–74 in the agricultural state of Nebraska, USA showed a much higher risk of mortality from leukaemia for farmers than for any other occupational group.[48] Farmers from counties where use of pesticides and fertilizers was heaviest tended to be at higher risk of contracting types of leukaemia than those from counties where less of these inputs was used.

In Britain an analysis of the health records of children born to agricultural workers, gardeners and groundsmen in England and Wales between 1974 and 1979 revealed above average rates of birth defects, especially in respect of cleft palates.[44].

## Circle of Poison

Whilst pesticide poisonings in Britain are sufficient cause for concern the situation worldwide is very much worse. Although Bhopal-type tragedies make the headlines, every day hundreds of people are routinely poisoned by pesticides. In 1972 the World Health Organisation conservatively estimated that half a million people were accidentally poisoned by pesticides each year, and of these some 9,000 or so died.[7] More than half of these casualties occur in the Third World.

Faced with increasing restrictions on sales of pesticides in the developed world, the multinational pesticide companies have reacted by exporting banned chemicals to the developing nations. Here they are used by an often illiterate labour force, unable to read the instructions on the labels. Spraying doses are frequently exceeded and scant regard is paid to operator safety. Protective clothing is hardly ever worn.

It is scarcely surprising that high pesticide residue levels occur in meat, cotton, coffee, bananas, rice and other major cash crops which account for the vast majority of all Third World sprays. These are usually meant for export. Hence the circle of poison, whereby substances banned as unsafe in the West are exported to the Third World and re-imported via the food we eat.[49]

## Nitrates

The problem of nitrate contamination of water supplies was touched upon in Chapter 1. Already levels exceed the maximum level as laid down by the EEC and would seem set to go higher still. What is perhaps less widely known is that most of the nitrate which enters our bodies does so in the food we eat rather than in our drinking water. In fact some four-fifths of total nitrate arrives by this route. Of this the nitrate in vegetables exceeds the total for all other food sources.[18] The question is, are nitrates harmful?

Apart from the risk of blue baby syndrome mentioned earlier there is a possible risk of stomach cancer. Basically nitrates, once ingested, are changed into nitrites. Nitrites can react with substances called secondary and tertiary amines to form nitrosamines which are known cancer-producing agents. Although each of these links has been demonstrated, and stomach cancers have been produced in laboratory animals, there is as yet no firm evidence for this happening in humans. Nevertheless, the potential is such that many authorities feel that a dramatic reduction in nitrate intake for humans is necessary.[50]

Some European governments, notably Switzerland and Austria, have made proposals for maximum tolerated nitrate levels in vegetables of between 2,500 and 3,000 p.p.m. Figures from Switzerland indicate a particular problem with salad crops grown over the winter and with those varieties that are bred to respond to nitrogen fertilizers. Average values of 2,700 p.p.m. of nitrate in head lettuce are not uncommon. This would mean that a 4 oz (100 gm) lettuce would supply 270 mg of nitrate, which exceeds the maximum daily intake of 255 mg of nitrate as laid down by the World Health Organisation for a person weighing 11 stone (70 kg). In the view of Dr H. Vogtmann of Kassel University, West Germany, nitrate levels in head lettuces grown during the winter are such that they should not be eaten, or if so the heart, which concentrates the nitrate, should be discarded.[50]

A further complication occurs where crops have been treated with any of the dithiocarbamate (DTC) sprays against fungal diseases. Nitrites are capable of reacting with the breakdown products of these sprays in the stomach to form powerful cancer-producing chemicals. This is but one example of the potential for damaging reactions brought about by the chemical cocktail of pesticide residues, food additives and other non-food substances in our bodies.

## Growth Promoters

It is a regrettable but true indication of human complacency that it takes a story such as the Milan meat scandal to jolt us into action. In 1980 mothers of young children aged six and under were horrified to notice their sons growing breasts and their daughters showing premature sexual development. The cause was traced to meat from veal calves which had received a high dose of diethylstilboestrol (DES), a hormone used to speed up the natural growth pattern. In Puerto Rico more than 1,000 children have suffered a similar fate as a result of farmers using DES and/or similar growth promoters.

It is as a result of such stories that the EEC has, from January 1988, banned the use of hormones in agriculture – against, it should be added, the wishes of the Ministry of Agriculture. Mr Michael Jopling, the Minister concerned, was the sole European representative to vote against the ban.

As usual we have been reassured that growth promoters, if used correctly, do no harm. The point is that it is almost impossible to monitor what the farmer is doing down on the farm. The temptation to overuse antibiotics and hormones in order to cash in on a quick liveweight gain must seem irresistible.

Such overuse means a bigger risk of excessive levels of these drugs ending up in the meat, and dairy produce, we eat. Organs such as the kidney and liver are likely to be most heavily contaminated. Only lamb can be expected to be relatively free from growth promoter residues.

## What Else?

In a book this size only a brief mention can be made of some of the contaminants which might be found in the food we eat. Nothing has been said of the veterinary products which are necessary to prop up a system of animal husbandry that puts so much stress on the livestock that they require almost continuous medication. Nor of the presence of organisms such as salmonella bacteria which are so prevalent now in factory-farmed chickens, and which are one of the commonest causes of food poisoning in Britain today.

The real worry to my mind, though, is the long-term health effect of taking in toxic substances, albeit in small quantities, such as pesticides and nitrates. Nobody can say with a clear conscience that they are harmless. We have much to learn, and we just do not know what the long-term consequences will be. In this respect we are all guinea pigs in a massive toxicological experiment.

Fears about the risks they may be running are one of the main reasons why more and more people are turning to organic foods. The next part of the book will look at exactly what is meant by organic farming and the food that derives from such methods.

# PART II

## ORGANIC FARMING – THE BIOLOGICAL ALTERNATIVE

## 4  WHAT IS ORGANIC FARMING?

Ask anyone what they understand by the term organic farming and the answer you are likely to get will be something to the effect that no chemicals are used. Press a little harder and this might be amplified to include the rejection of pesticide sprays and artificial fertilizers. This is usually seen as being a 'good thing' in theory, but in practice of course we must have fertilizers and sprays, despite all the harmful side-effects, because otherwise we wouldn't be able to feed ourselves. The view that agrochemicals are vital to efficient food production is assiduously, and to a large extent successfully, promoted by fertilizer and pesticide manufacturers, aided by the Ministry and the agricultural establishment.

My aim in this part of the book, now that I have pointed out the negative effects of modern agricultural practices, is to demonstrate that organic farming is a viable method of producing food. Indeed, I would go as far as to say that only an agricultural system based on organic methods can take us forward into the twenty-first century and beyond. Conventional farming methods are just not sustainable either in terms of the pollution and destruction of the natural environment or in their wasteful use of resources.

It is easy to forget that until this century almost all farms operated a system which could be termed organic, and that the wholesale revolution that has affected British agriculture is largely a post-World War II phenomenon. So it is rather amusing to be dismissed by disciples of modern chemical methods as having an untried 'muck and magic' philosophy, for it is the proponents of the organic approach who have the historical pedigree, not they. This is not to say that we wish to turn the clock back. Rather, we take as our basis the wisdom accumulated over the centuries and graft on to it selected modern techniques of biological pest control and of non-chemical weed control, and use of disease-resisting plant varieties and modern equipment. Uppermost in our minds is the need to develop an agriculture which works with Nature rather than against her.

So, what are the main points that distinguish organic farming from its conventional chemical counterpart? No artificial fertilizers are used. Nor are any of the modern synthetic sprays, although some traditional pesticides are permitted. Livestock are kept under as natural conditions as possible – battery houses are not permitted – and feed additives are banned. Instead of relying on chemicals, organic farmers concentrate on building up healthy soils through the use of compost, animal manures, clovers and deep-rooting herbs. Plants grown on such soils are better able to withstand diseases, which in turn are discouraged through the use of crop rotations.

In short, organic farming doesn't mean abandoning chemicals and doing nothing. On the contrary it is all about building up a thriving living soil in which, and from which, a dynamic balance between harmful and beneficial organisms emerges, leading to the growth of strong, health-giving crops.

## How Are Pests and Diseases Controlled?

The late Sam Mayall used to tell a story about an occasion on which he was conducting a group of scientists on a tour around his farm. At one point a couple detached themselves from the main party, only to reappear at the latter end of the walk.

When asked to account for their absence they replied that they had been looking for pests. 'And did you find any?' asked Sam. 'Oh yes,' replied the scientists, 'but they didn't seem to be doing any harm.' When questioned, Sam pointed out that his aim was to support a wide range of pests on his land, but at levels at which they would do no appreciable damage. How is this achieved?

Many farmers in the process of converting from chemical-based to organically based regimes notice that as their soils improve so does the ability of the crops to withstand attack from pests and diseases. Exactly why this should be so is as yet not understood, but recognition that the phenomenon occurs is at the heart of the organic approach to the problem.

In an unsprayed environment there will, of course, be a natural build-up of beneficial creatures. These can include insects such as ladybirds, hoverflies, lacewings, a large number of parasitic wasps, predatory ground beetles and other species too numerous to mention. Other animals such as frogs, toads, hedgehogs and birds all exert a useful controlling effect on the pests.

Then there is the use of introduced biological controls. These are specific organisms which attack only the pest or disease in question and so avoid one of the chief problems of pesticides – their lack of selectivity. Most biological controls have been developed for use in greenhouses, as for example the parasitic wasp Encarsia formosa which attacks whitefly, or the predatory mite Phytosieulus persimilis which keeps the red spider mite under control. In both cases these insects are introduced with the aim, not of eliminating the pests, but of maintaining a balance between pest and prey such that no economic damage is done to the crop. To this end growers often introduce the *pests* into greenhouses early on in the season to give the predators something to feed on.

Outside, there is now a natural bacterial control for cabbage white and other caterpillars. A parasitic fungus has also been developed which will cure silver leaf disease of fruit trees and which has an effect against Dutch Elm Disease.

More and more conventional growers are turning to biological controls as a way of dealing with pests that are rapidly becoming resistant to pesticides. Using biological controls demands a more sophisticated approach to pest control than that of the 'If it's Tuesday, let's spray 'em' brigade, but in the end it is far more effective.

This is not to say that organic growers have all the answers. There are quite a number of problem areas which have to be addressed. Some farmers respond to the knowledge that pests will do some damage by simply sowing seed at a higher rate than average and accepting the loss.

## Crop Rotations and Weed Control

When modern farmers complain that they could not farm without the use of pesticides, the problem that worries them most is weeds. More weedkillers are used than all other pesticidal products put together. Of the 29.6 million kilograms of pesticides used in Britain in 1984, over 19 million kilos were classified as herbicides.[6]

You may wonder, since weedkillers have only been with us on any scale for the last three decades, how farmers managed without them. The answer is they practised crop rotations. It is a biological fact of life that if you keep on growing the same crop on the same land year after year, not only will you build up pests and diseases but you will also encourage weeds that compete with the crop. Our ancestors coped with this circumstance by moving their crops around the farm so that diseases, weeds and pests did not get a chance to build up in the soil. However, under our modern scientific chemical agriculture, farmers are encouraged to dispose of crop rotations and to deal with the resultant weed and fungal problems by drenching the crops with chemicals instead.

It would not be appropriate here to go into technical details about the type of crop rotations that organic farmers use. The basic principle, however, is to have the land part of the time under grass and the rest of the time under cereals such as wheat and barley. The time spent under grass, where it is grazed by cattle or sheep, is used to build up soil fertility. Usually after three or four years the grass is ploughed up and the resultant fertility is 'cashed in' to grow cereals for a couple of years. Then it is back to grass again.

Crop rotations apart, the other key techniques in the struggle against weeds mainly involve mechanical cultivations. At the simplest level this means hand hoeing. This is just not practicable for a farmer with a large acreage, who instead might take advantage of some of the new equipment that is being developed, particularly on the Continent. A spring-tined cultivator, for example, can be towed behind a tractor through a field of wheat to pull out any weeds that might be competing with the crop.

Flame weeding also finds favour with some growers. Timing is all-important. Though seed is sown into a prepared seedbed, inevitably weeds germinate first so that there may already be a light green covering of weed growth before the crop emerges. The grower, however, knows how long it takes for each seed to germinate and appear. A day or so earlier he drives over with his tractor pulling a device which lightly scorches the weeds – not enough to incincerate the leaves but enough to burst the plant cell walls and kill them. The crop can then emerge into a completely clear seedbed which may give it sufficient advantage to outgrow the weeds completely.

## Doing without Fertilizers

Organic farming is mixed farming. It involves a blend of animal and crop enterprises that are mutually dependent. Manure from the livestock is returned to the land, either directly by the grazing animals or indirectly as strawy compost or treated farm slurry. This is the basis for the improvement of soil fertility which enables crops to be grown without the use of artificial fertilizers. The same reliance on animal manure obliges organic market gardeners, who don't have the acreage to keep livestock, to import manure and other animal by-products from outside.

Attempts have been made to try and farm organically without livestock by making use of the nitrogen-fixing potential of clover, peas and beans. If successful this might make it possible for the many continuous cereal farmers we have in Britain today to grow organic crops. However, the results so far have not been especially encouraging and to my mind the very idea goes against the basic principles of organic farming. Sir Albert Howard, one of the pioneers of organic methods, commented that in his experience crops grown with manure-free compost did not possess the same pest- and disease-resisting qualities. For him animal manure was an absolute essential.

This is not to say that clovers and the like do not have a place in organic practice. On the contrary, farmers rely very heavily on the abilities of clovers and legumes to provide nitrogen whilst other plants, especially deep-rooting herbs, are used to exploit the vast amounts of minerals that are available in the subsoils of most British land. It is just that a holistic approach to fertility-building requires both animals and plants.

One of the regrettable side-effects of our industrial society has been that human sewage is no longer readily available for use in agriculture. The Chinese have maintained systems of farming for over 4,000 years in which a key element has been the recycling of human waste. Indeed it has been estimated that if all sewage were combined with household rubbish, then some 5.5 million tons of compost would be available for use.[21]

As it is, the sewage sludge cannot be used because of the lead and cadmium content, derived from vehicle emissions washing into the drains together with the discharges from various industrial processes. Consequently almost all of this huge reserve of nutrients is lost to tipping either on land, in rivers or at sea. Only a small proportion is returned to agriculture as liquid tanker waste and even in this highly diluted form it has to be carefully monitored to prevent excess metals from accumulating in the soil.

Household rubbish, collected at great expense from our homes, instead of being screened and recycled, is either burned or tipped. A policy of segregating difference types of waste at source, sifting out recyclable elements at a collection centre and composting all the decayable material with sewage sludge to produce a valuable fertilizer would be a great step forward in the move to a sustainable society. At present there is to my knowledge only one municipal composting plant operating in Britain.

Other fertilizers, used by organic growers, include animal by-products such as hoof and horn, bonemeal and dried blood, plant by-products such as straw and vegetable wastes, seaweed meals and some mineral fertilizers. Gypsum, limestone, ground chalk, dolomite, rock potash and granite dust are all examples of minerals that might be used. When using fertilizers such as these the main consideration is whether or not the soil is improved by their addition, for it is a basic tenet of organic growing that plants should be fed indirectly through the agency of the soil rather than directly, as happens with artificial fertilizers.

## Aren't Crop Yields Lower?

This is not quite as easy a question to answer as might at first be thought. A great many factors are involved, and the ways in which comparisons are usually made tend to weight the scale against the organic farmer.

Amongst conventional growers an average value of wheat, say, produced from an acre of land for the country as a whole will hide enormous farm-to-farm variations. There are obvious regional differences such as soil, geography and climate. Crop yields can vary significantly from season to season. One farmer might choose to put on more fertilizer than his neighbour or might have more of a weed problem. A good farmer will in any event get more from the land than a less successful farmer, even if their inputs and methods are very similar, simply because of an intuitive feel for the work.

There are as yet not enough organic farms in Britain for an average yield to have much meaning and any farm-by-farm comparison is going to introduce the problems of interpretation I have indicated. Then there are other difficulties. Organic farmers usually grow wheats for bread-making whilst most conventionally grown wheat is used for animal feeds. Wheat varieties used in milling generally have a higher protein content, but lower yield, than varieties developed for stockfeed. Many modern varieties are bred to respond to high levels of fertilizers so that organic growers are at an immediate disadvantage. Even where a straight comparison of yield is possible there are further complications which will be discussed in the next chapter. Water content of organic crops is usually lower than that of their chemically grown counterparts so higher yield can often mean just more water. Keeping quality is much better with organically grown crops so a lower yield at harvest might convert to a higher yield at the end of a period of storage.

The general view to be drawn from the limited number of studies that have been undertaken so far, however, is that whilst organic production can never achieve the record yields of high input conventional farming it can frequently attain and often improve upon typical yields. Overall, many commentators accept that some yield reduction, of the order of 10 per cent, would be the price to be paid for switching to organic methods. Admittedly there is a reduction but hardly a recipe for mass starvation!

# 5   ORGANIC FOOD – IS THERE ANY DIFFERENCE?

Why are people willing to pay more for organic produce? Is it that the food tastes that much better? Or are they worried about the possible effect of pesticide and other residues on their health? Perhaps they object to factory farming methods, or the way that the countryside is being destroyed by modern farming, and wish to strike a blow for a saner agriculture?

At least in the latter case they can be sure that organic farming is better for animal welfare and the countryside in general. But are they kidding themselves about the taste? Is organic food any better for us?

Unfortunately there is not a great deal of scientific evidence on the subject, but what does exist is generally supportive of the claim that organic produce is superior to its non-organically grown equivalent.

## Nutritional Composition

One of the main findings that crops up time and again when chemically produced food is compared analytically with organic food is the higher water content in the former. It is not unusual for the dry matter content of organically grown food to be 20 per cent higher than equivalent non-organically grown food.[21] This is because fertilizer produces lusher growth which has a higher moisture content. It also means that the consumer, when buying produce by weight, is actually paying for extra water.

The best long-term experiment which has been carried out comparing vegetables grown with compost, stable manure, or artificial fertilizer undoubtedly finds in favour of the organic produce. Schuphan over a twelve-year period discovered that nutritionally valuable substances were generally higher, whilst undesirable substances were lower, in the organic produce than in the conventional produce.[51] Protein was up by an average of 18 per cent, vitamin C by 28 per cent, total sugars by 19 per cent, the amino acid methionine by 23 per cent, potassium by 18 per cent, calcium 10 per cent, and phosphorus 13 per cent. By contrast, nitrates were 93 per cent lower, free amino acids 42 per cent lower and sodium 12 per cent lower.[21]

This is extremely important scientific work, for only when crops have been grown for a number of years under organic methods do the full effects begin to show. It is unrealistic to expect much, if any, difference in crop quality, lack of residues apart, one or two years after conversion from chemical systems.

A comparison of blackcurrants grown under contrasting production systems showed a similar increase in desirable components for crops grown organically. Sugar content was up by 18 per cent, vitamin C by 5 per cent. Calcium, magnesium, phosphate, copper and iron all showed increases over the chemically grown blackcurrants.[22] Similar findings have been reported for spinach (more iron) and carrots (3.5 times as much vitamin C and 2.3 times as much carotene).[22]

Incidentally, the higher sugar levels – almost one-fifth more for organic produce – may give a clue to the generally held view that organic food tastes better. Sweetness is often one of the characteristics that people refer to. The higher water content in conventional produce would also help to explain the tastelessness which is so noticeable in much of our food, particularly fruits such as tomatoes and strawberries.

Before leaving the subject of the composition of food it is worth making the point that an analysis merely tells you the quantities of the substances you are looking for when you carry out the analysis. If you don't ask the question, an analysis won't provide the answer. It might be that organic produce contains significantly higher quantities of trace elements – those vital minerals that are essential to our health. Indeed, with conventional crops being produced from ever-depleted soils using bagged fertilizers containing only major nutrients such as nitrogen, potassium and phosphorus, it would be most unlikely if this were not the case.

Then, of course, an analysis will not tell you about the substances, or non-substances, about which at present we know nothing. This may sound pretty esoteric but we don't have to go back very far to discover a time when vitamins were not known to exist. Those who suggested such factors were present in food invited ridicule. Can we really rule out as absurd those who claim, as does the biodynamic school of agriculture, the presence of a life force in food, as in all things, which can have an important bearing on whether or not such food can sustain us, helping to keep us healthy? In other words is food more than merely an agglomeration of chemical nutrients? Time will tell.

## Keeping Quality

One of the disadvantages of a crop's having a high moisture content is that the produce is more likely to shrivel in store. Sir Albert Howard noticed that organically produced tomatoes kept much better, even in the hot climate of India, than did chemically grown fruits.[52] Other scientists have noted that organic produce stores better; for example there is a 3–5 per cent water loss for organic celery compared with 20–25 per cent for conventional celery.[21]

Organically grown potatoes, because of their better keeping qualities in store, can overcome any initial yield disparity with chemical produce. A three-year experiment in Sweden bears this out. Initial potato yields in October were just over 15 per tons an acre for conventionally grown potatoes and just under 13.5 tons an acre for biodynamically grown ones (see p. 205 for a description of the biodynamic approach). However, storage losses were 30 per cent for the conventional produce but only 12.5 per cent for the biodynamic produce, resulting in a marketable yield the following April of less than 10.5 tons an acre compared with 11.75 tons respectively.[53] The authors of the report went on to describe the better cooking characteristics of the biodynamic potatoes (less browning), higher vitamin C content (17 per cent) and better taste, as established by a tasting panel.

Another experimenter found that it was easier to grow moulds on vegetables produced using conventional methods as compared to organically grown vegetables.[54]

This difference disappeared if the vegetables were cooked. He concluded that in vegetables grown organically there is an anti-fungal factor which breaks down at high temperatures. Could this help to explain the observation, made by many organic farmers, that their plants show a better resistance to attack by fungal diseases? This same researcher reached broadly the same conclusions regarding storage losses in fresh vegetables, which varied from 45 to 60 per cent for conventional produce as compared with 30 to 35 per cent for biologically grown produce.

Clearly, it is somewhat simplistic to express differences between organically grown and conventionally grown produce purely in terms of yield at harvest without reference to water content or storage-keeping qualities.

## Pesticide and Other Residues

Let me dispel a misconception right away. There can be no such thing as guaranteed pesticide-free produce. In our polluted world air, water and soil are inevitably contaminated by pesticides so that it is just not possible to produce crops, even organically, that can be guaranteed free of pesticide residues. This is not to say that organic food does not contain considerably less pesticides, as one would expect if pesticides had not been used in the growing operation.

It would not be unreasonable to speculate that whereas between a third and a half of all fresh produce grown non-organically contains detectable levels of pesticides the figure for organically grown produce would be very much less. In fact as far as I am aware, none of the spot checks that have been carried out by trading standards officers on organic foods offered for sale has yet revealed the presence of pesticides. That lower levels of pesticide residues are to be found in the breast milk of mothers who have a high proportion of organically grown food in their diet is just one of the interesting findings of the French research worker Claude Aubert.[55]

The position with regard to nitrates is less clear. Again there is very little hard information to go on. Research carried out in Switzerland indicates that nitrate levels in summer-grown organic salad crops are approximately one-third that of those that receive artificial fertilizers. (However, if winter lettuce are compared there is virtually no difference at all.)[50] As a general rule, the higher the inorganic nitrogen level applied, the higher the level of nitrate in the crop. It can be expected that, with declining soil fertility of conventional farms being offset by increased use of fertilizers, nitrate levels will increase.

## Other Considerations

Just as there are differences in the mineral content of food grown organically as compared with food grown conventionally, so these differences also show up in fodder grown for livestock feed. Pasture fertilized with artificially derived nitrogen and potassium, whilst often high in potassium, can be so depleted of sodium, calcium and magnesium as to produce mineral deficiencies in grazing cattle. Livestock fed on biologically produced feeding stuffs require up to 15 per cent less feed than they do of the equivalent grown using chemical methods, and more often than not are more productive into the bargain.[38]

There are also indications that the way in which food is grown can affect fertility rates. In one experiment a group of bulls kept for artificial insemination were fed fodder from land which had experienced increasing amounts of fertilizers. The result – a drastic drop in semen quality over three years. By comparison, bulls fed during the summer on manured pastures had almost twice the semen quality of bulls fed on intensively fertilized pastures.[21] It is well known that dairy cattle under organic regimes generally have more lactations and are less prone to calving difficulties than intensively reared beasts.

Feeding trials with rabbits – one group fed conventionally

and the other fed with fresh organic produce – gave interesting results. Though the initial birth rate was higher for the conventionally fed rabbits (6.6 compared with 4.8 rabbits per female) the survival rate at 90 days was 3.3 compared with 3.5 rabbits per female respectively. It goes without saying that all other factors in the experiment were as near as possible identical.[22]

Whilst none of this makes for a cast-iron case in favour of organically grown produce, nonetheless the indications are favourable. It remains for much more scientific work to be done.

I will leave this section with one of my favourite stories. It concerns a TV appearance I made on Granada TV early in 1986. The subject was organic food. To illustrate the discussion a selection of fresh organic produce bought from the local supermarket had been piled up next to some chemically grown food purchased from the same source. During the course of the programme I made the usual points about pesticide residues, flavour being superior and so on in front of a somewhat disbelieving floor crew. At the end of the show, as the set was being dismantled, the most sceptical of the technicians picked up and ate one of the chemically grown tomatoes – no surprises here. Then I invited him to try one of the organic ones – he just could not believe the difference in flavour. I think that one example – he then went around the whole set telling everyone how good the organic produce was – had more effect than any amount of scientific evidence or persuasion on my part. So if you are still not convinced after reading this, why not go out and try some for yourself?

# 6 SOME PRACTICAL EXAMPLES

Most farmers are individualists. Organic farmers are no exception to this rule – perhaps they are more so, having jibbed against current orthodoxy. It is very difficult, if not impossible, to think of examples of farms which might be considered typical. Nevertheless a choice has to be made, and the following four examples have been picked to cover the main spectrum of farming activities, viz. dairying, beef and cereals, mixed, and market gardening. On reflection I have probably picked the most atypical farms, but since they are each in their own way fascinating I have decided to include them nonetheless.

## Cherry Trees Farm, Herts

Michael Bell's conversion to organic farming methods began rather suddenly and violently in an event which almost killed him. Back in 1971, as a young farm apprentice, he was given the task of standing on the back of a seed drill making sure that the barley seed which was being sown spread evenly across the hopper. Not a demanding task, perhaps, but one which

69

meant that he had to frequently dip his hand into the seeds to remove any blockages. Unbeknown to him, the seed had been dressed with an organophosphate compound which throughout the day was being steadily absorbed through his skin. By the early evening he was in a very sorry state – dizzy, nauseous and badly dehydrating. He was rushed into hospital where by a happy coincidence he was treated by a junior doctor who had been studying pesticide poisoning and who immediately recognized the symptoms. Had he not been quickly diagnosed it is unlikely that he would be alive today.

Such a traumatic event might have put anyone off farming for life, but Michael was determined to get his own farm. He began a haulage business from scratch and by working all hours he was able gradually to build up his capital. Eventually in 1976 he acquired 30 acres of land in Hertfordshire from a shipping broker. All of the dwellings on the erstwhile farm had been sold off to private individuals leaving the bulk of the farm without a farmhouse. So a pre-fabricated wooden building had to be purchased and used as a home, which is still the position today.

The next problem was how to make a living from the land. The banks advised intensive pig-rearing and were more than happy to lend the money needed to put up the buildings. Within seven years the herd had expanded to 100 sows. But all was not well. The pigs were forever suffering from meningitis and antibiotics were constantly applied to the feed. Michael admits that he would not eat the meat himself but that he was trapped by the cyclical nature of the pig business and the need to pay off the debt to the bank. He recounts a story about a woman who asked to look around the farm, saying that she loved pigs. Some minutes later he found her in tears and when pressed to explain what was wrong she said, 'How can you do this to them?'

It was about this time that Mary, who had been a family friend for many years, came into his life. She agreed to live on the farm only if the intensive pig enterprise was abandoned. 'If a piglet escaped from the pens,' she said, 'it behaved like a condemned man who has suddenly been freed – rushing around, hardly believing its good fortune. Pigs are such intelli-gent and sensitive animals, I couldn't be part of a system that treated them so barbarically.' So in the teeth of opposition from the bank, and with great uncertainty, they sold off all the pigs and began the enterprise that is Cherry Trees Farm today.

What a sight greets the eyes of a visitor to the farm. There can be scarcely another scene like it in all England. Passing up the long drive to the car park the field on the left is full of chickens. Hundreds of them clucking about pecking at the grass, milling amongst the beef cattle which help to keep the long grass down. As you pass through the farm gate a calf pokes its head out from inside a barn and a posse of black spotted piglets hurtle towards you to be scratched. In the middle distance a small flock of Dorset ewes graze another field and a huge black sow roots around amongst the dilapidated but still standing old pig buildings.

Picturesque it most certainly is, but anachronistic or uneconomic it definitely is not. The main enterprise on the farm is the free-range hen flock. Over 1,000 birds are kept, but what marks this out from other free-range hen concerns is the feedstuff. Only organically grown layers' mash is used, made up from feed wheat, fishmeal, limestone flour plus minor ingredients. The birds are all hybrids bought in at point of lay. Ex-battery birds have been tried but although they are cheap they bring the feather-pecking vice with them and can't get out of the habit even when removed from the stultifyingly boring battery conditions which cause it.

Beef cattle are reared naturally on grass, taking 2½–3 years to finish, by which time the meat has an exquisite flavour. They are just beginning to build up the pigs again, using Gloucester Old Spots, a Welsh Black and more recently a Masterboar hybrid. The piglets roam free but are able to return to their mothers, whilst the fattening is done in open straw yards. Needless to say disease is virtually non-existent and the annual veterinary bill is less than £100.

The pig muck is spread on to the land, which is used for growing barley, at the rate of about 10 tons an acre. When I visited the farm in the summer of 1986, apart from a few thistles the crop was entirely free of weeds and from the spring sowing the Bells expected at least 30 cwt an acre.

Though the farm is self-supporting a useful extra income is provided by on-farm tourism. The farm is open to the public

71

from Wednesday to Sunday, and as might be expected is proving to be very popular. A cafe on-site serves home produce and visitors are encouraged to collect their own eggs! Asked about vandalism the Bells said that though they had had parties of children from the roughest parts of inner London the only time there had been any trouble was when a group of agricultural students had engaged in an egg fight. They are keen to develop the various aspects of the farm and are sure to provide inspiration for many years to come.

## Montague Organic Gardens, Somerset

Deep in the heart of Somerset lies the little village of Shepton Montague where can be found a most remarkable system of organic growing. Montague Organic Gardens is the brainchild of Charles Dowding who organically cultivates his seven acres, surrounded by the hundreds of acres of mixed farm run by his brother, Oliver.

At present only vegetables are grown on a series of long narrow raised beds separated by walkways which are covered in straw. There is no livestock, and apart from initial cultivations no machinery is used at all – everything is done by hand. The first task when starting off new beds is to rotavate in the existing pasture during the autumn months. The soil is fairly light and the beds, which are 1.5 metres wide and 45 metres long, are shaped by hand with spades, scooping the soil from the paths. It takes about 3 hours to construct each bed, which means that an acre of beds comprising 50 beds takes some 150 hours to construct. Overall, almost 10 miles of beds have been laid down.

Once constructed, plants can be grown much closer together because there is no need to walk between the rows to harvest and without walking on the soil there is access all year round. Great use is made of mulching materials to keep down weeds, including straw, 'Hortopaper' and discarded residues, though compost heaps are also made.

Fertility is maintained through the use of imported straw, horse manure and yarded cattle manure. Charles also buys in calcified seaweed and is experimenting with the use of clovers and other legumes.

Such is the vigour of the plants grown at Montague that pests and diseases rarely cause problems. Charles refuses to use any sprays at all, including even those that are authorized under the organic standards, and instead prefers to compost any that are sickly. The worst problem is carrot root fly, though this is largely controlled through the use of crop rotations. Blackfly is sometimes a problem on the broad beans, but is eliminated by pinching out the tops of the beans. Slugs are a persistent nuisance, especially under rotting vegetation, and for this no real answer has yet been found other than replanting seedlings.

It must be said that the system requires a great deal of labour. Quite apart from the task of constructing the beds, the maintenance of some ten miles of vegetable beds takes some doing. At present Charles enlists students, usually from the Continent, who are keen to learn organic methods. He provides full board and pays £40 a week for work which in summer can mean a 5 am–5 pm day. On average there are two full-time workers during the winter months and five during the summer.

By not using fertilizers and pesticides his input costs are kept down, so that the main expenses are seeds, labour, manure and mulching materials and packaging. Since the land is family-owned there is no mortgage to worry about. The enterprise turns over approximately £5,000 an acre and yields a net income in the region of £5,000, which is not a great deal considering all the effort that goes into it.

Montague Organic Gardens is not at all typical of most organic market gardening enterprises. Indeed I can think of only one other grower using similar methods, and in his case a machine is used to actually construct the beds and lay a black polythene mulch. Most growers employ a variety of machinery and considerably less labour. Here we have an example of an ecologically sound high-yielding system of growing food which enhances the soil and environment but which, since it is heavily dependent on labour, is at odds with currently prevailing economic criteria.

# Kite's Nest Farm, Hereford and Worcestershire

The mixed farm is the basis of organic farming. Kite's Nest Farm, run by the Young family, is one of the finest examples of the successful organic farm to be found in the country today. Of its 420 acres of Cotswold hillside, approximately 170 acres are down to permanent grassland, the remainder operating on a seven-year rotation of four years of temporary grassland, followed by three years of cereals.

Whilst the land is under pasture and being grazed by the beef herd it is building up fertility, both from the animal droppings and from the organic matter in the grass and clover mixture. Compost made from the strawy farmyard manure, produced by the cattle which are brought into yards in the winter, is also spread over the grass. Consequently, when it is ploughed in after year four there is a great bank of fertility to provide the nutrients for the succeeding cereal crops. These usually comprise two years of winter-sown wheat followed by winter oats or barley.

The great delight of the farm, though, is the livestock. It supports over 200 head of animals, counting calves, followers and fattening cattle, with a permanent stock of 70 suckler cows. For a calf born at Kite's Nest its subsequent life must be as near natural as is possible, given the inevitable constraints of a farming system. Each calf is allowed complete access to its mother's milk for up to a year, or until the cow is put into calf again. After weaning the calf will stay with the herd right up to slaughter. It is fascinating to observe the way the animals stay in family groups, even when the calves are completely independent. No cereals are used in fattening the cattle, which are entirely grass-fed throughout their lives. Finally, the beasts are slaughtered locally and Richard Young personally travels with each beast to the slaughterhouse to minimize stress. Indeed, it is the lack of stress in the entire farming operation that probably accounts for the long life of the cows, which averages twenty-two years compared with the national average of seven, and for the virtually negligible veterinary bills. When illness does strike, homoeopathic remedies are tried first and are usually successful. Only in exceptional circumstances will antibiotics be used. Needless to say, the beef produced under this regime is exceptional indeed. Quite simply it has to be tasted to be believed! The Youngs have a farm shop and all meat is retailed through it.

When it comes to the cereal crops, the problem of weeds is dealt with using very thorough seedbed cultivation. Grassland is broken up using a rotavator in July and then left for three or four weeks. During this time fresh seeds germinate and the chopped-up grass begins to re-grow. A second pass with the rotavator in early August gets rid of most of this, but often a third pass is required towards the end of August. Even so, with most British summers being too wet to ensure a complete kill of weeds and grass, the field gets a final ploughing in early September. Apart from a final harrowing to prepare the seedbed, this should be enough to make certain that the corn emerges into clean soil. Sowing rates are higher than average, to cope with loss to pests and to ensure smothering of weeds. Once sown, nothing need be done to the crop until harvest the following year.

At the Conference on Organic Farming, held at Stoneleigh in March 1986, Richard Young described the farming methods used at Kite's Nest and referred to the income from the farm as being 'very good, almost to the point of embarrassment'. It is without doubt a striking example of a farming enterprise based on a deep love of, and commitment to, the environment and the animals in the Youngs' stewardship, which in addition is financially rewarding.

## Brynllys Farm, Dyfed

I first became aware of Brynllys Farm back in the early 1970s when I heard Dinah Williams speak at a conference on organic growing. At that time Brynllys was one of the very few organic farms in the country, and I was struck by the passion and commitment in this small yet strong Welsh woman.

Now the farm has passed on to Dinah's daughter Rachel, and her husband Gareth Rowlands. It is a 254-acre holding on the edge of the Welsh coast, with fine views over Borth near Aberystwyth, and it has been farmed organically for three generations. Brynllys is a mixed livestock farm with the emphasis on dairying. This is based on 70 pedigree Guernsey milking cows and a similar number of followers. They also have a flock of over 100 breeding ewes from which they usually get around 200 lambs each year. A few pigs and chickens are also kept.

Like Kite's Nest they also grow a proportion of cereals, though in their case it is a smaller percentage of the overall farm area. Some 45–50 acres of spring cereals are sown each year, usually wheat, oats and barley.

The farm is not entirely self-sufficient for cattle food, relying to a small extent on outside purchased feed. Compared with an orthodox dairy operation, however, there are striking differences at Brynllys. For instance, all calves are reared for four months on the cow, unlike the usual practice where cow and calf are separated almost immediately. Inter-mammary antibiotics are never used. Mastitis, the scourge of conventional dairy farmers, is controlled by detailed management and when necessary by a cold water treatment discovered by Dinah. Nor do the Rowlands use wormers routinely, either for their cattle or sheep. Compulsory sheep-dipping with organophosphate insecticides presents problems for organic farmers, and at Brynllys they are used – though none of the lamb is marketed as organic. As with all the examples mentioned above, veterinary costs are very low at Brynllys, amounting in 1985 to £650 over the whole range of livestock.

Most of the milk is processed on-site to produce butter, cream, a range of yoghurts, buttermilk, and a soft lactic cheese. This is sold at the farm gate under the 'Rachel's Dairy' label. More recently it has found its way into other retail outlets around the country and, as might be expected, is much in demand. Surplus milk is sold to the West Wales Co-op for use in 'Pencarreg', the new and delicious organic soft fat cheese from West Wales.

In addition, some field vegetables are grown, including carrots, cabbages, potatoes and leeks. These are sold both from the farm gate and through the Welsh subsidiary of Organic Farm Foods.

Gareth Rowlands, speaking at the 1986 Stoneleigh Conference, listed his objectives as: (1) To be part of the community, to employ labour from the community and to secure a future for the family. (2) To produce quality food by means of a practical, economic and modern organic farming system. Summing up he added: 'At a time when farming faces an uncertain future with many problems, it is comforting for me to know the consumer is increasingly on my side. Comforting because without a solid, financially viable and growing market, in my opinion the future for conventional family farming is bleak.'

# 7   AN ORGANIC FUTURE?

## How Much Longer Can We Go on Like This?

At the 10 July 1986 meeting of the European Parliament, a plan was presented to save the Common Agricultural Policy. The most notorious feature of the CAP is its encouragement of production. Everything that is grown by farmers throughout the countries of the Community, if not sold, is bought up and either stored, sold off cheap, or destroyed. This has given farmers carte blanche to produce and produce, irrespective of demand. During 1986 it is likely that the EEC Farm Policy will gobble up in total more than £13,000 million. Just how fast this is rising can be seen by reference to previous years' figures. In 1985 the UK contribution to farm support was £1,157 million, yet one year earlier the cost had been one-third of this at £414 million.[56] So much for cheap food, when for every £100 that the farmer produces more than £200 is provided by the taxpayer! More than half of this money goes on storing and subsidizing the sale of surplus food. At the last count the EEC had nearly 17 million tonnes of grain, half a million tonnes of skimmed milk powder and almost a million tonnes of beef in store.

At the July meeting a request was made for yet more funds – a further £660 million, which was to be partly paid for by a cut in development aid for the Third World. Most ludicrous of all was the suggestion that the 1.2 million tonne butter mountain, obtained through feeding dairy cattle vast amounts of rich concentrated food, could be reduced by feeding the butter back to the cows. Even this, crazy as it sounds, makes more sense than the fate that awaits much EEC surplus food. During 1983 over 200,000 tonnes of apples, half a million tonnes of oranges and lemons and 10,000 tonnes of pears were destroyed.[58] In fact, anything which doesn't store especially well is just dumped. Vegetables such as cauliflowers and tomatoes are tipped into huge pits where they are covered in oil to make them inedible.

A few weeks earlier the *Observer* newspaper[59] had carried an article on an official Government report that had been withheld from publication because 'policies for protecting Britain's fast-vanishing countryside are in a shambles – and farmers are using them to rip off the taxpayer'. The report was referring to payments made under the 1981 Wildlife and Countryside Act whereby a farmer has only to state that he intends to fell a wood, drain a swamp, or plough up a special site in order to grow cereals to become entitled to a free annual handout, equivalent to the value of the crop not grown, in perpetuity. According to the *Observer*, the report states that farmers are being dishonest. 'Some are threatening to carry out damaging work merely to claim compensation. Under the Act it is impossible to detect such cheating and virtually impossible to call the landowner's bluff.' Figures in excess of £10,000 a year have already been paid out to some farmers.

The lid has finally been blown on the farm payments scandal thanks to the efforts of Tory MP Richard Body[60] and others. The public are beginning to wake up to the cost. For how much longer will they be prepared to pay taxes to subsidize farmers who are producing unsaleable surpluses at the same time as they are destroying the environment? To add insult to injury, money is to be claimed back that was promised to drought-stricken Africa and elsewhere in the Third World. How must that seem to all those who joined Bob Geldof's army who 'ran the world', or who contributed to any of the many Aid events in 1986?

## Could Organic Farming Do Any Better?

Without a doubt a changeover from conventional to organic methods of agriculture would give great environmental benefits. It is self-evident that the pollution from pesticides and fertilizers would cease to exist. Although there would still be some leaching of nitrogen from organically cultivated fields it would be considerably less than that which is currently putting our drinking-water supplies at risk.

Undesirable practices such as intensive livestock rearing in battery houses would disappear and the consequent need for animal bedding and feed would lead to the elimination of the anti-social and wasteful practice of straw-burning.

The need to integrate livestock enterprises back into arable farms would also have a dramatic effect on the landscape. Free-ranging animals have to be kept on the farm. Whilst this would initially be done with wire or electric fences, the sensible long-term solution would rest with the return of hedges. The need for shelter belts would also result in the planting of many more trees. In short, there would be a return to the traditional British landscape whose passing is much lamented. With it would come a flourishing of wildlife along the hedges and in the trees and unsprayed pastures as new sympathetic habitats were created.

Soil erosion, too, would cease to cause alarm. Organic farming practices directly aid soil conservation. The increase of soil organic matter content traps water and prevents run-off, whilst helping to bind light soils together to reduce erosion by wind. Hedges, too, have a helpful role to play in reducing wind erosion. Putting much more of the land under grass, and attempting to keep land either cropped or covered with a surface mulch for most of the time also does much to stop erosion from taking place. Of course, there will always be some erosion. That is entirely natural, but what is of concern is the unnatural rates of erosion under modern circumstances.

From the consumer's point of view, not only would organically grown food be more appetizing but it would eliminate the

Russian Roulette-like uncertainty of not knowing the long-term consequences of pesticide and other residues on our health.

One could also argue that it is high time we set an example to the Third World. It is overseas where the worst effects of modern intensive agriculture can be seen. Developing countries have been sold the notion that agricultural progress lies along the road of high fertilizer and pesticide applications, high-yielding seed varieties and monoculture on the Western model. The consequences are appalling. Pesticide abuse is rampant and soil erosion is a major problem. Furthermore, having become hooked on the chemical approach many countries are finding that they can't afford the price of the next fix. Since the principles behind organic agriculture are essentially the same as those on which most peasant farming methods are based, is it not more realistic to develop an efficient and self-sufficient biological husbandry system in Third World countries rather than try to impose Western methods on them?

## But Is It Possible?

Reading the preceding section one might feel that both the logical and ethical case for organic farming is so strong that it is inconceivable that it would not now be busily being put into practice by governments, agriculturalists and farmers everywhere. Yet the fact of the matter is that apart from a small but admittedly growing number of farmers, organic farming is making slow progress. If anything things are getting worse. 'Progress' is taking us in the opposite direction. Why should this be? Is there some serious disadvantage, some terrible snag that I have not mentioned which makes a transition to organic methods so difficult?

Before any change can begin to take place, the *idea* of such a transition must first become generally accepted. But this would be directly against the interests of some very interested parties, and in agriculture there must be more vested interests than almost anywhere else. Pesticide and fertilizer manufacturers are, perhaps, the most obvious examples. Their vast profits enable them to conduct sophisticated advertising campaigns in all of the farming magazines, and to keep a small army of reps on the road. These unofficial farming advisers who turn up at the farm gate with regular frequency are not short on advice, particularly where it results in the purchase of their products. Until recently the threat posed from organic agriculture was small enough for its proponents to be dismissed as cranks. Coverage of organic topics in the farming press was cursory and generally unfavourable because, quite apart from anything else, no editor likes to upset major advertising sponsors. Now that the organic lobby has become so vocal that it cannot be ignored, the agrochemical giants have gone on to the offensive with public 'information' campaigns such as the ICI attempt last summer to point out the benefits of using fertilizers.

Pesticide and fertilizer manufacturers are but part of the enormous range of agricultural suppliers that have an interest in seeing the gravy train continue. A less obvious party is the agricultural academic community. Over the years the research establishments, universities, agricultural colleges and the like have absorbed and promoted the conventional view of things. Agricultural progress meant one thing, and that was technological farming – more intensification, higher outputs from higher inputs, using less labour. In this they were, of course, helpfully advised by the agrochemical companies who were never at a loss to supply free materials for testing purposes.

Those scientists who had their doubts about the wisdom of this approach, whilst often uttering sympathetic noises about organic methods in private, would never dream of going into print, for that way lay professional suicide. Being a maverick may work in other industries but it won't do in educational establishments if you want to get on.

Nobody likes admitting they're wrong and if the admission relates to a lifetime of work it will be resisted to the end. Consequently, you will find few senior academics or research administrators prepared to say more than a token good word for organics, though younger entrants into the system may see the way the wind is blowing and mark time until the picture is clearer.

This same credibility factor applies equally to the civil servants who help form agricultural policy. Having promulgated one particular line for years on end, and having set up an advisory service to back it up, such a radical turnaround in attitudes is going to take some swallowing. A recent report, following a visit to Europe by Government scientists to view developments in organic farming, which recommended the setting up of an experimental research unit in organic husbandry has been quietly shelved.[61] Their political masters, the politicians of the member EEC states, are no better. All the time that the public remains reasonably quiescent on the farm budget issue it is easier to cave in to pressure from farm lobbyists. In any event no one appears to be able to see a way out of the mess we have got ourselves into. Everyone admits the farm policy is absurd, everyone admits it can't go on without bankrupting the EEC, and yet otherwise responsible and reasonable men and women react by wringing their hands, asking for more money, and crying that there is no way of stopping it.

You may be wondering when I'm going to get round to including the farmers in my list of vested interests. Surely they more than most have a desire to keep the ship afloat? Surprisingly, perhaps, in view of what I've said in earlier chapters, I see the farmer as something of a helpless victim. Certainly, many farmers have done exceedingly well out of the system. These are primarily the big perpetual cereal barons of the eastern counties. Not surprisingly they are well represented on the National Farmers' Union (NFU) and are most vocal in calling for a continuation of existing policies. Whilst these farmers have flourished on generous tax handouts, many smaller farms, particularly the mixed family farm, have gone out of business. Those that haven't are balanced on a knife-edge of profitability. Having been encouraged by successive governments to expand production they have borrowed heavily and now find that with costs rising and farm gate prices fixed they cannot meet the interest repayments. With shrinking capital assets as land prices plummet they can't even get out because nobody wants to buy while the present uncertainty lasts.

The average farmer is not responsible for the direction of agricultural policy. He has not unreasonably responded to the carrots dangled before him by the Ministry of Agriculture. Now the rug is about to be pulled from under him. It's not the average farmer who is to blame for our predicament – the responsibility rests squarely on the shoulders of the mandarins and academics, the politicians and elements of the NFU, urged on by the oil giants that dominate the trade in agrochemicals.

## Practical Problems

Although vested interests are a nuisance they are by no means the most intractable of the problems that would be faced in a transition from a chemically based to a biologically based agriculture.

There would be the enormous problem of revitalizing denuded soils. It is just not possible for a farmer hooked on chemicals to stop using them overnight. The withdrawal symptoms would be too painful. A phased approach would be required, gradually taking more and more of the farm into the organic regime. One large cereal farmer I know of has a twenty-year conversion plan. Some soils have been so polluted with agrochemicals and are so totally devoid of life that it could take decades to restore them. Wall-to-wall deserts would be an apt description of such places.

Much more serious, though, is the present disposition of land. Hand in hand with the specialization of agriculture over the last forty years has been the swallowing up of small family farms into ever-larger holdings concentrated into fewer and fewer hands. Not only have farm labourers (down from 750,000 in 1946 to less than 100,000 in 1985) been driven from the land as a result of mechanization, but farmers themselves have also had to go.[62]

Now, as we have seen in an earlier chapter, the basis of organic farming is the mixed farm. This is something of a rarity today. In order to re-establish mixed farms we would have to divide up and enclose the enormous prairie fields of the lowlands. Houses would have to be built in the green belt in order to accommodate the extra workers and their families that an organic approach would demand. The mind boggles at the legal and planning implications. It would require not only a mixture of positive tax incentives and penalties, access to grants, and other financial inducements but also a complete re-think of rural development policy.

What would be the economic implications of a shift to

organic methods? This question has been barely addressed at all, though an interesting article appeared in the *Guardian* on 15 September 1983. David Pimental is an American specializing in energy budgeting. That is, instead of looking at a manufacturing or agricultural process in terms of financial costs and returns, the budget instead considers the energy value of what is put in compared with the energy obtained. We are so used to thinking in terms of cash that this approach may seem a little academic. Yet we would do well to remember that fossil fuel energy in the form of oil and natural gas will become rare if not in our lifetime, then in our children or grandchildren's lifetimes.

What Pimental and others have shown is that the energy used in organic agriculture is about one-third of that used in conventional agriculture. In Britain, approximately a quarter of all energy consumed goes in the production, processing and distribution of food. Pimental's research in the States, if applied to the UK, could, according to the article in the *Guardian*, lead to the following conclusions: 'If the labour requirement for wheat-growing in Britain increased from 4.5 hours/hectare [1 hectare = 2½ acres] to 8.4 hours/hectare as in the US study this could generate 3,400 more agricultural workers' jobs on Britain's wheat hectareage. If organic farming of barley – Britain's major cereal, occupying 2,222,000 hectares – needed a somewhat similar increase in labour, a further 4,500 jobs could be created. The savings in synthetic fertilizer, herbicide, insecticide and fungicide costs (presently heavily subsidized by the British taxpayer) and in unemployment and related benefits could easily outweigh the costs, at present pay rates, of employing several thousand more agricultural workers.'

To which I would add that such an increase in the agricultural labour force, if applied to all sectors of agriculture, could act as the engine for much greater rural revitalization.

Undoubtedly, the present economic system which favours the capital-intensive, low-labour farm discriminates against the organic farm. Most if not all tax incentives encourage the purchase of machinery and buildings. Hence the popularity of factory farming. By contrast the more extensive, labour-demanding methods that characterize organic farming offer little scope for tax handouts. Despite massive unemployment there are no positive measures which discriminate in favour of enterprises requiring more labour. Whereas new buildings can be set against tax the purchase of land for free-ranging chickens or pigs cannot.

It is beyond the scope of this book to go into the economic arguments in any depth. In any event, I am an ecologist not an economist and others are more able to advance the discussion of economic factors. But the increasing number of practising organic farmers and growers in itself disproves the theory that this is the quickest road to ruin. I am certain that organic farming methods can be successful both at the personal level and at the national level, even under today's (to an ecologist) distorted economic values.

## Do We Have Any Choice?

Even as I write the geneticists are hard at work producing new varieties that will give even higher yields from even higher doses of fertilizer. Hedges are being grubbed up and trees felled in the race for more surpluses to pile up in Europe. Engineers at the National Institute of Agricultural Engineering are devising robots that will drive tractors, plant seeds and spray crops.[63] They are even working on a robotic apple-picker that can decide whether or not the fruit is ripe enough to pick. On dairy farms the search is on for an automated system that will do away with the stockman altogether. Each cow will wear a computerized necklace which will determine its food ration and when it should be milked. Getting a robot to put the sucking device on to the teats is proving tricky – magnets surgically implanted into the udder have been tried and found wanting – though researchers expect to have cracked it within the next five years. Meanwhile, at a training course for Government agricultural advisers held in the North of England in the winter of 1983, Mr Jack Panes, the head of microbiology at the Agricultural Development and Advisory Service, is reported as suggesting that farm animals of gigantic proportions could be bred as a result of the successful isolation of the human growth hormone.[64] One can almost imagine the headlines if a monster chicken breaks loose and terrorizes the population! With the cream of our agricultural scientists pursuing their technological fantasies and the whole weight of the agricultural establishment committed to the chemical approach what hope is there for organic farming?

The choice is clear. We can continue following our present shortsighted course of increased production whatever the cost – just keep on shutting our eyes to the environmental degradation and hope it will go away. The problem of surpluses can be overcome by paying farmers not to produce food and taking land out of production. Land that is not cropped can instead be used for recreation and wildlife whilst the land that is cropped will be pushed to the limit. Although in the long term it solves nothing, this is probably the easiest and therefore the most attractive choice politically, short of doing nothing at all.

Alternatively we can take the biological path. There are immense political difficulties. Much research still remains to be done if existing organic methods are to be improved. Nevertheless we would be setting agriculture on a course which would not place it in conflict with the environment; a sustainable path that we could pass on to our children confident in the knowledge that their food security would be safeguarded. Are we far-sighted enough to accept the challenge? For their sakes, I hope so.

# PART III

## WHERE TO BUY ORGANIC FOOD

## 8   ORGANICALLY GROWN FOODS TO BE FOUND IN THE SHOPS

Without doubt, shops selling whole, natural and health foods have been one of the great success stories of recent years. Their numbers have so mushroomed that there can be few places that do not boast an establishment of one sort or another, as a glance under 'Healthfood and wholefood shops' in any Yellow Pages will show. Such shops have concentrated on providing food that is whole, additive-free and as little processed or refined as possible. They can vary greatly in character and in the type of goods they stock. Some may have a particular section devoted to organic foods or even specify that they stock only organically grown natural foods. You may also find, as well as the increasing range of dried, packed and processed organic foods, a few organically produced – often local – vegetables, and maybe milk products. And of course, health-food and wholefood shops usually have a fairly strict policy concerning the general quality of foods they stock. You will not find highly processed foods on the shelves, and foods containing white sugar and white flour are not encouraged. You can also expect to find fewer chemical food additives such as stabilizers, emulsifiers, preservatives, colourings and artificial flavourings. However, it still makes sense to read the ingredients list which is now printed by law on all packaged foods. (*E for Additives* by Maurice Hanssen is an excellent guide for deciphering the meaning of E numbers.)

The natural food shopkeeper is usually an authority on the foods in stock and those that are available, and should be able to answer any queries you have about organic produce. Many shops are happy to order specific items or larger quantities for customers, or will direct you to another outlet that can help.

As has been the case with a number of basic wholefoods such as wholemeal spaghetti or brown rice, organically grown foods are also finding their way on to some supermarket shelves and into smaller corner shops. Both fresh fruit and vegetables and prepacked goods labelled as organic would not be a surprising find on a visit to a Sainsbury, Safeway or Tesco supermarket.

Wherever you have bought an organic product the basic ingredient will probably be whole and natural. *How* it has been 'organically grown' is a question which should always be asked. Where possible the consumer should look for recognizable marks of authenticity and an explanation of that standard on any 'organically grown' foods (although this may be difficult with some imported products). In particular, beware of the fact that some manufacturers sell organic and non-organic versions of the same product, often in confusingly similar packaging. Alternatively, only one product in a manufacturer's range may be organic, so you will have to check the label. The generally accepted interpretation of the meaning of 'organic' on a label is explained in Appendix 1.

You will also almost certainly notice a difference between the price of conventional commodities and of their organic counterparts. The organic versions will usually be dearer. Producing organically grown crops is a more labour intensive and at present very specialized area of farming, which enjoys none of the subsidies or benefits bestowed on conventional farming. Higher prices do not automatically mean higher profits but are simply the going rate for the best quality unadulterated foods available.

The basic wholefood commodities which are available are sometimes labelled OG or ORG, which means organically grown. They include whole cereals, cereal flakes and flours, beans, lentils and pulses, dried fruits and some nuts. These are distributed nationally through several different wholesalers serving natural food shops. You may also find a surprising variety of organic processed and packaged foods from oils and jams to fruit juices and baby foods, not to mention vegetables and dairy produce. Organically produced meat and meat products are also coming on to the market but are unlikely to be found in healthfood shops, which tend to be largely vegetarian.

Under various headings below some guidelines are given as to the kind of organically grown produce which is available from retail outlets. These notes are a general reference rather than a definitive list, and with pressure from you, the consumer, the type, variety and status-guarantee of organically produced foods will increase and become more widely distributed.

## Meat

Organic farming requires a balanced system of crop and livestock rotation, one of the products of which is naturally reared meat. However, there is as yet no centralized system of distribution and it remains unlikely that one will be established in the near future, although one or two farmers already marketing meat products can be expected to expand their operations.

The demand for organically reared meat is again buoyant, with a good demand for farm gate sales. Farmers will want to sell you half or part of an animal and you may have to pay extra to have it butchered (or be prepared to do it yourself). One or two advertise that they will send your requirements by post or by rail to the nearest station. Try this directory and the back pages of healthfood magazines for addresses.

An increasing number of outlets offer 'additive-free' or 'hormone-free' meat and meat products. These would not meet the strict standards for organic livestock products, which require that 80 per cent of all animal feed should be organically grown, but they nonetheless constitute a step in the right direction. Use the information in the chapter on 'Food Fit for Animals' to establish from the farmer just what is meant by the description 'additive-free', etc.

Some organic meat products such as sausages and pies are

produced on a local farmhouse basis but none as yet carries a recognized guarantee, or has any national availability.

## Dairy Produce

You will not find unpasteurized organically produced milk (the old green top) on sale in any shops, since the Government ban of November 1985. It is now only available direct from the farmer. Cream and yoghurt from unpasteurized organic sources is, however, not affected by this rule and may be available locally.

Organically produced cheese from unpasteurized milk is also coming on to the market. Look out for Pencarreg, a full-fat soft cheese produced to organic standards, and a variety of soft and hard goats' cheeses.

Some of these dairy products will be on sale in natural food stores which have a chilled cabinet, but an equally good supply is becoming available in the growing number of cheese and dairy shops which are springing up.

## Fresh Fruit and Vegetables

For a number of years the occasional box of organic carrots could be found languishing in the odd healthfood shop. Just why it was there was probably a question asked by quite a few customers, as the contents slowly shrivelled and the box was finally tossed out. This state of affairs has now become a thing of the past, with the arrival of the excellently organized Organic Growers' Association, which helps and supports the growers, and the setting up of Organic Farm Foods, the first wholesaling and distribution network for organically grown foods in Great Britain. The Organic Growers' Association has created a much-needed lifeline for the countless, previously isolated, organic vegetable growers in this country. A range of Organic Growers' Association packaging, for bulk and retail sales, was developed for use by members, and their waving leaf symbol and 'Eat Organic' message is now well known by those in the healthfood trade. The arrival of Organic Farm Foods to wholesale and distribute the available produce at last brought status and salvation to a variety of excellent-quality organically grown vegetables which previously were lost on the regular commercial market, with customers who wished to buy unable to obtain supplies.

Now Organic Farm Foods – with depots in Scotland and Wales – Clean Foods of Birmingham, and a number of other organic wholesalers, stock a wide variety of produce from farmers and growers all over Britain, importing from abroad where necessary. Availability will remain seasonal with organic produce, which is not produced in the intensive and artificial agricultural systems sometimes employed to lengthen a cropping season. Nevertheless, about twenty basic lines are available throughout the year, with hundreds more available according to season.

Good packaging and an efficient delivery service mean that quite a number of natural food stores now stock a welcome and wide range of organically grown fruit and vegetables. They should easily compensate in freshness, flavour and keeping quality for the extra you pay. Some supermarkets, especially Safeways, are also starting to stock organically grown vegetables. It is likely that both range and availability will quickly increase.

## Fruit and Vegetable Juices

Aspall's organic apple juice and organic cyder vinegar are the oldest-established and most widely available products of British manufacture. Make sure you look at the label to get the organic variety. Quite a number of other juices are imported, mainly from Europe. Although it is very expensive, apple juice concentrate from organic apples is available and some shops will buy in bulk and bottle it under their own label.

A variety of juices from other organically grown and Demeter quality fruits are available under a number of different labels. For other fruit and vegetable juices look out for the Eden label and Biotta label. Biotta juices are naturally preserved using a lactic fermentation process which you cannot taste, rather than artificial intervention. Apart from the Aspalls products which have excellent national distribution to a range of shops, other individually imported or locally available organic fruit and vegetable juices will also be found in natural food shops.

# Wine

In Europe – France, Germany and also Italy – an increasing range of wines is now produced to organic standards. Guarantees are available but do not always appear on the labels because of EEC regulations. These guarantees relate not only to how the grapes are grown, but also to the process of vinification, for which detailed standards have been drawn up. Chemical aids – preservatives, stabilizers, etc. – too often used in commercial wine production, are avoided.

A number of small wine merchants/importers now stock a few such 'organic' lines which are worth looking out for, and there are also a number of importers who distribute wholesale. Infinity Foods of Brighton and Real Foods of Edinburgh have wine lists whose 'organic' authenticity they have investigated. They only sell direct to the public in their own shops, but on receipt of an s.a.e. should send addresses of their stockists in other areas. Other importers whose lists are exclusively organic are West Heath Wine, West Heath, Pirbright, Surrey, and Wholefood, 24 Paddington Street, London W1.

# Whole Grains, Flakes and Other Cereal Products

A good variety of organically grown grains and cereal products are produced in this country and more are imported from abroad. They are more likely to be found in your natural food store than in a supermarket. The label on the packet will most probably be that of the retailer who has bagged it himself, so do ask about the source and organic guarantee. If it is produce of this country it should carry the Soil Association symbol or may indicate that it is produced by Organic Farmers and Growers Ltd. You may also be able to establish the name of the mill it was processed at which is a further guarantee (for example Hofels or Pimhill or another in this directory).

The range of imported organic cereal products is very good, but they may not be widely available unless you ask for them. They will be of special interest to anyone on a gluten-free diet who is also trying to eat organic produce. Millet flakes, maize flakes, rice flakes, buckwheat flour, couscous and bulghur are all imported into this country. However, this imported produce is likely to carry even less information about its organic status than UK cereals, so you may have to take the retailer's or importer's word as to its quality for the time being.

## Rice

Long-grain and short-grain organically grown brown rice is imported into this country from Italy and America. The availability of these rices varies at different times of the year, but short-grain organic Italian is the most consistently available.

Natural food retailers are most likely to buy this product in bulk and pack it down themselves, although organic rice is pre-packed under several labels. Supermarket brown rice is not generally organically grown. Neither will you find organically grown refined rice.

A ready-to-eat Savoury Rice and Vegetables, made with organic brown rice, is available under the Whole Earth label. Organic rice flour, as well as rice flakes, are also available.

## Breakfast Cereals

Both muesli and muesli base (a variety of flaked cereals on their own) are available from a number of wholesaling sources and are generally packed down by natural food shopkeepers themselves. Some shops also buy the individual ingredients and mix their own organic muesli and pack it under their own label. A variety of sizes could be available according to demand in the shop, and the label used should indicate whether all or some of the ingredients are organic. If unsure, ask.

## Flour

Organically grown flour has very good availability throughout the country in natural food shops, local groceries, bakeries and some supermarkets. If you are lucky you may even have a choice of brands, and with those nationally available, year-round supply is uninterrupted. Wholemeal (100 per cent extraction) is the most usual find, but brown flour (81–85 per cent extraction) is very occasionally available.

Since wholemeal flour is the product of milling clean wheat with nothing added and nothing taken away, the organic option is a wise one. Pesticide residues from conventional farming can remain on the endosperm or outer layers of the wheat grain, and are not removed by either the milling or baking process.

Do study the description on the packet to see what you are buying, because some millers sell both organic and non-organic flours in similar bags. Some small farms grind their own wheat and supply one or two local stockists. All mills sell flour by the sack which may be re-bagged by retailers. Ask what standards the organic wheat has been grown to, and ask if the flour carries any kind of organic certification mark which you can recognize.

If you do a lot of home baking and require larger amounts of flour, many natural food shops may stock behind the counter, or can order for you, a 15 kg bag of organic flour. When baking with organic flour you will undoubtedly notice a superior flavour but your loaf may have less volume, which is normal.

## Bread

Quite a number of individual Master Bakers are developing an interest in switching their regular wholemeal loaf for one baked with organically grown wholemeal flour. Traditional bakeries are always rewarding when you manage to seek them out, as their fresh breads are generally quite unlike those available in supermarkets. This kind of local bakery may well also supply other outlets such as healthfood shops and delicatessens. Do ask who made the organic flour used to bake the bread and you should either recognize the mill, and/or be able to check what kind of organic guarantee they offer.

On supermarket shelves hunt out either Springhill Bread or Doves Farm organic bread. Springhill bread is made from organic grains which are milled and baked to a special recipe at Springhill Farm. This dense wholesome bread is sliced and specially wrapped for long keeping: excellent for the store cupboard. Goswells produce an uncut 1 lb and a sliced 2 lb loaf wrapped in a polythene bag labelled Goswells and Doves Farm, whose organic wholemeal is used to bake the bread. They will freeze well if you wish to buy several at a time.

## Pasta

The variety of organic wholemeal pasta on sale in healthfood shops and supermarkets is now very good. A range of shapes (spirals, alphabets, hoops, shells) is available as well as the more common spaghetti, macaroni and lasagne. The Ugo and Waymill varieties are made in England and others including Euvita and Lima products are imported. Organic buckwheat noodles may also be available in natural food shops stocking a good variety of international and Japanese foods.

## Dried Fruit and Nuts

In general terms the dried fruits available in natural food shops have been particularly carefully selected for their quality. You may find some fruits are kiln- or sun-dried and not further preserved (for example – with sulphur dioxide). These fruits will tend to be darker in colour than those which have been treated with a preservative. Some dried fruits will seem more sticky than the supermarket varieties, and this is usually because they have not been sprayed with oil to help keep them separate. If oil is used, care will also have been taken in the selection of a vegetable oil rather than a mineral oil.

Organically produced dried fruits are available within a limited range and you may have to ask your shopkeeper specifically if it would be possible to obtain supplies. America, Greece, Israel, Italy and Turkey are all sending organic dried fruits to this country. Some Moroccan produce is labelled as organic, but it will almost certainly have been sprayed at least once before shipping, as this is mandatory in Morocco. Some organically produced raisins may be available in supermarkets, but their authenticity is unchecked.

The availability of organically produced nuts is much more patchy. Almonds are coming from Spain, hazelnuts from Italy and sunflower seeds from the USA. More should follow.

## Beans and Pulses

Quite a variety of beans, lentils and pulses of organically grown quality are imported into this country. Again, these products remain the exclusive domain of the natural food stores and you may have to encourage your shopkeeper to stock the organic option when it is available. It is possible to buy either in bulk or pre-packed under such labels as Suma, Infinity or Hawthorne Vale. Quite a few beans and pulses will have a recognized symbol of organic authenticity printed on to the sack, but when packed down usually only carry the merchant or packer's guarantee.

## Baby Foods

The range of organic baby foods available to natural food shops is both highly recommended and of very good quality. All are imported from Switzerland and produced to biodynamic standards. There are three Holle cereal foods for very small babies and Holle rusks. The Johanus range of ten ready-prepared meals for babies from four months are the next best thing to preparing your own. Sold in quite large glass jars, the food is very palatable either hot or cold and should do for two or three meals. Four further and more sophisticated varieties of baby food are available for babies of 10 months onwards. Don't forget the range of ordinary organic, and concentrated organic fruit juices available.

None of these baby foods is available at chemists or supermarkets. Indeed you may have to persuade your natural food shop that there is a demand, or ask them to order a whole case specially for you.

## Other Processed Foods

These will fall into two broad categories. Those which are made entirely of guaranteed organic ingredients and those of which some or the larger part is of organic origin. Check the label thoroughly and carefully and complain to the manufacturers if their description is confusing or incomplete.

The following notes on various foods indicate what is available to or stocked in natural food shops, mainly in the South of England. However, organically produced and processed foods generally appeal to a wider range of consumers and shops than unprocessed wholefoods, and may also be found on supermarket shelves next to the chain's own-label olive oils or digestive biscuits.

Amongst cereal-based foods look out for the Living Foods range of rice cakes, biscuits by Doves Farm Flour, crispbreads by Fertilia and Lima and cakes from Springhill Bakery.

Various vegetable pâtés are available under the Springhill Bakery, Living Foods and Euvita labels and a range of tofu spreads are available from Living Foods and from Infinity Foods. (Tofu is a kind of creamy soyabean cheese.) The first soya milk made from organic soya beans is available in 500 ml cartons from Living Foods.

Soyanaise, an alternative mayonnaise based on organic soyabean tofu, is marketed under the Infinity label.

Very occasionally you may find Euvita olive oil or Infinity sunflower oil labelled as organic.

Organically grown black olives can be found under the Euvita label and various other pickles and vegetable products with either Eden, Demeter, Lima or Infinity labels.

Organic barley malt syrup, a delicious alternative sweetener, is available under two or three labels, and one or two jams are labelled as organic but this probably refers to the fruit used rather than the sugar content.

Few of these products labelled as organic will be found to carry any symbol of verification, which is a poor record for the very reputable manufacturers concerned, but this situation should improve in the near future. Both the range of products on offer and the availability will also undoubtedly increase and improve.

# 9 A GUIDE TO OUTLETS

The addresses in the following list range from small producers with a little surplus produce for sale to large 1000-acre farms; from wholefood shops to supermarkets.

Some are open for just a few hours a week whilst others adopt normal shop hours. There are even some places which stay open during daylight hours for seven days a week. Most welcome callers at any reasonable time, but where set opening times are known they have been published in the text. Some growers insist on being phoned first and where this is the case it is indicated in the text. In any event the rule is 'phone first' if only to check that someone will be in when you arrive and that they have what you want. They will also let you know if you have to place a minimum order. Not everyone, particularly a busy farmer, will welcome a break in the daily routine in order to sell you a lettuce.

I have tried to be as accurate as possible in describing the produce available at each outlet. Remember, however, that seasons vary, and what may have been in glut last year might be in short supply this year. Because it is easily possible to vary the type of vegetables that are grown, I have made no attempt to itemize specific vegetables, the availability of which could change from week to week. Since fruit requires more of a commitment, involving the long-term planting of trees and bushes, I have itemized fruits, where known.

Customers purchasing eggs, dairy produce, meat or other animal products should be aware of the problems involved in livestock husbandry, as set out in earlier chapters. There are very few farmers who are self-sufficient to the extent that all of their livestock feed can be produced on the farm. Some feeding stuffs, particularly concentrates, may be bought in and these will usually not be organically grown. Farmers can, however, try to ensure that their feed is 'additive-free', and a lot of the meat mentioned on subsequent pages falls into this category. In these cases the onus is on consumers to ensure that they know what they are buying. If in doubt, ask. If you don't like what you hear, don't buy. An informed public is the key to getting more organic produce.

The location of many farms is self-evident from the address, but where a place is difficult to find we have included directions. It is, perhaps, as well to check the route at the time of phoning.

The entries have been divided up on a regional basis and apart from a few areas there should be outlets within easy reach of most people. If not, you might consider growing your own (see the entry for Henry Doubleday Research Association in Appendix 2).

You will find reference in the lists to Safeway Food Stores Ltd. This company has a commitment to buying organically grown fruit and vegetables from reputable sources. A wide variety of fresh organic produce can usually be obtained from any of its stores.

## Is the Food Genuinely Organic?

What guarantees do we have that the food labelled as organic is in fact grown without the use of artificial fertilizers and synthetic pesticides?

In many, but not all cases, the word 'organic' on a label or package refers to some definite set of standards to which any member of the public should be able to refer. In some European countries, for example France and Switzerland, and in some American states, such as California and Oregon, this is now legally obligatory. Under their consumer protection laws it has been held that use of the word 'organic' (or the equivalent of 'biological' in German or French) without precise definition of what is implied could mislead the public into payment of premium prices which might be unjustified and thus fraudulent. In this country we have had no such legal constraints.

Internationally there is a basic standards document that has been produced by IFOAM (International Federation of Organic Agriculture Movements). Individual countries usually take this document as their basis and adapt it according to their own particular circumstances. In Britain this has led to a unified standard produced by the British Organic Standards Committee (BOSC) (see Appendix 3).

There are three British bodies which conform to this standard and whose symbol on the produce packaging indicates that the food within has been grown to BOSC requirements. These are the Soil Association, Organic Farmers and Growers, and the Bio-Dynamic Agricultural Association. Look out for their symbols as follows:

Soil Association     Bio-Dynamic Agricultural     Organic Farmers &
                           Association                    Growers

Where a farm or market garden meets any of these standards the appropriate symbol is indicated in the text. Although you will not see symbols against shop entries this does not mean that symbol produce cannot be obtained from such sources. Many shops have an extremely strict buying policy and will only sell vegetables or fruit that come from symbol farms. Others sell a mixture of produce from holdings that do have a symbol and from those who claim their produce is organic yet have not bothered to apply for a symbol. This is to be discouraged. Again the consumer holds the key to improving the situation by insisting that all organically grown food should carry a recognized symbol.

Produce coming from abroad is likely to be identified in a number of ways. The Demeter sign is international and can be thoroughly depended on. You might see a label marked Biodyn which indicates farms in conversion to full biodynamic, i.e. Demeter status. A similar conversion grade is under consideration by the British Organic Standards Committee.

## A Note on the Listings

Entries have been listed alphabetically on a regional basis under first their county and then the nearest town, or where more appropriate, the nearest village. In case the ordering of counties under the nine separate regions of England is not immediately obvious the following list is included:

| | |
|---|---|
| Avon | South West |
| Bedfordshire | London and the Home Counties |
| Berkshire | London and the Home Counties |
| Buckinghamshire | London and the Home Counties |
| Cambridgeshire | East Anglia |
| Cheshire | North West |
| Cornwall | South West |
| Cumbria | North West |
| Derbyshire | East Midlands |
| Devon | South West |
| Dorset | Southern England |
| Durham | North East |
| East Sussex | South East |
| Essex | East Anglia |
| Gloucestershire | West Midlands |
| Hampshire | Southern England |
| Hereford and Worcester | West Midlands |
| Hertfordshire | London and the Home Counties |
| Humberside | North East |
| Kent | South East |
| Lancashire | North West |
| Leicestershire | East Midlands |
| Lincolnshire | East Midlands |
| Merseyside | North West |

| | |
|---|---|
| Norfolk | East Anglia |
| North Yorkshire | North East |
| Northamptonshire | East Midlands |
| Northumberland | North East |
| Nottinghamshire | East Midlands |
| Oxfordshire | London and the Home Counties |
| Shropshire | West Midlands |
| Somerset | South West |
| South Yorkshire | North East |
| Staffordshire | West Midlands |
| Suffolk | East Anglia |
| Surrey | South East |
| Tyne and Wear | North East |
| Warwickshire | West Midlands |
| West Midlands | West Midlands |
| West Sussex | South East |
| West Yorkshire | North East |
| Wiltshire | Southern England |

# THE SOUTH WEST

## AVON

### Bath

Mr and Mrs J. E. Pillinger
Roseland Nursery
Bailbrook Lane
Bath
Avon
(Tel. 0225 313301)
*Open* Daily 9am–7pm
*Produce* Fruit and vegetables

Harvest Natural Foods
37 Walcot Street
Bath
Avon
(Tel. 0225 65519)
*Open* Monday 11.30am–5.30pm;
Tuesday–Saturday
9.30am–5.30pm
*Produce* Wholefoods, vegetables,
lemons, oranges, pears and
apples (in season)

Neills of Bath
10 Caroline Buildings
Pultney Road
Bath
Avon
(Tel. 0225 337652)
*Open* Available any time by
telephone, deliveries only
*Produce* Hen eggs, butter, cheese,
ewe's cheese, beef, pork, lamb,
poultry, meat products

Allens Wharf
2 Prior Park Road
Widcombe
Bath
Avon

Tel. 0225 316696)
*Open* Monday–Friday
9am–6.30pm; Saturday
9am–5pm; Sunday 9.30am–1pm
*Produce* Vegetables, fruit, hen
eggs, dairy produce (cow, goat
and sheep), wholefoods

Seasons Wholefoods and
Takeaway
10 George Street
Bath BA1 2EH
(Tel. 0225 69730)
*Open* Monday–Saturday
9am–5.30pm
*Produce* Vegetables, fruit, dairy
produce (cow, goat and sheep),
eggs, wholefoods, organic wine

Radford Mill Farm
Timsbury
Nr Bath
Avon
*Produce* Vegetables,
wholefoods, dairy produce
(cow), eggs (duck and hen),
meat, fish (carp)

### Bristol

Radford Mill Farm Shop
41 Picton Street
Montpelier
Bristol
(Tel. 0272 45360)
*Open* Monday–Saturday
8.30am–6.45pm; Sunday
10am–1.30pm
*Produce* Vegetables, eggs (duck
and hen), dairy produce (cow
and goat), wholefoods, beef,
mutton, lamb, ham, pork and
meat products

Windmill Hill City Farm
Doveton Street
Bedminster
Bristol
(Tel. 0272 633252)
*Produce* Eggs (hen and duck),
goat's milk, cheese, yogurt, pork,
lamb, kid, chicken, duck, turkey,
occasionally quail and guinea
fowl

The Rowan Tree
Berkeley Place
The Triangle
Bristol
(Tel. 0272 277030)
*Open* Monday–Saturday
9am–5.30pm
*Produce* Vegetables, apples, pears,
lemons and oranges, eggs (hen
and occasionally duck),
wholefoods

St Werburgh's City Farm
Watercress Road
St Werburgh's
Bristol BS2 9YJ
(Tel. 0272 428241)
*Open* Daily 9am–5pm
*Produce* Vegetables, apples and
oranges, eggs (hen and duck),
goat's milk, yogurt and cream
(cow), pork, lamb and poultry,
herbs

Safeway Food Stores Ltd
Broadwalk Shopping Centre
Knowle
Bristol BS4 2QN
(Tel. 0272 771324)

Ron Elliot
9 Regent Street
Clifton
Bristol BS8 4NW
(Tel. 0272 735223)
*Open* 9am–5.30pm; early closing
Wednesday 2pm
*Produce* Vegetables, fruit, eggs,
wholefoods

Beans and Greens
88 Colston Street
Bristol
(Tel. 0272 28961)
*Open* Monday–Friday
8.30am–6pm; Saturday
9am–5pm
*Produce* Vegetables, fruit, dairy
produce (cow and goat), eggs,
wholefoods

Bartrum Wholefoods
12 Clevedon Terrace
Cotham
Bristol BS6 5TX
(Tel. 0272 41183)
*Open* Monday–Saturday
9.30am–7pm; Sunday
10am–2pm
*Produce* Vegetables, fruit, eggs
(hen and goose), dairy produce
(cow, goat and sheep),
wholefoods

The Mango Tree
224 Gloucester Road
Bristol BS7 8NZ
(Tel. 0272 46589)
*Open* Monday–Friday
9am–5.30pm; early closing
Wednesday 1pm; Saturday
9am–5pm
*Produce* Vegetables, fruit, dairy

produce (cow, goat and sheep), eggs, wholefoods

Carols
129 Coldharbour Road
Westbury Park
Bristol
(Tel. 0272 48732)
*Open* Monday–Saturday
8.30am–7.30pm; Sunday
9.30am–1pm
*Produce* Vegetables, fruit, dairy produce (cow, goat and sheep), eggs (hen, duck and goose), meat

Roger Thomas
37 North View
Bristol BS6 7PY
(Tel. 0272 734255)
*Open* Monday–Saturday
8.30am–5.30pm
*Produce* Vegetables and fruit, eggs

## Midsomer Norton

Safeway Food Stores Ltd
High Street
Midsomer Norton
Avon
(Tel. 0761 412848)

## Thornbury

Safeway Food Stores Ltd
St Mary's Street
Thornbury
Avon
(Tel. 0454 419480/412366)

## Winscombe Hill

Janet Arnold
Holly Croft
Winscombe Hill
Avon BS25 1DQ
(Tel. 0934 84 2578)

*Open* 24 hours' notice required
*Produce* Vegetables, apples, raspberries, currants, hen eggs, lamb by arrangement

# CORNWALL

## Falmouth

Harvest Wholefoods
16 High Street
Falmouth
Cornwall
(Tel. 0326 311507)
*Open* Monday–Saturday
9am–5.30pm
*Produce* Vegetables, apples, bananas, oranges, mandarins or clementines or satsumas (in season), eggs (duck, goose and hen), wholefoods and dairy produce

## Launceston

Food for Thought
4A Market Street
Launceston
Cornwall
(Tel. 0566 4300)
*Open* Monday–Saturday
8.30am–5pm
*Produce* Eggs (hen and duck), dairy produce, wholefoods

## Liskeard

Mr and Mrs C. Woolf
Woodfield
Merrymeet
Liskeard
Cornwall PL14 3LS
(Tel. 0579 43347)
*Open* Please telephone first
*Produce* Vegetables, apples, hen and duck eggs, goat's milk and yogurt

*Directions* Just off the A390 between Merrymeet and St Ives. Turn at the bottom of the hill through the gate beside Steart Cottage and follow the track for a quarter of a mile

Peter Byrne and Lesley Martin
Market Stall
Courts Arcade
Fore Street
Liskeard
Cornwall
*Open* Saturday only 8am–4pm
*Produce* Vegetables, wide range of fruit, hen and duck eggs

## Looe

Keveral Farm
St Martins by Looe
Cornwall
(Tel. 0535 215)
*Open* Daylight hours
*Produce* Vegetables, strawberries, raspberries, blackcurrants, gooseberries, duck and hen eggs, herbs
*Directions* 4 miles east of Looe off the B3253

## Marazion

Justin Brooke
Chymorvah Vean
Marazion
Cornwall TR17 0DQ
(Tel. 0736 710468)
*Open* Please telephone first
*Produce* Vegetables

*Directions* 100 yds east of Fire Engine public house

## Newquay

Mr D. M. Coles
Newlands Organic Farm
Fiddlers Green
Newlyn East
Newquay
Cornwall TR8 5NJ
(Tel. 087 254 467)
*Open* May 31st–November 30th, Tuesday–Saturday inclusive, 10am–5.30pm. Please telephone at other times
*Produce* Vegetables, strawberries
*Directions* On the Zelah Road from Newlyn East

## Penryn

Mr B. D. Broadbank
Menallack Farm
Treverva
Penryn
Cornwall TR10 9BP
(Tel. 0326 40333)
*Produce* Vegetables, raspberries (pick your own), strawberries, blackcurrants, gooseberries, cream and milk and butter (cow and goat), pork, lamb, poultry, beef
*Directions* On B3291 three-quarters of a mile from village of Treverva going towards Gweek

Mr E. J. Brown
Trenance Round Ring
Penryn
Cornwall
(Tel. 0326 74800)
*Open* Monday–Saturday 9am–5.30pm
*Produce* Vegetables, hen eggs, goat's milk, yogurt

and cheese, cow's cheese, poultry
(duck, chicken, turkey), honey

## Penzance

Richards Health Foods
Bread Street
Penzance
Cornwall
(Tel. 0736 62828)
*Open* 9am–5.15pm; early closing
Wednesday 1.15pm
*Produce* Vegetables, apples,
oranges, hen eggs, dairy produce
(cow, sheep and goat), wholefoods

The Granary Traditional Foods
15D Causeway Head
Penzance
Cornwall
(Tel. 0736 61869)
*Open* Monday–Saturday
9am–5pm; closed on Wednesday
*Produce* Wholefoods, vegetables,
eggs, cream

## Perranporth

Robert Burns
Lovely Vale,
Higher Penwartha
Perranporth
Cornwall TR6 0BA
(Tel. 0872 573863)
*Open* Daylight hours
*Produce* Vegetables,
strawberries, hen eggs,
goat's milk
*Directions* Opposite RSPCA
Centre

## St Austell

D. B. Pascoe and F. A. Edwards
Stoneybridge Organic Nursery
Tywardreath
Par

Cornwall PL24 2TY
(Tel. 072 681 3858)
*Open* March–mid-October
9am–8pm
*Produce* Vegetables, herbs,
apples and pears,
strawberries, raspberries,
gooseberries and blackcurrants,
hen eggs
*Directions* 1 mile from the B3269
Fowey Road signposted
Stoneybridge

## Truro

R. and F. B. H. Bowcock
Polsue Cottage
Ruan High Lanes
Truro
Cornwall TR2 5LU
(Tel. 0876 501576)
*Open* Please telephone first; closed
Sundays
*Produce* Vegetables,
strawberries, goat's milk

Carley and Co.
35–36 St Austell Street
Truro
Cornwall TR1 1SE
(Tel. 0872 77686)
*Open* Monday–Saturday
9am–5.30pm
*Produce* Vegetables, oranges,
apples, lemons, grapefruit,
peaches, nectarines, eggs, Gouda
and Staffordshire cow cheese,
wholefoods

P. J. and J. Curd
Lanhay
Portscatho
Truro TR2 5ER
(Tel. 087 258 282)
*Open* Daily 8am–8pm

Produce Vegetables, soft
fruit, apples, Jersey milk,
cream and soft cheeses

# DEVON

## Ashburton

C. Staniland
The Gardens
Buckland-in-the-Moor
Ashburton
Devon TO13 7HN
(Tel. 0364 53169)
Open May–September 10am–6pm
Produce Vegetables,
strawberries,
blackcurrants, hen eggs, goat's
milk, yogurt and cheese,
strawberry jam and honey

## Ashwater

B. and P. Veltman
Uphill Farm
Ashwater
Devon EX21 5DL
(Tel. 040 921 405)
Open Weekends
Produce Vegetables,
strawberries

## Barnstaple

E. W. and J. C. Morrish
East Acland Farm
Landkey
Nr Barnstaple
Devon EX32 0LD
(Tel. 0271 830216)
Open Please telephone first
Produce Potatoes, Bramley
apples, beef and lamb

## Bideford

L. A. Cosgrove
Little Braddons

Buckland Brewer
Bideford
N. Devon EX39 5ND
(Tel. 02375 383)
Open Any reasonable time
Produce Vegetables, soft
fruit, eggs

## Brixham

Pine Pantry Health Foods
7 Bolton Street
Brixham
Devon
(Tel. 08045 6140)
Open Monday–Friday
9am–5.30pm; early closing
Wednesday 1.30pm; Saturday
9am–4pm
Produce Vegetables, some fruit,
hen eggs, goat's milk,
wholefoods

## Budleigh Salterton

Tilburys
24 High Street
Budleigh Salterton
Devon EX9 6LQ
(Tel. 039 54 2304)
Open Monday–Saturday
8am–6pm
Produce Vegetables and
fruit

## Chudleigh

J. N. Farr
Crammers Farm
Chudleigh
Devon
(Tel. 0626 853107)
Open Weekdays 9am–5pm
Produce Vegetables,
fruit

**Crediton**

B. Kellett
Skylands
Thelbridge
Crediton EX17 4SJ
(Tel. 0884 860 844)
*Open* Any reasonable time
*Produce* Vegetables

**Exeter**

T. and J. Deane
Northwood Farm
Christow
Exeter
Devon EX6 7PG
(Tel. 0647 52915)
*Produce* Vegetables, apples,
hen eggs

Richard Kerswell
4 Leighton Terrace
Exeter
Devon EX4 6AZ
*Open* Daylight hours
*Produce* Vegetables
(especially unusual
vegetables), herbs

Seasons
8 Well Street
Exeter
Devon
(Tel. 0392 36125)
*Open* 9.30am–5.30pm
*Produce* Vegetables, apples,
oranges, lemons, hen eggs,
yogurt (cow, goat and sheep),
wholefoods

City Ditch Foods
14 South Street
Exeter
Devon

(Tel. 0392 50925)
*Open* Monday–Saturday
9.30am–5.30pm
*Produce* Vegetables and fruit, hen
eggs, wholefoods

Bowhay Wholefoods
Shillingford Abbot
Exeter
Devon
(Tel. 0392 832300)
*Open* Please telephone first
*Produce* Vegetables, plums,
flour

Round the Bend Wholefood Shop
53 The Strand
Exmouth
Devon
(Tel. 0392 264398)
*Open* Monday–Saturday
9.30am–5.30pm; early closing
Wednesday
*Produce* Vegetables, soft fruits
when in season, hen eggs, sheep
and goat's milk, wholefoods

W. J. and A. F. Clack
Lower Thornton Farm
Kenn
Exeter EX6 7RH
(Tel. 0392 833434)
*Open* 8am–dusk
*Produce* Vegetables,
Bramley apples

**Hartland**

Colin Marshall
Cranham Farmhouse
Hartland
Bideford
Devon
(Tel. Morwenstow 351)
*Open* Please telephone first

*Produce* Vegetables, strawberries, eggs (hen and duck), poultry and beef

*Directions* Turn off the A39 at the West Country Inn, towards the coast. First left over the moor, signposted to Wembsworthy. Follow to the end, down an unmetalled road, through the farmyard and down a concrete drive – 3 miles in all

## Honiton

Elliots Farm Shop and Nursery
Osswell
Honiton
Devon EX14 9RT
(Tel. 0404 83549)
*Open* Daily 9am–10pm
*Produce* Vegetables and fruit, hen eggs

## Kingsbridge

Mr B. Stone
South Allington Kitchen Garden
c/o The Flat
Halwell Farm
South Pool
Kingsbridge
S. Devon
(Tel. 054 853 320)
*Open* Friday morning from Dartmouth Market only
🌐 *Produce* Vegetables, apples

## Newton Abbot

Linda Phelps and Gordon Strutt
Moorfoot Organic Garden
Denbury
Nr Newton Abbot
Devon
(Tel. 0803 813161)
*Open* Tuesdays and Saturdays 10am–1pm and 2pm–4pm; market stall every Friday at Totnes

🌐 *Produce* Vegetables, apples, pears, oranges, strawberries, raspberries, lemons, melons, peaches

*Directions* From the A38 take the turn off to Denbury and Woodland, keep on this road two and a half miles, turn right at Moorfoot Cross

J. Reddaway
Lower Rixdale
Luton
Ideford
Nr Newton Abbot
S. Devon
(Tel. 062 67 5218)
*Open* Six days a week, 8am–6pm, but please telephone first
🌐 *Produce* Cider

## Ottery St Mary

Food on the Hill
2b Cornhill
Ottery St Mary
Devon
(Tel. 040 481 2109)
*Open* Monday–Saturday 9am–5.30pm; early closing Wednesday 1pm
*Produce* Vegetables, apples, eggs (hen and duck), goat's milk and cheese, yogurt (sheep and cow), wholefoods

## Plymouth

Barbican Wholefoods
Citadel Ope (off Southside
  Street)
The Barbican
Plymouth
Devon
(Tel. 0752 660499)
*Open* Monday–Saturday
9.30am–6pm
*Produce* Vegetables, raspberries,
strawberries, blackcurrants,
grapes, apples, oranges, lemons,
clementines, peaches, pears,
eggs (duck and hen), dairy
products, wholefoods

## Tavistock

Timothy Clark
Kilworthy House School
Tavistock
Devon
(Tel. 0822 2610)
*Open* Tuesday to Saturday; early
closing Wednesday 12 noon
  *Produce* Vegetables and fruit
  are sold at Kilworthy
Kapers Wholefood Shop, Tel.
0822 5039

T. M. Clark
Rumleigh Organic Gardens
Rumleigh
Bere Alston
Nr Yelverton
Devon PL20 7HN
(Tel. 0822 840557)
*Open* Please telephone first
  *Produce* Salad vegetables,
  herbs, strawberries,
blackcurrants
*Directions* Take Tavistock–Bere
Alston road. Turn right 1 mile
before Bere Alston at the sign for
Rumleigh Tuckermarsh. Down
hill on left at second crossroads

Kilworthy Kapers
11 King Street
Tavistock
Devon PL19 0DS
(Tel. 0822 5039)
*Open* Monday–Saturday
9am–5.30pm; early closing
Wednesday 1pm; Tavistock
pannier market, Friday
*Produce* Most varieties of
vegetables and fruit in season,
eggs (duck and hen), dairy
produce (goat, cow and sheep),
wholefoods

N. and M. Willcocks
Higher Birch
Bere Alston
Yelverton
Devon PL20 7BY
(Tel. 0822 840257)
*Open* Please telephone first
  *Produce* Beef and
  lamb

## Tiverton

Joan and Peter Berger
Castle Barn
Exeter Hill
Tiverton
Devon EX16 4PL
(Tel. 0884 254573)
*Open* Please telephone first
*Produce* Goat's milk, cheese (semi-
hard and hard)

Reapers Wholefoods
23 Gold Street
Tiverton
EX16 6QD

(Tel. 0884 255310)
*Open* Monday–Saturday
8.45am–5.15pm; early closing
Thursday
*Produce* Vegetables and fruit, hen
eggs, dairy produce (goat and
sheep), wholefoods

Angel Food
1 Angel Terrace
Tiverton
Devon
(Tel. 0884 254778)
*Open* Monday–Saturday
9am–5.30pm; early closing
Thursday 2.30pm
*Produce* Vegetables, hen eggs,
dairy produce (cow, goat and
sheep), wholefoods

## Totnes

Charles and Janet Riggs
Weston House Organic Fruit
    Farm
Totnes
Devon
(Tel. 0803 862066)
*Open* 10am till dusk; closed
Fridays; Totnes Market,
Fridays; Newton Abbot Market,
Wednesdays and Saturdays
*Produce* Vegetables, raspberries,
strawberries, loganberries, black
and red currants, top fruit,
melons, grapes, eggs

Sacks Wholefoods
High Street
Totnes
Devon
(Tel. 0803 863263)
*Open* Daily 9am–5pm
*Produce* Watercress, vegetables,
wholefoods, eggs

### Welcombe

Yarner Trust
Welcombe Barton
Welcombe,
Nr. Bideford
Devon
(Tel. 028 883 482)
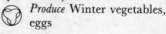 *Produce* Vegetables, eggs
(hen and duck), dairy
produce (cow)
*Directions* 2 miles off the A39 near
Welcombe Church

### Winkleigh

Martin and Julia Kuhn
Woodroberts
Winkleigh
Devon
(Tel. 083 783 301)
*Open* All day
*Produce* Winter vegetables,
eggs

# SOMERSET

### Bridgwater

Wyvern Farm Organics
Cossington Lane
Nr Bridgwater
Somerset TA7 8LU
(Tel. 0278 723019)
*Open* Monday–Saturday
8am–5.30pm; Sunday 8am–1pm
*Produce* Vegetables and fruit,
meat

### Castle Cary

Old Bakehouse
High Street
Castle Cary
Somerset
(Tel. 0963 50067)
*Open* 9.30am–5.30pm; early
closing Thursday 1.30pm

*Produce* Vegetables, hen eggs

## Frome

The Wholefood Shop
Cork Street
Frome
Somerset
(Tel. 0373 73334)
*Open* Monday–Saturday
9.30am–5.30pm
*Produce* Vegetables, fruit, eggs
(duck and hen), wholefoods

Safeway Food Stores Ltd
King Street
Frome
Somerset BA11 1BH
(Tel. 0373 4063)

## Glastonbury

Phoenix Wholefoods
4 High Street
Glastonbury
Somerset
(Tel. 0458 31004)
*Produce* Vegetables, fruit, eggs,
dairy produce (cow, goat and
sheep), wholefoods

## Langport

A. V. R. Cracknell and Son
Free Range Poultry Farm
Huish Episcopi
Langport
Somerset TA10 9EY
(Tel. 0458 250731)
*Open* Weekdays but please
telephone first
*Produce* Hen eggs, goat's milk,
chicken, ducks and geese, lamb
*Directions* Half a mile down lane
off the Langport to Somerton
Road, one and a half miles out of
Longford

## Minehead

A. C. Oakes
Howtown House
Winsford
Nr Minehead
Somerset
(Tel. 064 385 245)
*Open* Please telephone first
    *Produce* Vegetables,
    lamb
*Directions* Off Dunster–Tiverton
Road, approximately 6 miles
from Dunster. Turn right at sign
for Winsford

The Whole Food Shop
3 Parks Lane
Minehead
Somerset
(Tel. 0643 6101)
*Open* Monday–Saturday
9am–5pm; early closing
Wednesday 2pm
*Produce* Vegetables, dairy produce
(cow, goat and sheep), hen eggs,
wholefoods

## Norton St Philip

F. R. Applegate
Brown Shutters Farm
Norton St Philip
Nr Bath
Somerset
(Tel. 022 122 3172)
*Produce* Eggs (hen, duck and
goose), poultry and game

## Shepton Mallet

Dr H. R. H. Tripp
Avalon Vineyard
The Drove
East Pennard
Shepton Mallet
Somerset BA4 6UA

(Tel. 074986 393)
*Open* Pick your own in June, July,
August. Thursday–Sunday
10am–5pm, otherwise please
telephone first
 *Produce* Strawberries,
raspberries, tayberries,
gooseberries, wine
*Directions* 5 miles south of Shepton
Mallet on A37. At Wraxall
crossroad take Glastonbury turn
for one and a half miles. Turn
right at sign

Wolffs Green Grocery
34 High Street
Shepton Mallet
Somerset
(Tel. 0749 2657)
*Open* 8.30am–5pm; early closing
Wednesday 1.30pm
*Produce* Vegetables and fruit, hen
eggs

## Somerton

J. M. Spiers
Turners Field
Behind Town
Compton
Dundon
Somerton
Somerset TA11 6PT
(Tel. 0458 42192)
 *Produce* Vegetables

Jane Procter
Little Coombe
Coombe Hill
Keinton Mandeville
Nr Somerton
Somerset TA11 6DQ
(Tel. 045 822 3215)
*Open* Please telephone first

 *Produce* Vegetables, apples,
plums, soft fruit, hen eggs

## Taunton

Natural Foods
18 Station Road
Taunton
Somerset
(Tel. 0823 88179)
*Open* Monday–Saturday
9am–5.30pm
*Produce* Vegetables and fruit, hen
eggs, wholefoods

## Watchet

Simon Passmore
28 Belle Vue
Washford
Watchet
Somerset
(Tel. 0984 40344)
*Open* Please telephone first
 *Produce* Vegetables

## Wellington

Bindon Home Farm
Langford Budville
Wellington
Somerset TA21 0RU
(Tel. 0823 400644)
*Open* By special arrangement only
 *Produce* Vegetables, hen
eggs, flour

Sunseed
24 High Street
Wellington
Somerset
(Tel. 082 347 2313)
*Open* 9am–5.30pm
*Produce* Wholefoods, vegetables
and fruit (when available)

## Wells

Good Earth Natural Food Store
4 Priory Road
Wells
Somerset
(Tel. 0749 78600)
*Open* Monday–Saturday
9am–5pm
*Produce* Wholefoods, eggs,
vegetables, dairy produce (goat),
flour

## Wincanton

Charles W. J. Dowding
Orchard House
Shepton Montague
Wincanton
Somerset BA9 8JW
(Tel. 0749 813319)
*Open* 24 hours' notice required

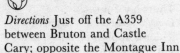 *Produce* Vegetables

*Directions* Just off the A359
between Bruton and Castle
Cary; opposite the Montague Inn

## Winscombe

Coombe Valley Nurseries
Eastwell Lane
Winscombe
Somerset BS25 1DA
(Tel. 093 484 3782)
*Open* Please telephone first
*Produce* Vegetables, hen eggs

## Yeovil

Safeway Food Stores Ltd
Quedam Centre
Yeovil
Somerset
(Tel. 0935 29233)

Symes Delicatessen
50 Princes Street
Yeovil
BA20 1EQ
(Tel. 0935 23763)
*Open* Monday–Friday
8.45am–5.15pm; Saturday
8.45am–4pm
*Produce* Vegetables

# SOUTHERN ENGLAND

## DORSET

### Blandford

Safeway Food Stores Ltd
West Street
Blandford
Dorset
(Tel. 0258 56368/56356)

### Bournemouth

Mustard and Cress
300 Holdenhurst Road
Bournemouth
Dorset BH8 8AY
(Tel. 0202 33137)
*Open* Monday–Saturday
8am–6pm
*Produce* Vegetables, apples, pears,
oranges, lemons, eggs, goat's
milk; yogurt and cheese (cow's)

Earth Foods Ltd
250 Old Christchurch Road
Bournemouth
(Tel. 0202 422465)
*Open* Monday–Saturday
9am–6pm
*Produce* Vegetables and fruit,
eggs, wholefoods

Safeway Food Stores Ltd
Parkway House
Avenue Road
Bournemouth
Dorset BH2 5SJ
(Tel. 0202 292240)

Safeway Food Stores Ltd
King John's Avenue
Bearwood
Dorset

(Tel. 0202 570639)

### Bridport

Fruits of the Earth
Victoria Grove
Bridport
(Tel. 0308 25827)
*Open* Monday–Saturday
9am–5pm; early closing
Thursday 1pm
*Produce* Vegetables, hen eggs,
dairy produce (sheep and goat),
wholefoods

### Dorchester

Down to Earth
18 Princes Street
Dorchester
Dorset
(Tel. 0305 68325)
*Open* Monday–Saturday
9am–5pm; early closing
Thursday 1pm
*Produce* Vegetables, oranges,
lemons, apples, bananas, plus
soft fruit when in season, hen and
duck eggs, goat's and sheep's
milk, wholefoods

Arthur and Josephine Pearse
Tamarisk Farm
West Bexington
Dorchester
Dorset DT2 9DF
(Tel. 0308 897 784)
*Open* All daylight hours. Visitors
welcome
⊘ *Produce* Vegetables and
fruit
*Directions* At West Bexington
close to the sea between
Abbotsbury and Burton
Bradstock

## Sherborne

Food for Thought
64 Cheap Street
Sherborne
Dorset DT9 3BJ
(Tel. 0935 814262)
*Open* Monday–Saturday
9am–5.30pm
*Produce* Vegetables, apples and
pears sometimes, hen eggs and
occasionally duck and goose eggs,
yoghurt and ice cream (cow's),
goat's milk, yoghurt and cheese,
imported Greek sheep's yoghurt
and cheese, wholefoods

B. and J. Brook
Claypitts Farm
Beer Hackett
Nr Sherborne
Dorset DT9 6QT
(Tel. 0935 872060)
*Open* Daylight hours
*Produce* Vegetables, soft
fruit
*Directions* Drive through Beer
Hackett leaving church on right.
Take first turn on left (cul-de-
sac). Farmhouse is on the right

## Shillingstone

C. C. G. Edwards
Burlton Cottage
Shillingstone
Dorset DT11 0SP
(Tel. 0258 860641)
*Open* Mail order only
*Produce* French and German
wines, olive oil, grape juices,
honey

## Southbourne

Earth Foods Ltd
75 Southbourne Grove
Southbourne
Dorset
(Tel. 0202 422465)
*Open* Monday–Saturday
9am–6pm
*Produce* Vegetables, fruit, eggs,
wholefoods

## Verwood

Safeway Food Stores Ltd
Manor Road
Verwood
Dorset
(Tel. 0202 822622)

## Wimborne

Sir Michael and Lady Hanham
Deans Court
Wimborne
Dorset
*Open* Thursday afternoons,
daylight hours
*Produce* Vegetables, top and
soft fruit, apples (wide
range) and raspberries, hen eggs

Riverside Organic Growers
Riverside Farm
Slough Lane
Horton Heath
Wimborne
Dorset
(Tel. Verwood 826509)
*Produce* Vegetables, strawberries

Robin and Lisa Walker
(Wimborne Organic Produce)
79 Leigh Road
Wimborne
Dorset
(Tel. 0202 881680)
*Open* At Wimborne Market
Fridays only 8am–2pm
*Produce* Wide range of vegetables

and fruit, hen eggs, yogurt and
cheese (cow's), poultry,
wholefoods

Spill the Beans
7 West Street
Wimborne
Dorset
(Tel. 0202 888989)
*Open* Monday to Saturday
9am–5pm; early closing
Wednesday 1pm
*Produce* Vegetables, wholefoods

Safeway Food Stores Ltd
92/94 Victoria Road
Ferndown
Wimborne
Dorset BH22 9JA
(Tel. 0202 877183)

Safeway Food Stores Ltd
Town Centre Development
Hanham Road
Wimborne
Dorset BH21 1ED

# HAMPSHIRE

## Andover

Safeway Food Stores Ltd
55/57 Bridge Street
Andover
Hants
(Tel. 0264 54081/63379)

## Christchurch

Safeway Food Stores Ltd
85 Station Road
New Milton
Hants BH2 6JD
(Tel. 0425 610072/616038)

## Eastleigh

Safeway Food Stores Ltd
105/111 Winchester Road
Chandlers Ford
Eastleigh
Hants B05 2GH
(Tel. 04215 66547)

Safeway Food Stores Ltd
Leigh Road
Eastleigh
Hants SO5 4FH
(Tel. 0703 610639/611489)

## Fareham

George and Dorothy Marshall
2 Burnt House Lane
Stubbington
Fareham
Hants PO14 2LQ
(Tel. 0329 662317)
*Open* Please telephone first
*Produce* Vegetables, hen eggs,
farmhouse cow's butter, cheese,
double cream, goat and ewe's
cheese, beef, lamb, pork and
poultry, meat products

## Fleet

David Wootton
Wood Farm
Brickhouse Hill
Eversley
Hants RG27 0PY
(Tel. 0734 733767)
*Open* Please telephone first
*Produce* Vegetables, raspberries,
gooseberries, blackcurrants and
rhubarb, hen eggs
*Directions* Half a mile south of
Eversley Church, on Eversley to
Fleet road

## Fordingbridge

Hockeys–Naturally
Newtown Farm
South Gorley
Fordingbridge
Hants SP6 2PW
(Tel. 0425 52542)
*Open* Monday–Saturday
9am–6pm (5.30pm Saturdays)
*Produce* Hen eggs, beef, pork,
lamb, chickens, meat products.
Available mail-order by Datapost
*Directions* Situated off A338
between Fordingbridge and
Ringwood

Richard and Susan Loader
Furzehill Farm
South Gorley
Fordingbridge
Hants SP6 2PT
(Tel. 0425 53361)
*Open* Please telephone first
*Produce* Vegetables, fruit,
goat's milk

Eden Cormack
Sandy Balls Organic Gardens
Sandy Balls Estate
Godshill
Fordingbridge
Hants SP6 2JX
(Tel. 0425 54743)
*Open* Any reasonable time
*Produce* Vegetables,
herbs

## Lymington

Safeway Food Stores Ltd
Standford Hill
Lymington
Hants
(Tel. 0590 78295/78494)

Mrs C. Ashby
Coronation Cottage
Main Road
East Boldre
Brockenhurst
Hants
(Tel. 059 065 336)
*Open* At weekends and weekdays
after 6pm
*Produce* Pork, eggs, cream, honey
(as available)

## Portsmouth

Safeway Food Stores Ltd
Anchorage Park
Portsmouth
Hants

## Southampton

Barbara Otto
Sharveshill Farm
Little Testwood
Totton
Southampton
(Tel. 0703 868503)
*Open* Please telephone first
*Produce* Summer vegetables,
goat's milk/cheese
*Directions* The farm is just off the
A36 between Totton and Ower

Southampton Community
Co-operative Ltd
92 St Mary's Road
Southampton SO2 0AM
(Tel. 0703 32583)
*Open* Monday–Saturday
9am–5.30pm (6pm Fridays)
*Produce* Vegetables, lemons,
oranges, apples

Safeway Food Stores Ltd
West End Road
Bitterne
Southampton
Hants
(Tel. 0703 433580/443940)

Safeway Food Stores Ltd
99 Queensway
Southampton
Hants SO1 1HJ
(Tel. 0703 24704)

### Stockbridge

S. L. and J. D. Tidy
The Anchorage
Salisbury Road
Broughton
Nr Stockbridge
Hants
(Tel. 079 430 234)
*Open* Please telephone first
*Produce* Vegetables, raspberries,
blackberries, blackcurrants, hen
eggs, pork and poultry
*Directions* Approximately 1 mile
south of A30 on B3084

### Waltham Chase

P. and E. Rainey
Oaklands Farm
Lower Chase Road
Waltham Chase
Hants SO3 2LH
(Tel. 04893 2394)
*Open* Please telephone first
*Produce* Eggs (hen and
goose), goat's milk

### Whitchurch

M. and J. Breen,
A. W. and D. M. Wright and
  families
Larks Barrow Market Garden

Kingsclere Road
Whitchurch
Hants
(Tel. 025 682 2253)
*Open* Daylight hours
*Produce* Vegetables, raspberries,
strawberries, pork
*Directions* 1 mile north of
Whitchurch on old A34, take
right turning to Kingsclere. Larks
Barrow is a quarter of a mile on
the left

# WILTSHIRE

### Bradford-on-Avon

Chris Jones
87 Trowbridge Road
Bradford-on-Avon
Wilts BA15 1EG
(Tel. 022 16 4792)
*Open* Monday–Saturday
9am–5.30pm
*Produce* Vegetables and fruit

### Malmesbury

Malmesbury Wholefoods
29 Abbey Row
Malmesbury
Wilts SN16 0AG
(Tel. 06662 2567)
*Open* 9am–5.30pm; early closing
Thursday 2pm
*Produce* Eggs (duck and hen),
goat's milk and cheese, yogurt
(sheep and cow), wholefoods

### Marlborough

Doves Farm Flour
Ham
Marlborough
Wilts
(Tel. 0488 4374)

*Open* Weekdays 9am–5pm
*Produce* Traditional French soft goat cheeses, flour, biscuits
*Directions* South of Hungerford, Berks. (See also under Wholesalers)

### Salisbury

Safeway Food Stores Ltd
8/10 Brown Street
Salisbury
Wilts
SP1 1HE
(Tel. 0722 28730/25674)

### Upavon

C. B. Wookey
Rushall Farms
The Manor
Upavon
Pewsey
Wilts
(Tel. 0980 630264)
*Open* Normal working hours
*Produce* Hen eggs, flour
*Directions* On A342 1 mile west of Upavon

### Warminster

Mrs L. Peddle
7 Beacon View
Warminster
Wilts
(Tel. 0985 214411)
*Open* By order only
*Produce* Hen eggs, cheese, beef, pork, lamb and poultry

Safeway Food Stores Ltd
Market Place
Warminster
Wilts BA12 9BT
(Tel. 09852 12072/14633)

# THE SOUTH EAST

## EAST SUSSEX

### Bexhill

B. Faulkner
16 Ninfield Road
Widley
Bexhill
East Sussex
(Tel. 0424 213643)
*Open* Monday–Saturday
7.15am–8pm; Sunday
8.30am–2pm
*Produce* Vegetables and fruit, eggs (duck, hen and goose), dairy produce (cow, goat and sheep), meat, wholefoods

### Bodiam

John Rigby and Yvonne Dhooge
Bramley Organic Farm
Staplecross Road
Bodiam
East Sussex TN32 5UJ
(Tel. 058083 566)
*Open* Weekends from May to December
*Produce* Vegetables, apples, strawberries, apple juice
*Directions* Quarter of a mile south of Bodiam Castle on the road to Staplecross

### Brighton

Infinity Foods Co-operative Ltd
25 North Road
Brighton
(Tel. 0273 603563)
*Open* Monday–Saturday
9.30am–5.30pm; Wednesday
early closing 2pm; late night
Friday 7pm

*Produce* Vegetables, oranges, apples, pears, avocados, pineapple, mangoes, lemons, grapefruit, hen eggs, yogurt, wholefoods

## Crowborough

Safeway Food Stores Ltd
Fernbank Shopping Centre
High Street
Crowborough
East Sussex TN6 2QB
(Tel. 08926 4390)

## East Grinstead

Safeway Food Stores Ltd
West Street
East Grinstead
East Sussex
(Tel. 0342 312630/314847)

## Eastbourne

Safeway Food Stores Ltd
High Street
Old Town
Eastbourne
East Sussex
(Tel. 0323 22587/27049)

## Forest Row

Walter J. Rudert
Tablehurst Farm
Forest Row
East Sussex
(Tel. 034 282 3536)
*Open* Please telephone first
*Produce* Vegetables, hen eggs, beef, flour
*Directions* Off A22 – 100m north of Forest Row

The Seasons
10/11 Hartfield Road
Forest Row
East Sussex
*Open* Monday–Friday
9am–5.30pm; Tuesday and
Saturday closed at 1pm
*Produce* Wholefoods, vegetables, fruit, eggs, untreated milk, cream cheese, yogurt, meat

## Hailsham

Graeme Fisk
The Granary
Prinkle Farm
Bodle Street
Hailsham
East Sussex BN27 4UD
(Tel. 0323 833541)
*Open* By appointment only
*Produce* Vegetables, blackcurrants, strawberries

R. C. Burfield
Pekes Farm
Nash Street
Hailsham
East Sussex BN27 4HD
(Tel. 0825 872480)
*Open* By appointment only
*Produce* Corn (*Soil Association Symbol*); beef, lamb
*Directions* Off A22 Gun Hill–Horam Road

## Lewes

Full of Beans
96–97 High Street
Lewes
East Sussex BN7 1XH
(Tel. 0273 472627)

*Open* Monday–Friday
9am–5.30pm; Saturday to 5pm
*Produce* Vegetables, citrus fruits
and apples, eggs (duck and hen),
goat's milk and yogurt, cheese
(cow), wholefoods

Lansdown House Health Foods
10 Lansdown Place
Lewes
East Sussex
(Tel. 0273 474681)
*Open* Monday–Friday
9am–5.30pm; Saturday
9am–1pm
*Produce* Vegetables, fruit, eggs,
dairy produce, wholefoods

Safeway Food Stores Ltd
Eastgate Street
Lewes
East Sussex BN7 2LP
(Tel. 0273 476980/476972)

## Mayfield

Mrs Jean Flintan
Clayton Farmhouse
Newick Lane
Mayfield
East Sussex TN20 6RE
(Tel. 0435 873476)
*Open* All day Monday-Saturday,
Sunday by arrangement, but
please telephone first
*Produce* Vegetables, hen
eggs, soft fruit, dairy
produce, beef, veal, pork, table
poultry, meat products
*Directions* From north, Newick
Lane is the first left out of
Mayfield, on A267 opposite
Railway Inn. Farm is 1 mile
along on right-hand bend. From
east, it is the first right after

Crown Inn, approaching
Heathfield on A265 – farm is then
3 miles along on left

## Peacehaven

Mrs Beaumont's Natural and
Organic Foods
9 Outlook Avenue
Peacehaven
East Sussex BN9 8XE
(Tel. 07914 5551)
*Produce* Vegetables, a wide range
of fruits, eggs (hen and duck),
chickens

## Robertsbridge

Roy Cook
Pine Ridge Vineyard
Staplecross
Robertsbridge
East Sussex TN32 5SA
(Tel. 058083 715)
*Open* May–September, daily
10am–6pm
*Produce* Vegetables,
strawberries, wine
*Directions* On A229 between
Hawkshurst and Sedlescombe,
1 mile north of Sedlescombe

## Rye

Lady Daphne Russell
Oak Cottage
Beckley
Rye
Sussex
(Tel. 079 726 265)
*Produce* Vegetables, soft fruit
mostly raspberries and currants

## Wadhurst

Wealden Wholefoods
High Street
Wadhurst
East Sussex

(Tel. 0892 88 3065)
*Open* Monday–Saturday
(9am–5pm); early closing
Wednesday and Saturday 1pm
*Produce* Vegetables, lemons,
apples, soft fruits in season, hen
eggs, dairy produce, wholefoods

Mrs J. V. Hamon
Old Granary Farm
Woods Green
Wadhurst
East Sussex
(Tel. 089 288 3302)
*Open* Daily 9.30am–9.30pm
*Produce* Vegetables,
strawberries, Jersey milk,
cream, butter, yogurt, goat's milk
and cheese (hard and soft), eggs.
Occasionally pork, bacon, beef,
goat meat, cheese

### Uckfield

Hamilton and Laurence Hill
Boathouse Farm
Isfield
Nr Uckfield
East Sussex TN22 5TY
(Tel. 082 575 302)
*Open* Daylight hours, but please
telephone first for meat
*Produce* Potatoes, hen eggs,
beef, lamb, flour
*Directions* Midway between Lewes
and Uckfield, half a mile off A26,
signed to Isfield. Do not cross
level crossing

# KENT

### Ashford

Safeway Food Stores Ltd
New Street

Ashford
Kent
(Tel. 0233 42974)

P. J. Zeen
Pollards Dane
Canterbury Road
Charing
Ashford
Kent
(Tel. 023371 2580)
*Open* Daily 9am–6pm
*Produce* Vegetables

M. D. and D. N. Rust
Tamley Nurseries
Hastingleigh
Ashford
Kent TN25 5HW
(Tel. 023 375 253)
*Produce* Vegetables,
raspberries, strawberries,
honey
*Directions* Take the lane from the
centre of Hastingleigh village to
'South Hill'. Look for Sycamore
Cottage on the left after 250
yards

### Beckenham

Safeway Food Stores Ltd
135/143 High Street
Beckenham
Kent BR3 1AG
(Tel. 01 650 0549)

### Biggin Hill

Safeway Food Stores Ltd
Main Road
Biggin Hill
Kent
(Tel. 0959 73222/75095)

**Broadstairs**

P. Challans
'All the Best'
16 The Broadway
Broadstairs
Kent
(Tel. 0843 604408)
*Open* 8.30am–5.30pm
*Produce* Hen eggs, cheese,
wholefoods, vegetables, apples,
damsons, figs, grapes, grapefruit,
lemons, oranges, greengages,
pears, plums

**Bromley**

Safeway Food Stores Ltd
23 Westmoreland Place
Masons Hill
Bromley
Kent BR1 1DS
(Tel. 01 460 8353)

Bromley Health Centre
54 Widmore Road
Bromley
Kent
(Tel. 01 460 3894)
*Open* Monday–Saturday
9am–5pm
*Produce* Vegetables, oranges,
lemons, pears, apples,
grapefruit, bananas, avocados,
hen eggs, goat's milk, wholefoods

**Canterbury**

Safeway Food Stores Ltd
St George's Place
Canterbury
Kent
(Tel. 0227 69335)

A. G. Brockman and Company
Perry Court Farm
Garlinge Green
Petham
Canterbury
Kent
(Tel. 0227 738449)
*Open* Wednesday and Friday
3–4.30pm or please telephone
first
   *Produce* Vegetables, hen
   eggs, flour

J. R. Sharman
Orchard View
Iffin Lane
Thanington Without
Canterbury
Kent CT4 7BE
(Tel. 0227 60680)
*Open* Please telephone first
   *Produce* Vegetables, apples,
   plums, eggs (hen, duck
and goose), honey

Gateways Wholefood Superstore
10 The Borough
Canterbury
Kent
(Tel. 0227 464623)
*Open* Monday–Saturday
9am–5.30pm
*Produce* Vegetables, fruit, eggs,
cheese, wholefoods

Dumbrells
15 Military Road
Canterbury
Kent
(Tel. 0227 464881)
*Open* Tuesday, Thursday, Friday
and Saturday 8.30am–5.30pm;
Monday and Wednesday
8.30am–1.30pm

*Produce* Vegetables and fruit

## Cranbrook

Healthy Way
1 St David's Bridge
Cranbrook
Kent
(Tel. 0580 712388)
*Open* Monday–Saturday
8.45am–5.30pm
*Produce* Vegetables, fruit, hen
eggs, dairy produce (cow and
sheep), wholefoods

## Gravesend

Good Health Wholefoods
22 High Street
Gravesend
Kent          *and*
142 Pelham Road
Gravesend
Kent
(Tel. 0474 358192)
*Open* Shops Monday–Saturday
9am–5.30pm; Friday to 7pm
*Produce* Vegetables, oranges,
lemons, grapefruit, hen eggs,
dairy produce (goat and cow),
meat, wholefoods

Safeway Food Stores Ltd
Anglesea Centre
New Road
Gravesend
Kent DA11 0AU
(Tel. 0474 60498)

## Herne Bay

Safeway Food Stores Ltd
Beach Street
Herne Bay
Kent CT6 5PF
(Tel. 02273 63890)

T. and C. Davis
3 Broomfield Road
Herne
Kent CT6 7AY
(Tel. 0227 372519)
*Open* Please telephone first
*Produce* Vegetables, rhubarb,
apples, hen eggs, honey

Manna Wholefoods
20 William Street
Herne Bay
Kent
(Tel. 02273 66660)
*Open* Tuesday, Wednesday,
Friday and Saturday
9am–5.30pm; Thursday
9am–4pm; Monday 9am–1pm
*Produce* Hen eggs, dairy produce
(goat and sheep), wholefoods

## Horsmonden

J. L. Orbach
Small's Farm
Horsmonden
Kent
(Tel. 089 272 2519)
*Open* Please telephone first
*Produce* Vegetables, apples,
grapes, figs
*Directions* Situated in School
House Lane

## Maidstone

Safeway Food Stores Ltd
London Road
Larkfield
Maidstone
Kent
(Tel. 0622 840282)

Safeway Food Stores Ltd
37 King Street
Maidstone
Kent ME14 1DD
(Tel. 0622 57548)

Safeway Food Stores Ltd
The Broadway
Maidstone
Kent
(Tel. 0622 672311)

The Pocket Garden
Museum of Kent Rural Life
Lock Lane
Sandling
Maidstone ME14 3AU
(Tel. 0622 63936)
*Open* Monday–Saturday
10am–4.30pm; closed
Wednesday; Sunday
2pm–4.30pm, April–October
*Produce* Vegetables,
rhubarb, soft fruit, herbs,
honey
*Directions* Junction 6, M20.
3 miles north of Maidstone off
Chatham Road

## Margate

No Frills Wholefoods
114 Northdown Road
Cliftonville
Margate
Kent
(Tel. 0843 297690)
*Open* Monday–Saturday
9am–7pm
*Produce* Vegetables, apples,
oranges, lemons, bananas, hen
eggs, cheese, wholefoods

## Orpington

Safeway Food Stores Ltd
The Walnuts Precinct
High Street
Orpington
Kent BR6 0TW
(Tel. 0689 20782)

Safeway Food Stores Ltd
330 Crofton Road
Farnborough
Orpington
Kent BR6 8NW
(Tel. 0689 52381)

## Petts Wood

Safeway Food Stores Ltd
Queensway
Petts Wood
Kent
(Tel. 0689 20548/34099)

## Rainham

Rainham Health Food Centre
28 Rainham Shopping Precinct
Rainham
Kent ME8 7HW
(Tel. 0634 362267)
*Open* Monday–Saturday
9am–5pm
*Produce* Vegetables, fruit, eggs,
dairy produce, wholefoods. Mail
order available

## Rochester

Safeway Food Stores Ltd
High Street
Strood
Rochester
Kent
(Tel. 0634 719279/718314)

## Sidcup

Safeway Food Stores Ltd
Westwood Lane
Sidcup
Blackfen
Kent DA15 9PS
(Tel. 01 303 8594)

## Thanet

Mrs S. Kulzer
Marsh Farm Organics
Marsh Farm
Gore Street
Monkton
Thanet CT12 4BU
(Tel. 0843 822318)
*Open* 8am–6pm
 *Produce* Vegetables, herbs,
strawberries, goat's milk,
pork
*Directions* On road to Wingham
(B2046) half a mile from the
A253 junction. Just over the
railway bridge

## Tonbridge

Safeway Food Stores Ltd
3/11 Quarry Hill Road
Tonbridge
Kent TN9 2RH
(Tel. 0732 350167)

## Tunbridge Wells

Natural Life
66 Grosvenor Road
Tunbridge Wells
Kent TN1 2AS
(Tel. 0892 43834)
*Open* Monday–Saturday
9am–5.30pm
*Produce* Vegetables, apples,
lemons, oranges, hen eggs,
yogurt, cheese, milk (cow, sheep
and goat), wholefoods

## West Wickham

Safeway Food Stores Ltd
High Street
West Wickham
Kent
(Tel. 01 777 5217/8308)

Farringtons
7–9 Beckenham Road
West Wickham
Kent BR4 0QR
(Tel. 01 777 8721)
*Open* Monday–Friday
9am–5.30pm; Saturday to 5pm;
early closing Wednesday 1pm
*Produce* Vegetables (Thursday
only), fruit, hen eggs, wholefoods

## Whitstable

Dilnots (Bakers)
77 High Street
Whitstable
Kent
(Tel. 0227 272747)
*Open* 7am–5pm; Saturdays to
4.30pm
*Produce* Bread

# SURREY

## Addlestone

Safeway Food Stores Ltd
Station Road
Addlestone
Surrey KT15 2PB
(Tel. 0932 55902)

## Chertsey

Mr W. E. Cattle
Linton Lodge
Fancourt Gardens
Longcross Road
Longcross
Chertsey
Surrey KT16 0DJ
(Tel. 093287 2571)
*Open* Please telephone first
*Produce* Vegetables,
blackcurrants, rhubarb,
raspberries
*Directions* Proceed along the
Longcross Road from Chertsey
towards Chobham. When double
white lines on bend and small hill
are encountered cross at the end
of these

## Croydon

Safeway Food Stores Ltd
24 Norfolk House
George Street
Croydon
Surrey CR0 1LG
(Tel. 01 688 8469)

## Egham

Health and Diet Centre
35 The Precinct
Egham
Surrey TW20 9HN
(Tel. 0784 36402)
*Open* Monday–Saturday
9am–5.30pm
*Produce* Vegetables, fruit, dairy
produce (cow and goat), hen
eggs, wholefoods

## Ewell

Roberts Fruiterers
178 Kingston Road
Ewell

Epsom
Surrey KT19 0SF
(Tel. 01 393 5658)
*Open* Monday–Friday 8am–6pm;
Saturday to 5.30pm; Sunday
9.30am–1pm
*Produce* Vegetables, apples,
oranges, lemons, grapefruit, soft
fruit, avocados, wholefoods

## Godalming

Health and Diet Centre
81 High Street
Godalming
Surrey GU7 1AW
(Tel. 04868 24353)
*Open* Monday–Saturday
9am–5.30pm
*Produce* Vegetables, fruit, dairy
produce (cow and goat), hen
eggs, wholefoods

## Guildford

Earthbound Wholefoods
10 Madrid Road
Guildford
Surrey GU2 5NT
(Tel. 0483 69611)
*Open* Tuesday–Friday
9.30am–5.30pm; Saturday to
5pm
*Produce* Vegetables, eggs (duck,
hen and goose), dairy produce
(sheep and goat), wholefoods

Loseley Park Farm Shop
Guildford
Surrey GU3 1HS
(Tel. 0483 571881)
*Open* June to September,
Wednesday–Saturday 2pm–5pm
*Produce* Vegetables,
strawberries, herbs, dairy
produce, wholefoods

*Directions* Take the B3000 turning off the A3 through Compton, signposted to Loseley. Also signed off the A3100 between Guildford and Godalming

David Priestley
Barn Field Market Garden
Franksfield
Peaslake
Guildford
Surrey GU5 9SR
(Tel. 0306 731310)
*Open* 9am–7pm but please telephone first

 *Produce* Vegetables, raspberries, gooseberries, blackcurrants, duck eggs
*Directions* Peaslake is 2 miles south of Shere which is midway between Guildford and Dorking. Ask for Franksfield in village

Piccards Farm Products
Conduit Farm
Sandy Lane
Guildford
Surrey GU3 1HJ
(Tel. 0483 63095)
*Open* Please telephone first
*Produce* Pork, sausages, lamb

## Hersham

Safeway Food Stores Ltd
Hersham Centre
Hersham
Surrey
(Tel. 0932 231150/231257)

## Kew

Real Life Foods
19 Maze Road
Kew

Richmond
Surrey TW9 3EB
(Tel. 01 878 4695 or 940 5299)
*Open* Home delivery service only
*Produce* Vegetables, apples, oranges, lemons, grapefruits, clementines, strawberries and other berries in season, pears, rhubarb, avocados, mangoes, melons, hen eggs, yogurt and cheese (cow) and goat's milk cheese, beef, pork, lamb, poultry goose, duck and meat products, wholefoods

## New Malden

Safeway Food Stores Ltd
126/130 High Street
New Malden
Surrey KT3 4EP
(Tel. 01 942 7498)

## Redhill

Safeway Food Stores Ltd
Queensway
Redhill
Surrey RH1 1QR
(Tel. 0737 64043)

## Sutton

Safeway Food Stores Ltd
167/169 High Street
Sutton
Surrey SM1 1JS
(Tel. 01 642 7557)

## Virginia Water

Richard's Fruiterers
6 Station Approach
Virginia Water
Surrey
(Tel. 099 04 3730)
*Open* Monday–Saturday
8.30am–5.30pm

*Produce* Vegetables, apples, oranges, bananas, lemons

## Walton-on-Thames

Safeway Food Stores Ltd
18/32 Church Street
Walton-on-Thames
Surrey
(Tel. 0932 220263)

## Woking

Mizen's Farm Shop
Mizen's Farm
Chertsey Road
Woking
Surrey
(Tel. 04862 29799)
*Open* Daily 9am–5.30pm
*Produce* Vegetables, apples, pears, oranges, lemons, and seasonal fruits, wholefoods

# WEST SUSSEX

## Haywards Heath

Toos Jeuken
Laines Organic Farm
47 Newbury Lane
Cuckfield
West Sussex RH17 5AA
(Tel. 0444 452663)
*Open* Daily 10am–6pm
*Produce* Vegetables, gooseberries, raspberries
*Directions* On A272–before entering the village of Cuckfield (going east) turn to right (signs on road)

## Henfield

Barrow Hill Farms
Henfield
West Sussex BN5 9DN

(Tel. 0273 492733)
*Open* Daylight hours
*Produce* Vegetables, hen eggs, goat's milk and sometimes cheese
*Directions* Half a mile from Henfield village on the Shoreham Road

## Horsham

The Country Basket
7 East Street
Horsham
West Sussex RH12 1HH
(Tel. 0403 65102)
*Produce* Vegetables, fruit, wholefoods

## Pulborough

F. W. Dougharty
Cattlestone Farm
Harbolets Road
West Chiltington
Nr Pulborough
West Sussex RH20 2LG
(Tel. 07983 3156)
*Open* Daily 9am till dusk
*Produce* Vegetables, apples, plums, hen eggs, herbs
*Directions* Near Broadford Bridge on the B2133

## Washington

R. D. Muntz
Barnard's Nursery
Rock Road
Washington
West Sussex RH20 3BH
(Tel. 0903 892320)
*Open* Please telephone first (not Sunday)
*Produce* Vegetables
*Directions* Half a mile up Rock

Road from the London Road, on
the right

### Worthing

Broadwater Produce Ltd
Southdownview Road
Broadwater Trading Estate
Worthing
(Tel. 0903 204274/34091)
*Open* Thursday, Friday, Saturday
9am–5.30pm
*Produce* Vegetables, fruit, eggs,
dairy products, wholefoods

# LONDON AND THE HOME COUNTIES

## BEDFORDSHIRE

### Bedford

Safeway Food Stores Ltd
Greyfriars
Bedford MK40 1HP
(Tel. 0234 54418)

### Sandy

Eleanor Hodges
Rosehaven
110 Cinques Road
Gamlingay
Sandy
Beds SG19 3NR
(Tel. 0767 50142)
*Open* Please telephone first
 *Produce* Vegetables,
raspberries and
blackcurrants, eggs (hen and
goose), lamb and poultry
*Directions* Half a mile west of
village centre on the St Neots
road

### Yelden

Yelden Manor Organic Growers
The Manor Cottage
Church Lane
Yelden
Beds MK44 1AV
(Tel. 0933 315660)
*Open* Please telephone first
*Produce* Vegetables, eggs
(hen and goose), herbs

# BERKSHIRE

## Maidenhead

New Morning Wholefoods
King Street Market
Maidenhead
Berks
(Tel. 0628 25592)
*Open* Friday and Saturday
9am–5.30pm
*Produce* Vegetables and fruit (full
range), hen eggs, goat's milk,
yogurt (cow's), meat (monthly
order), meat products,
wholefoods

## Reading

Aidan Carlisle and Peggy Ellis
64 Blenheim Road
Caversham
Reading
Berks RG4 7RS
(Tel. 0734 473159)
*Open* Please telephone first
between 8pm and 9.30pm
*Produce* Vegetables,
strawberries, raspberries,
gooseberries, blackberries,
blackcurrants, eggs (hen and
duck), goat's milk, rabbits and
hens

Garlands Organic Farm Shop
Garlands Farm
Gardeners Lane
Upper Basildon
Reading
Berks
(Tel. 0491 671556)
*Open* Monday–Saturday
9am–4pm
*Produce* Vegetables, apples,
pears, oranges, lemons,
grapefruit, raspberries,

strawberries in season, hen eggs,
dairy produce (cow, sheep and
goat), beef and pork, poultry,
wholefoods

Springalls Farm Ltd
Trowes Lane
Swallowfield
Reading
Berks RG7 1RN
(Tel. 0734 883736)
*Open* June–November, Fridays
and Saturdays 10am–4pm
*Produce* Vegetables, hen
eggs

Hardwick Farm Produce
Path Hill Farm
Whitchurch
Nr Reading
Oxon
(Tel. 07357 2365)
*Produce* Vegetables, dairy
produce (Guernsey cow),
pork, beef, lamb, table poultry

## Sandhurst

Safeway Food Stores Ltd
Yorktown Road
Sandhurst
Berks
(Tel. 0276 33243)

## Thatcham

Thatcham Health Foods
Shop 3
16 High Street
Thatcham
Berks
(Tel. 0635 61017)
*Open* Daily 9am–5.30pm; early
closing Wednesday
*Produce* Eggs (hen, duck and

goose), meat products, dairy produce (sheep and goat)

## Windsor

Oasis Wholefoods
96 Peascod Street
Windsor
Berks
(Tel. 0753 860618)
*Open* Monday–Saturday
9am–5.30pm
*Produce* Vegetables, fruit, hen eggs, dairy produce (cow, goat and sheep), wholefoods

## Wokingham

Safeway Food Stores Ltd
Woosehill Centre
Woosehill
Wokingham
Berks
(Tel. 0734 794140)

# BUCKINGHAMSHIRE

## Amersham

Amersham Wholefoods
156 Station Road
Amersham
Bucks
(Tel. 02403 6752)
*Open* Monday–Saturday
9am–5.30pm
*Produce* Vegetables, fruit, duck eggs, dairy produce (cow, sheep and goat), wholefoods

## Aylesbury

Springhill Farm Foods
Gatehouse Close
Aylesbury
Bucks HP19 3DE
(Tel. 0296 25333)

*Open* Monday–Friday 9am–5pm
*Produce* Vegetables, hen eggs, bread, cakes, pâté, wholefoods
*Directions* Just off the Ring Road

## Chalfont St Peter

Only Natural
41 St Peter's Court
Chalfont St Peter
Bucks
(Tel. 0753 889441)
*Open* Monday–Saturday
8.30am–5.30pm
*Produce* Vegetables, apples, oranges, grapes, lemons, hen eggs, dairy produce (sheep, cow and goat), wholefoods

## Chesham

Miles of Wholefoods
Sunnyside
Chesham
Bucks
(Tel. 0494 774185)
*Open* Monday–Saturday
9.15am–6pm
*Produce* Vegetables, fruit, hen eggs, wholefoods

# HERTFORDSHIRE

## Barnet

C. R. G. Shewell-Cooper
Arkley Manor Farm
Rowley Lane
Arkley
Barnet
Herts EN5 3HS
(Tel. 01 449 7944)
*Open* Monday–Friday 9am–5pm
*Produce* Vegetables, fruit, hen eggs, wholefoods

## Berkhamstead

Cooks Delight
360–362 High Street
Berkhamstead
Herts HP4 1HU
(Tel. 04427 3584)
*Open* Tuesday 8am–5.30pm;
Wednesday 8.30am–3.30pm;
Thursday and Friday 8am–9pm;
Saturday 8am–3.30pm; Sunday
9.30am–5.30pm
*Produce* Vegetables, apples,
oranges, lemons, grapes,
bananas, pears, plums, peaches,
avocados, Staffordshire cheese,
wholefoods

## Hemel Hempstead

Only Organic Ltd
56 High Street
Hemel Hempstead
Herts
(Tel. 0442 47555)
*Open* Monday–Saturday
9am–5.30pm
*Produce* Vegetables, apples,
oranges, mandarins, tomatoes,
pears, bananas, lemons, hen eggs,
dairy produce (cow and goat),
pork, lamb, beef, kidmeat,
venison, chicken (all to order),
grains

## Hitchin

Safeway Food Stores Ltd
18/19 Banecroft
Hitchin
Herts SG5 1JQ
(Tel. 0462 34883)

## Letchworth

Fairhaven Wholefoods
Unit 27
Jubilee Trading Centre
Letchworth
Herts SG6 1SP
(Tel. 0462 675300)
*Open* Mail order only
*Produce* Vegetables, fruit, hen
eggs, dairy produce (goat),
wholefoods


Fairhaven Wholefoods
Unit 9
Letchworth Market Hall
Letchworth
Herts
*Open* Saturday 8.30am–5pm
*Produce* Vegetables, fruit, hen
eggs, dairy produce (goat),
wholefoods

## Potters Bar

B. J. Donaldson
Leggatts Park
Potters Bar
Herts
(Tel. 0707 44838)
*Open* Please telephone first
*Produce* Vegetables, pork
sausages, 'bread free'
sausages available to special
order

## Rickmansworth

Michael and Mary Bell
Cherry Trees Farm
Olleberrie Lane
Belsize
Sarrat
Rickmansworth
(Tel. 09277 68289)
*Open* Daily 9am–5pm, but please
telephone first
*Produce* Vegetables, hen
eggs, beef, pork, poultry

## Royston

Wholefoods
Market Hill
Royston
Herts SG8 9JF
(Tel. 0763 44785)
*Open* Monday–Saturday
9am–5.30pm
*Produce* Vegetables, apples, soft
fruit, dairy produce (goat), meat,
wholefoods

## Ware

Down to Earth Wholefoods
7 Amwell End
Ware
Herts
(Tel. 0920 3358)
*Open* Monday–Saturday
9am–5.30pm; early closing
Thursday 1.30pm
*Produce* Vegetables, oranges,
lemons, hen eggs, goat's yogurt
and milk, wholefoods

# LONDON

## E6

Safeway Food Stores Ltd
66 High Street North
East Ham
London E6 2HJ
(Tel. 01 472 8684)

## E17

Only Natural
108 Palmerston Road
Walthamstow
London E17 6PZ
(Tel. 01 520 5898)
*Open* Monday, Tuesday and
Saturday 9am–5.30pm; early
closing Wednesday 1pm;

Thursday 9am–7pm; Friday
9am–6pm
*Produce* Vegetables and fruit (full
range in season), hen eggs, dairy
produce (cow and goat),
wholefoods

## EC1

Clear Spring Natural Grocer
196 Old Street
London EC1V 9BP
(Tel. 01 250 1708)
*Open* Monday–Friday
10.30am–7pm; Saturday to 5pm
*Produce* Vegetables, apples, pears,
citrus and local soft fruits in
season, hen eggs, goat's milk,
yogurt and cheese, sheep cheese,
wholefoods

Safeway Food Stores Ltd
Cherry Tree Walk Shopping
   Centre
Whitecross Street
London EC1
(Tel. 01 628 2317)

## N6

Earth Exchange
213 Archway Road
London N6
(Tel. 01 340 6407)
*Open* Friday–Tuesday 11am–7pm
*Produce* Vegetables, apples, pears,
lemons, oranges, hen eggs, cow's
yogurt, full fat and low fat,
wholefoods

## N7

Safeway Food Stores Ltd
81/83 Seven Sisters Road
Holloway
London N7 6BU
(Tel. 01 272 8543/7023)

## N8

Haelan Centre
41 The Broadway
Crouch End
London N8 8DT
(Tel. 01 340 4258)
*Open* Monday to Friday
9am–6.30pm; Saturday to 6pm
*Produce* Vegetables and fruit (full
range), hen eggs, dairy produce
(cow), wholefoods

## N16

Safeway Food Stores Ltd
1 Amherst Park
London N16 5LW
(Tel. 01 800 2686/802 1401)

## NW3

Peppercorn's Wholefood and
    Granary
2 Heath Street (Entrance in
    Perrins Lane)
Hampstead
London NW3
(Tel. 01 431 1251)
*Open* 10am–6.30pm; Sunday
11am–5pm
*Produce* Vegetables, oranges,
grapefruit, grapes, lemons,
pears, apples and seasonal fruit,
hen eggs, yogurt, wholefoods

## NW6

Peppercorn's Wholefood and
    Granary
193/195 West End Lane
West Hampstead
London NW6
(Tel. 01 328 6874)
*Open* Monday–Saturday
10am–7pm
*Produce* Vegetables, oranges,
grapefruit, grapes, lemons,
pears, apples and seasonal fruit,
hen eggs, yogurt, wholefoods

Safeway Food Stores Ltd
142/144 Kilburn High Road
London NW6 4JD
(Tel. 01 328 0191)

## NW9

Safeway Food Stores Ltd
Blackbird Hill
Wembley
London NW9 8SD
(Tel. 01 205 3551)

## SE3

Safeway Food Stores Ltd
17 Stratheden Parade
Blackheath
London SE3 7SX
(Tel. 01 858 2331)

## SE13

Safeway Food Stores Ltd
40 Riverdale
Lewisham
London SE13 7EP
(Tel. 01 852 1507/1526)

## SE19

Safeway Food Stores Ltd
Westow Street
Upper Norwood
London SE19
(Tel. 01 771 7639)

## SE25

Safeway Food Stores Ltd
18/20 Station Road
South Norwood
London SE25 5AJ
(Tel. 01 653 4853)

## SE26

Safeway Food Stores Ltd
74/78 Sydenham Road
Sydenham
London SE26 5QE
(Tel. 01 778 0518)

## SW1

Harrods Ltd
(Health Food Department,
  Lower Ground Floor)
Knightsbridge
London SW1
*Produce* Vegetables, fruit,
wholefoods

## SW3

Safeway Food Stores Ltd
35/37 Kings Road
Chelsea
London SW3 4NB
(Tel. 01 730 9150/9370)

## SW4

Nature Freight
63 Tremadoc Road
London SW4 7NA
(Tel. 01 622 1210)
*Open* Please telephone first
*Produce* Vegetables and fruit in
season, hen eggs, cheese,
wholefoods

## SW6

Olivers Wholefood Store
243 Munster Road
London SW6
(Tel. 01 381 5477)
*Open* 10am–7pm
*Produce* Vegetables, apples, pears,
lemons, avocados, grapefruit,
wholefoods

## SW14

Safeway Food Stores Ltd
284/288 Upper Richmond Road
  West
East Sheen
London SW14 7JE
(Tel. 01 876 8222)

## SW16

Safeway Food Stores Ltd
194 Streatham High Road
London SW16 1BB
(Tel. 01 769 0039)

Safeway Food Stores Ltd
350/372 Streatham High Road
London SW16
(Tel. 01 769 0825/0691)

## SW19

Safeway Food Stores Ltd
Lyon House
The Broadway
Wimbledon
London SW19 1QB
(Tel. 01 946 9981/6105)

## W1

Cranks Health Foods
8 Marshall Street
London W1
(Tel. 01 439 2915)
*Open* Monday–Friday 9am–6pm;
Saturday 9.30 am–5.30 pm
*Produce* Vegetables, apples,
oranges, pears, kiwi and
strawberries, hen eggs, dairy
produce (cow, sheep and goat),
wholefoods

Wholefood
24 Paddington Street
London W1M 4DR
(Tel. 01 935 3924)

*Open* Tuesday–Friday
9am–6.30pm; Monday to 6pm;
Saturday to 1pm
*Produce* Vegetables, fruit, wide
range of dairy produce,
wholefoods

Wholefood Butchers
31 Paddington Street
London W1M 4DR
(Tel. 01 486 1390)
*Open* Monday–Thursday
8.30am–6pm; Friday to 6.30pm;
Saturday to 1pm
*Produce* Duck and hen eggs, beef,
lamb, pork and poultry

## W2

Safeway Food Stores Ltd
159/169 Edgware Road
London W2 2HR
(Tel. 01 723 8965/1946)

## W5

Cornucopia Wholefoods
64 St Mary's Road
Ealing
London W5 5EX
(Tel. 01 579 9431)
*Open* Monday–Saturday
9am–5.30pm
*Produce* Vegetables, avocados,
apples, oranges, pears, lemons,
grapefruits, hen eggs
(occasionally duck), dairy
produce (cow, sheep and goat),
wholefoods

Safeway Food Stores Ltd
Ealing Broadway Centre
Ealing
London W5
(Tel. 01 840 3502/3517)

## W6

Safeway Food Stores Ltd
2/3 Kings Mall
Hammersmith
London W6
(Tel. 01 748 0092/0137)

## W8

Safeway Food Stores Ltd
150/158 Kensington High Street
London W8 7RL
(Tel. 01 937 4345)

## WC1

Safeway Food Stores Ltd
23/37 Brunswick Centre
Bloomsbury
London WC1N 1AF
(Tel. 01 837 0039/2784)

## WC2

Neal's Yard Wholefood
  Warehouse
21/23 Shorts Gardens
London WC2
(Tel. 01 836 5151)
*Produce* Oranges and apples,
wholefoods

Farm Shop
No. 1 Neal's Yard
Covent Garden
London WC2
(Tel. 01 836 1066)
*Open* Monday–Saturday
11am–6pm; Sunday (summer
only)
*Produce* Very wide range of
vegetables and fruit (in season),
dairy produce (sheep, goat and
cow), pork, lamb, beef and
poultry, wholefoods.

# MIDDLESEX

## Harrow

Safeway Food Stores Ltd
356 Pinner Road
Harrow
Middlesex HA2 6DZ
(Tel. 01 427 5812)

## Northwood

Moorpark Fruiterers
12 Main Avenue
Moorpark
Northwood
Middlesex
(Tel. 092 74 21707)
*Produce* Vegetables, pears,
avocados, apples, oranges and
any fruit in season

## Pinner

Safeway Food Stores Ltd
Bridge Street
Pinner
Middlesex HA5 3HZ
(Tel. 01 886 1747/429 2679)

## Staines

Mrs Andrea Levell
Willowslea Farm
Spout Lane
Stanwell
Staines
Middlesex
(Tel. 0753 685571)
*Produce* Vegetables, fruit, hen
eggs, dairy produce (sheep and
goat), all meat, also fish

## Stanmore

Safeway Food Stores Ltd
Broadway House
The Broadway
Stanmore
Middlesex
(Tel. 01 954 2883)

## Twickenham

Gaia
123 St Margaret's Road
Twickenham
TW1 2LH
(Tel. 01 892 2262)
*Open* Monday, Wednesday,
Thursday, Friday, 9.30am–7pm;
Tuesday and Saturday
9.30am–5pm (summer school
holidays – closed Monday all
day, Thursday 2pm)
*Produce* Vegetables, fruit, hen
eggs, dairy produce (cow, sheep
and goat), wholefoods

# OXFORDSHIRE

## Chipping Norton

A. and E. V. Henderson
Oathill Farm
Enstone
Oxford OX7 4ED
(Tel. 060 872 236)
*Produce* Additive-free pork

## Henley

Diana Seidl
Pond House
Kiln Lane
Binfield Heath
Henley
Oxon
(Tel. 0734 478511)
*Open* Please telephone first
*Produce* Apples and raspberries

## Princes Risborough

Tanya and Ugo d'Onofrio
Icknield Nurseries
Kingston Stert
Chinnor
Oxford OX9 4NL
(Tel. 0844 52481)
*Open* Daylight hours,
May–October
*Produce* Vegetables, strawberries,
apples, autumn raspberries
*Directions* Between Sydenham and
Kingston Blount

## Wallingford

The Wholefood Shop
26 High Street
Benson
Oxford OX9 6RP
(Tel. 0491 38727)
*Open* Monday–Saturday
9am–5.30pm; Friday to 7pm
*Produce* Vegetables, lemons,
apples, oranges, pears, grapes
and others in season, hen eggs,
cheese (sheep, goat and cow),
meat, wholefoods

# THE WEST MIDLANDS

# GLOUCESTERSHIRE

## Brookthorpe

Brentlands Cotswold Beef
Brentlands Farm
Brookthorpe
Glos
(Tel. 0452 813447)
*Open* Please telephone first
*Produce* Beef. Home delivery
available


Jenny Beer
Gilbert's
Brookthorpe
Nr Gloucester
(Tel. 0452 812364)
*Open* Please telephone first
*Produce* Vegetables, soft
fruit, plums, apples, hen
eggs, cottage cheese, lamb, beef,
veal, Christmas chickens, honey
*Directions* First house on right
down lane opposite Brookthorpe
Filling Station near bridge over
M5 on A4173


## Circencester

P. R. Haley
'High Anvil'
Winstone
Nr Cirencester
Glos GL7 7JZ
(Tel. 0285 82546)
*Open* Please telephone first
*Produce* Vegetables,
strawberries, raspberries,
blackberries, herb plants

Hatherop Gardens
Hatherop
Nr Cirencester
Glos.
(Tel. 028 575 326)
*Open* Thursday, Friday and
Saturday 9.30am–5pm, or by
appointment
*Produce* Vegetables, soft and
top fruit, grapes, all in
season, citrus fruits as available,
hen eggs

### Gloucester

Safeway Food Stores Ltd
Glevum Shopping Centre
Heron Way
Abbeydale
Gloucester GL4 9BL
(Tel. 0452 68118/68128)

### Newnham-on-Severn

M. and P. Horsley
'Ambleside'
Cinderford Road
Elton
Newnham-on-Severn
Glos
(Tel. 045 276 309)
*Open* Please telephone first
*Produce* Vegetables, plums,
apples, eggs

### Stonehouse

N. L. Jeffery
Tiled House Farm
Oxlynch
Stonehouse
Glos GL10 3DF
(Tel. 045 382 2363)
*Open* 9am–5pm
*Produce* Potatoes,
swedes

### Stow-on-the-Wold

Wye Organic Foods
The Square
Stow-on-the-Wold
Glos GL54 1AB
(Tel. 0451 31004)
*Open* Monday–Saturday
9.30am–5pm
*Produce* Vegetables and fruit in
season, beef, eggs, poultry,
wholefoods, dairy produce, herbs

### Uley

Peter Perry
Marsh Mill House
Shadwell
Uley
Glos GL11 5BN
(Tel. 0453 860784)
*Open* Summer, daily 9am–6pm;
winter Wednesday–Saturday
*Produce* Vegetables, eggs,
herbs

# HEREFORD AND WORCESTERSHIRE

### Alvechurch

Mrs D. Senior
Sunny Bank Farm
Stoney Lane
Alvechurch
Worcs
(Tel. 021 445 1106)
*Open* To order only
*Produce* Hen eggs, goat's milk,
pork, lamb, pigs, honey
*Directions* Between Alvechurch
and Bromsgrove

## Broadway

H. A. Young
Kite's Nest Farm
Broadway
Worcs WR12 7JT
(Tel. 0386 853320)
 *Produce* Carrots, totally
organic beef
*Directions* First driveway on left
after last house of Broadway
along Snowshill Road

## Bromyard

Muttons Organic Growers
Elm Grove
Thornbury
Bromyard
Herefordshire HR7 4NJ
(Tel. 08854 204)
*Open* Monday–Saturday
9am–5pm, but please telephone
first
 *Produce* Vegetables, herb
plants

## Evesham

Mrs V. Roberts
Domestic Fowl Trust
Honeybourne Pastures
Honeybourne
Nr Evesham
Worcs WR11 5QJ
(Tel. 0386 833083)
*Open* 10.30am–5pm daily, except
Fridays
*Produce* Eggs (duck, hen and
turkey, goose in season), pork,
lamb, beef, poultry

## Hay-on-Wye

Hay Wholefoods and
Delicatessen
Lion Street
Hay-on-Wye

Herefordshire
(Tel. 0497 820708)
*Open* Monday–Saturday
9.30am–5.30pm
*Produce* Vegetables, oranges,
apples, pears, eggs, sheep's
yogurt, cheese (cow), wholefoods

## Hereford

Green Door Produce
89 East Street
Hereford
(within 'Gaffers' Wholefood
Cafe)
*Open* Tuesday–Saturday
10am–4.30pm
*Produce* Vegetables and fruit in
season, eggs (duck and hen),
wholefoods

David and Sheila Jenkins
Green Acres
Dinmore
Hereford HR4 8ED
(Tel. 056884 7045)
*Open* Daily 9am–6pm
 *Produce* Vegetables,
strawberries, apples,
plums, pears, raspberries,
damsons, greengages, herbs, hen
eggs, cheese, yogurt, poultry,
honey
*Directions* 6½ miles from both
Leominster and Hereford, on
A49 trunk road south side
Dinmore Hill

## Ledbury

David and Jane Straker
Frome Organic Growers
Canon Frome Court
Canon Frome
Ledbury HR8 2TD
(Tel. 053183 534)

*Open* Please telephone first
*Produce* Vegetables, beef, lamb
occasionally
*Directions* Canon Frome is off
A417, between Trumpet and
Newtown crossroads

Canon Frome Co-op
Canon Frome Court
Canon Frome
Ledbury
Hereford HR8 2TD
(Tel. 053 183 328)
*Produce* Vegetables, eggs, meat

## Leominster

Helen Woodley
Willows Nurseries
Newtown Lane
Leominster
Hereford
(Tel. 0568 4041)
*Open* Please telephone first
*Produce* Young brassica and leek
plants in season, young trees,
herb plants
*Directions* The nursery is located
2 miles south-west of Leominster
and most easily approached by
taking the first lane left (half a
mile) off the A4112 from Barons
Cross (A44 junction)

Linda Kaye
Brewer's Basic
15A Broad Street
Leominster
HR6 8BT
(Tel. 0568 2154)
*Open* Monday–Saturday
9am–5pm
*Produce* Vegetables, fruit, hen
eggs, dairy produce, meat and
poultry

## Ross-on-Wye

J. and E. Lambe
Castle Farm
Upton Bishop
Ross-on-Wye HR9 7UW
(Tel. 098 985 215)
*Open* By appointment only
*Produce* Lamb

## Stourbridge

H. and T. Clement
2 Cottage Farm
Broome
Nr Stourbridge
Worcs
(Tel. 0562 700147)
*Open* Tuesday–Saturday
10am–5.30pm
 *Produce* Vegetables,
citrus fruits, apples,
etc. according to season, hen
eggs, cheese, wholefoods
*Directions* Turn off A456 at Cross
Keys Garage at West Hagley on
to A450, second turning left to
Broome, second turning right,
farm on left

## Worcester

Safeway Food Stores Ltd
Blackfriars Square
Worcester WR1 3NJ
(Tel. 0905 21534)

Shirley Elwell
122 Goldsmith Road
Blackpole
Worcester WR4 9JT
(Tel. 0905 55684)
*Open* Please telephone first
*Produce* Vegetables, fruit, cheese,
hen eggs

# SHROPSHIRE

## Craven Arms

Guy and Jean Smith
The Wain House
Black Hill
Clunton
Craven Arms
Shropshire SY7 0JD
(Tel. 05884 551)
*Open* Daily
*Produce* Vegetables, eggs (hen and turkey), goat's milk, turkeys
*Directions* Take Woodside Road out of Clun, first left before church; 1½ miles on this road on top of hill

## Ellesmere

P. Jennings
The Orchard Nursery
Greenhill Bank
Ellesmere
Shropshire
(Tel. 069 175 295)
*Open* Telephone first. Stall at Ellesmere market each Tuesday
*Produce* Vegetables
*Directions* Two and a half miles from Ellesmere on the Ellesmere–St Martins Road to Dudleston Heath

## Ludlow

Mr J. L. Greenhall
Earthworks
22 Corve Street
Ludlow
Shropshire SY8 1DA
(Tel. 0584 2010)
*Open* Monday–Saturday 9am–5.30pm
*Produce* Vegetables, raspberries, blackberries, apples, oranges, lemons, clementines, plums, damsons, hen eggs, yogurt (cow and goat), cream and cheese, wholefoods

## Market Drayton

A. Hollins
Fordhall Farm
Market Drayton
Shropshire TF9 3PS
(Tel. 063083 255)
*Open* Please telephone first
*Produce* Beef, lamb, pork, veal, duck, chicken, goose

## Oswestry

Anna Doggart
The Poplars
Gwern-y-Brenin
Oswestry
Shropshire SY10 8AR
(Tel. 0691 652166)
*Open* Please telephone first
*Produce* Vegetables, damsons, cooking apples
*Directions* Two and a half miles south of Oswestry

Honeysuckle Wholefood Co-operative
53 Church Street
Oswestry
Shropshire SY11 1BD
(Tel. 0691 653125)
*Produce* Vegetables and fruit in season, eggs (duck and hen), goat's yogurt and cheese, wholefoods

Richard Juckes
Pentre Mawr
Penybont
Oswestry SY10 7JL
(Tel. 069 181 453)

*Open* Weekdays 2pm–6pm
*Produce* Vegetables

*Directions* Half a mile south of
B4396 at Penybont

M. J. R. Kearns
Ysgwennant
Llansilin
Oswestry SY10 7JL
(Tel. 09170 411)
*Open* Please telephone first
*Produce* Beef, table
birds
*Directions* Take Oswestry/
Llansilin Road, 1 mile before
Llansilin turn right for
Llangadwaldr

### Shrewsbury

Crabapple Wholefoods
1–2 Castle Gates
Shrewsbury
Shropshire
(Tel. 0743 64559)
*Open* Monday–Saturday
9.30am–5.45pm
*Produce* Vegetables, apples,
lemons, oranges, seasonal soft
fruit, wholefoods

S. Mayall and Son
Pimhill Produce
Lea Hall
Harmer Hill
Shrewsbury
Shropshire SY4 3DY
(Tel. 0939 290342)
*Open* Monday–Friday 8am–5pm;
Saturday 9am–12.30pm
*Produce* Vegetables, hen and
bantam eggs, cheese,
wholefoods
*Directions* We are on the A528,

5 miles north of Shrewsbury,
5 miles south of Wem on the
outskirts of Harmer Hill – sign
on road

A. and B. Myers
Bird Farm
Back Lane
Worthen
Nr Shrewsbury SY5 9HN
(Tel. 074383 342)
*Open* Please telephone first
*Produce* Potatoes, honey
*Directions* Worthen is on B4386.
Take lane opposite garage,
second gate on left (70 yards)

Safeway Food Stores Ltd
173/175 Abbey Foregate
Shrewsbury
Shropshire SY2 6AL
(Tel. 0743 53436)

### Whitchurch

Jackie and John Gunton
Green Gorse Wood
Whitchurch Road
Prees
Shropshire SY13 3JZ
*Open* Stall at Whitchurch Market,
Friday mornings from 8am
*Produce* Vegetables, soft fruit,
some top fruit in season, eggs
*Directions* Market is held at the
Civic Centre, Whitchurch

Mr C. Hobday
Roden House
Dobsons Bridge
Whixall
Whitchurch
Shropshire SY13 2QL
(Tel. 094 875 243)
*Open* Please telephone first

*Produce* Vegetables,
strawberries

# STAFFORDSHIRE

## Aldridge

Safeway Food Stores Ltd
High Street
Aldridge
Staffs WS9 8QR
(Tel. 0922 53624)

## Eccleshall

Rodney and Elizabeth Leaper
Wootton Lodge
Newport Road
Wootton
Eccleshall
Staffs ST21 6HU
(Tel. 0785 850629)
*Open* Wednesday–Friday
afternoons only; all day Saturday
 *Produce* Vegetables, goat's
milk
*Directions* On A519, one and a half
miles from Eccleshall, going
towards Newport

## Kingswinford

Safeway Food Stores Ltd
Charterfield Shopping Centre
Stallings Lane
Kingswinford
Staffs DY6 7DT
(Tel. 0384 280233)

## Newcastle-under-Lyme

M. and B. Deaville
New House Farm
Acton
Newcastle
Staffs ST5 4EE
(Tel. 0782 680366)

*Open* Tuesday, Thursday, Friday,
Saturday 9am–6pm
 *Produce* Vegetables, hen
eggs, cheese and yogurt
(cow's)
*Directions* Half a mile from A53 at
Whitmore

## Pattingham

Mr Chris McLean
Grange Farm
Hollies Lane
Pattingham
Staffs WV6 7HJ
*Open* Weekdays trade only; farm
shop Saturdays only 10am–5pm
 *Produce* Vegetables, lamb,
beef

## Rugeley

Pauline Kitson
Wholefood Grocery Store
25 Albion Street
Rugeley
Staffs
(Tel. 088 94 70364)
*Open* Monday–Saturday
9am–5pm; early closing
Wednesday 12 noon
*Produce* Vegetables, apples,
oranges, lemons, hen eggs, goat's
milk, yogurt, cottage cheese,
cow's cheese, poultry, pork,
wholefoods, herbs

## Stafford

Staffordshire Organic Growers
Newhaven Farm
Billington
Stafford
(Tel. 0785 851453)
*Open* Friday 10am–6pm;
Saturday 10am–2pm

*Produce* Vegetables, fruit,
hen eggs, cheese

The Good Food Store
15 Salter Street
Stafford
(Tel. 0785 55777)
*Open* Monday–Saturday
9am–5.30pm; early closing
Wednesday 2pm
*Produce* Vegetables, fruit, cheese,
hen eggs, wholefoods

### Uttoxeter

Mike Moore
Crowtree Farm
Loxley
Uttoxeter
Staffs ST14 8RX
(Tel. 08893 5806)
*Open* Please telephone first
 *Produce* Vegetables,
gooseberries, strawberries,
hen eggs
*Directions* The holding is on the
A518, 3 miles south of Uttoxeter

# WARWICKSHIRE

### Rugby

The Wholefood Shop
St Andrews Church House
Church Street
Rugby
Warks
(Tel. 0788 67757)
*Open* Tuesday, Thursday, and
Friday only, 9am–5pm
*Produce* Vegetables, apples,
strawberries, raspberries,
blackcurrants, eggs (duck and
hen), wholefoods

### Ryton-on-Dunsmore

Ryton Gardens (Shop)
National Centre for Organic
Gardening
Ryton-on-Dunsmore
Coventry CV8 3LG
(Tel. 0203 303517)
*Open* May–September daily
10am–6pm; October–April
10am–4pm
*Produce* Vegetables, fruit,
wholefoods, dairy products,
meat and meat products

### Shipston on Stour

Hawkins and Son
Market Place
Shipston on Stour
(Tel. 0608 61207)
*Open* Monday–Saturday
8am–5.30pm
*Produce* Vegetables

### Sutton Coldfield

Safeway Food Stores Ltd
Lichfield Road
Mere Green
Sutton Coldfield
Warks B74 2UW
(Tel. 021 308 6957)

The Health Store
10A Burnett Road
Streetly
Sutton Coldfield B74 3EJ
(Tel. 021 353 4169)
*Produce* Vegetables, fruit, hen
eggs, wholefoods

### Stratford-upon-Avon

Safeway Food Stores Ltd
8 Greenhill Street
Stratford-upon-Avon
Warks CV37 6LF

(Tel. 0789 204312/204305)

Don Burton
110 Maidenhead Road
Stratford-upon-Avon
Warks CV37 6XT
(Tel. 0789 204163)
*Open* Please telephone first
*Produce* Apples, pears, plums

### Warwick

Warwick Health Foods
40A Brook Street
Warwick
(Tel. 0926 494311)
*Open* Monday–Saturday
9am–5.30pm
*Produce* Vegetables, apples,
oranges, lemons, grapefruit,
eggs, goat's milk, yogurt,
wholefoods

# WEST MIDLANDS

### Aldridge

Harvest Health Foods
34 The Square
Aldridge Shopping Centre
Aldridge WS9 8QS
(Tel. 0922 51219)
*Open* Monday–Saturday,
8.30am–6pm; Friday to 7pm
*Produce* Vegetables, fruit, dairy
produce, hen eggs, wholefoods

### Birmingham

Mrs J. Warner
51A Barkers Lane
Wythall
Nr Birmingham B47 6BY
(Tel. 0564 824877)
*Open* Please telephone first
*Produce* Goat's milk

Safeway Food Stores Ltd
Warwick Road
Acock's Green
Birmingham 27
(Tel. 021 708 0248/707 8444)

Safeway Food Stores Ltd
High Street
Erdington
Birmingham B24 6RS
(Tel. 021 382 0111/1017)

Safeway Food Stores Ltd
Vivian Road
Harborne
Birmingham B17
(Tel. 021 427 4523)

Safeway Food Stores Ltd
Alcester Road South
Kings Heath
Birmingham B14 7JG
(Tel. 021 444 5545)

The Health Food Centre
236 Centre Court
Bull Ring Shopping Centre
The Bull Ring
Birmingham 5
(Tel. 021 643 4040)
*Open* Monday–Saturday
9am–5.30pm
*Produce* Vegetables, fruit, hen
eggs, dairy produce (goat),
wholefoods

Food for Thought
Martineau Square
Birmingham B2 4UB
(Tel. 021 236 0148)
*Open* Monday–Friday
8.30am–6pm; Thursday to 7pm;
Saturday to 5.30pm

*Produce* Vegetables, fruit, hen eggs, vegetarian cheese, wholefoods

Natural World
566 Bearwood Road
Smethwick
Warley
Birmingham B66 4BW
(Tel. 021 420 2145)
*Open* Monday–Saturday
9am–5.30pm
*Produce* Vegetables, fruit, hen eggs, vegetarian cheese, wholefoods

## Coventry

Mrs J. E. Burton
Good Heart Organics
Little Heartland
Station Hill
Tamworth Road
Fillongley CV7 8ED
(Tel. 0676 40283)
*Open* Please telephone first
*Produce* Vegetables, apples, plums, damsons and gages, cherries, raspberries, redcurrants, blackcurrants, gooseberries, strawberries, eggs (duck and hen), goat's milk, poultry, honey, herbs, home-made preserves
*Directions* On B4098, one and a quarter miles north-west of Fillongley, right-hand side of the road

Drop in the Ocean
74A Walsgrave Road
Coventry CV2 4EB
(Tel. 0203 459936)
*Open* Monday–Saturday

9am–5.30pm; early closing Thursday 2pm
*Produce* Vegetables, apples, oranges, wholefoods

Mr J. Sargent
'High Croft'
Wall Hill Road
Corley Moor
Nr Coventry CV7 8AP
(Tel. 0676 40970)
*Open* Please telephone first
*Produce* Vegetables, blackcurrants, gooseberries, rhubarb, duck eggs, goat's milk

The Farm Shop
Kings Hill Lane
Finham
Coventry CV3 6PS
(Tel. 0203 411486)
*Open* Saturday 9am–4pm
*Produce* Vegetables, rhubarb, apples, pears, plums, blackcurrants, raspberries, eggs, goat's milk, pork, beef, wholefoods

Mr and Mrs B. Whiteley
Brantwood
Waste Lane
Balsall Common
Coventry CV7 7GG
(Tel. 0203 469097)
*Open* Daily
*Produce* Vegetables, apples, pears, strawberries, raspberries and gooseberries, hen eggs
*Directions* Follow A4023 Coventry–Redditch Road. We are 1 mile before Balsall Common

## Solihull

Anthony's
16 Drury Lane
Solihull B91 3BG
(Tel. 021 705 7979)
*Open* Monday–Friday
9am–5.30pm; Saturday
8.30am–5.30pm
*Produce* Vegetables, fruit, hen eggs

The Health Food Centre
20 High Street
Solihull B91 3TB
(Tel. 021 705 0134)
*Open* Monday–Saturday
9am–5.30pm
*Produce* Vegetables, fruit, hen
eggs, wholefoods

New Millennium Ltd
20/22 High Street
Solihull
*Produce* Vegetables, citrus fruit,
hen eggs, wholefoods

## Stourbridge

Uhuru
Crown Centre Retail Market
Stourbridge
(Tel. 0384 376485)
*Open* Tuesday–Saturday
9am–5pm
*Produce* Vegetables, fruit, eggs
(duck and hen), cheese,
wholefoods

## Wolverhampton

Roots Two Wholefoods
77 Darlington Street
Wolverhampton
(Tel. 0902 712785)
*Open* Monday–Saturday
8am–6pm

*Produce* Vegetables, apples, pears,
oranges, lemons, grapefruit, kiwi
fruit, eggs, cheese (cow, goat and
sheep), wholefoods

Safeway Food Stores Ltd
Pendeford Shopping Centre
Blaydon Road
Wolverhampton
West Midlands
(Tel. 0902 783500)

# THE EAST MIDLANDS

## DERBYSHIRE

### Ashbourne

Mr J. and Mrs M. Hadfield
Acre Field Farm
Wyaston
Ashbourne
Derby
(Tel. 033 523 594)
*Open* Please telephone first
*Produce* Vegetables,
wheat
*Directions* Edge of Wyaston
village, 200 yds south of 'Shire
Horse', two and a half miles
south of Ashbourne


R. and A. Hughes
The Priory
Woodeaves
Fenny Bentley
Ashbourne
Derby DE6 1LF
(Tel. 033 529 238)
*Open* Please telephone first
*Produce* Eggs (duck and hen),
pork, lamb and beef, honey

### Bakewell

Bakewell Health Food
Hebden Court
Bakewell
Derby
(Tel. 062 981 4332)
*Open* Monday–Saturday
9.30am–5pm
*Produce* Vegetables, wholefoods

### Chesterfield

The Happy Nut House
Low Pavements
Chesterfield
Derby
(Tel. 0246 32536)
*Open* Monday–Saturday
9am–5.30pm
*Produce* Hen eggs, dairy products
(goat), wholefoods

### Derby

Judith Hunt
Meadows End Cottage
Mercaston Lane
Turnditch
Derby DE5 2LU
(Tel. 077389 703)
*Open* Please telephone first
*Produce* Beef, pork, lamb,
chickens, meat products

### Glossop

Glossop Wholefood Co-op Ltd
8 Henry Street
Glossop
Derby SK13 8BW
(Tel. 045 74 65678)
*Open* Monday–Saturday
9.30am–5pm; early closing
Tuesday 1pm
*Produce* Vegetables in season; to
order: bananas, grapefruit,
lemons, avocados, apples; hen
eggs (duck occasionally), goat's
milk and cheese, Staffordshire
cheese, wholefoods

## LEICESTERSHIRE

### Leicester

Whole Meal
58 Hinckley Road
Leicester LE3 0RB
(Tel. 0533 558414)
*Open* Monday–Friday 9am–6pm;
Saturday to 5.30pm

*Produce* Vegetables, apples, strawberries, cherries, grapefruit, avocados (in season), hen eggs, goat's milk and yogurt, wholefoods

Whole Meal
158 Queens Road
Clarendon Park
Leicester LE2 3FS
(Tel. 0533 703617)
*Open* Tuesday to Friday
9am–5.30pm; Saturday to 5pm
*Produce* Vegetables, apples, strawberries, cherries, grapefruit, avocados (in season), hen eggs, goat's milk and yogurt, wholefoods

## Loughborough

Safeway Food Stores Ltd
8 Charnwood Precinct
Loughborough
Leics LE11 1AJ
(Tel. 0509 216230/213909)

## South Kilworth

Mrs Ruth Daltry
Chevelswarde Organic Growers
Chevel House
The Belt
South Kilworth
Lutterworth
Leics LE17 6DX
(Tel. 085 881 309)
*Open* Daylight hours (meat sales by arrangement, please telephone first)
*Produce* Vegetables, soft fruit including strawberries, blackcurrants, gooseberries, pork (to order)
*Directions* 'The Belt' is a lane on the south side of B5414 between North and South Kilworth

# LINCOLNSHIRE

## Boston

Pam and Rick Bowers
Strawberry Fields
Scarborough Bank
Stickford
Boston
Lincs PE22 8DR
(Tel. 0205 78 490)
*Open* Please telephone first
*Produce* Vegetables, strawberries, eggs, lamb (to order)
*Directions* 1 mile off the A16 between Stickford and Stickney

M. Randerson
Clover Cottage
Station Road
Leake Commonside
Boston
Lincs
(Tel. 0205 870 049)
*Open* Daily 8am–8pm
*Produce* Vegetables, goat's milk, soft fruit, eggs

## Gainsborough

Dr T. D. Organ
East Farm
Normanby by Stow
Gainsborough DN21 5LQ
(Tel. 0427 788629)
*Open* Please telephone first
*Produce* Vegetables, rhubarb, beef, pork, honey
*Directions* On the B1241 between Stow and Willingham-by-Stow

## Lincoln

Greens Health Foods
175 High Street
Lincoln LN5 7AF
(Tel. 0522 24874)
*Open* Monday–Saturday
8.30am–5.30pm
*Produce* Vegetables, apples and
other fruit as available (oranges,
lemons, pears, etc.), hen eggs,
goat's yogurt, wholefoods

## Louth

Pamela and Peter Mansfield
84 Tinkle Street
Grimoldby
Louth
Lincs LN11 8TF
(Tel. 0507 82 655)
*Open* Please telephone first
⊘ *Produce* Vegetables, hen
eggs (spring and summer)
*Directions* North of double-bend in
main street of village

The Wholefood Co-op
7 Aswell Street
Louth
Lincs
(Tel. 0507 60411)
*Open* Monday–Saturday
9am–5pm
*Produce* Vegetables, apples, other
fruit in season, hen eggs, goat's
milk, yogurt (goat and cow),
wholefoods

## North Scarle

F. A. and J. Jones and Son
Red House Farm Butchers Shop
Spalford Lane
North Scarle
Lincs LN6 9HB
(Tel. 052277 224)

*Open* Wednesday, Thursday,
Saturday 9am–5pm; Friday to
7pm but please telephone first to
order
*Produce* Vegetables (*Soil
Association Symbol*); also pork, beef,
lamb, meat products

# NOTTINGHAMSHIRE

## Mansfield

Wild Oats
31a Church Street
Mansfield
Notts
(Tel. Mansfield 654121)
*Open* Monday–Saturday
9am–5.30pm
*Produce* Vegetables, lemons,
avocados, apples, oranges,
mango, pears, eggs (duck and
hen), yogurt (goat and sheep),
cheese (goat and vegetarian),
wholefoods

## Nottingham

Hiziki Wholefood Collective
15A Goosegate
Hockley
Nottingham
(Tel. 0602 505523)
*Open* Tuesday–Friday
10am–6pm; Monday
9.30am–2pm; Saturday
9.30am–5pm
*Produce* Hen eggs, goat's milk,
wholefoods

Ouroboros Wholefood Collective
37a Mansfield Road
Nottingham
(Tel. 0602 49016)
*Open* Monday–Saturday
9am–5.30pm; closed Thursday

*Produce* Vegetables, apples,
oranges, lemons, pears,
grapefruit, hen eggs,
Staffordshire cheese, wholefoods

Phil Corbett
5 Colville Villas
Nottingham NG1 4HN
(Tel. 0602 474977)
*Open* Please telephone first,
evenings
*Produce* Vegetables, pears,
raspberries, blackcurrants,
strawberries, rhubarb, herbs and
herb plants

# EAST ANGLIA

## CAMBRIDGESHIRE

### Cambridge

Sue McVey Catering
Unit 1
176 High Street
Cottenham
Cambridge CB4 4RX
(Tel. 0954 51861)
*Open* Monday–Friday
9am–1.30pm; Saturday
9am–12.30pm
*Produce* Wholefoods, baked
organic products

Arjuna
12 Mill Road
Cambridge CB1 2AD
(Tel. 0223 64845)
*Open* Monday, Tuesday,
Wednesday, Friday
9.30am–6pm; Thursday to 2pm;
Saturday to 5.30pm
*Produce* Vegetables, fruit, eggs,
dairy produce (goat), wholefoods

### Great Abington

Peter and Peggy Clark
30 South Road
Great Abington
Cambs
(Tel. 0223 893804)
*Open* Please telephone first,
between 8–9am and 5–6pm
*Produce* Vegetables, hen eggs
*Directions* South Road is exactly
two and a half miles north of
Stump Cross roundabout on A11

## Isleham

Will and Sheila Taylor
Karma Farm
8 Fen Bank
Isleham
Cambs CB7 5SL
(Tel. 063878 701)
*Open* Daylight hours daily, please
telephone 1–2pm
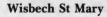 *Produce* Vegetables, apples,
pears, raspberries,
strawberries, hen eggs, beef, goat,
poultry, turkey
*Directions* Past Isleham Marina,
end of Fen Bank Road, then 300
yds along Flood Bank

## Peterborough

Brocklehurst Wholefoods
26 Leighton
Orton Malborne
Peterborough PE2 0QB
(Tel. 0733 238239)
*Open* Market stalls at St Ives
(Mondays), Market Deeping
(Wednesdays), Oundle
(Thursdays), Peterborough
(Fridays)
*Produce* Vegetables (ordered in
advance), wholefoods

## Soham

Downfield Windmill
Fordham Road
Soham
Cambs
(Tel. 0353 720333)
*Open* Sunday 11am–5pm and
Bank Holiday Mondays
*Produce* Flour

## Wisbech St Mary

M. J. Feeney
The Elms
High Road
Wisbech St Mary
Cambs
(Tel. 0945 81 335)
*Open* Please telephone first
*Produce* Garlic, apples,
plums, pears, hen eggs,
lamb, pork to order

# ESSEX

## Benfleet

Safeway Food Stores Ltd
London Road
Hadleigh
Benfleet
Essex SS7 2RD
(Tel. 0702 553654/555433)

## Brentwood

Hazel Collinson
Wealdcote
Wigley Bush Lane
S. Weald
Brentwood
Essex
(Tel. 0277 226432)
*Open* Third Thursday in the
month
*Produce* Vegetables, eggs, game,
turkey, pork, lamb, poultry, beef,
trout

## Brightlingsea

David Scott
Ford Farm
Brightlingsea
Colchester
Essex
(Tel. 0206 304854)

*Produce* Vegetables, strawberries, hen eggs

Cornflower
49 High Street
Brightlingsea
Colchester
Essex
(Tel. 0206 304854)
*Open* Monday–Saturday
9am–5pm; early closing
Thursday 1pm
*Produce* Vegetables, apples, pears, plums, hen eggs, wholefoods

## Chelmsford

Finest Wholefoods
The Barn
Southridge Farm
Highwood
Chelmsford
Essex
(Tel. 0245 48 220)
*Open* Home delivery service
*Produce* Vegetables, apples, soft fruit, imported fruit (including citrus fruit), eggs, wholefoods

Chris and Helen Goldsmith
Mill Farm
Purleigh
Chelmsford
Essex CM3 6PU
(Tel. 0621 828280)
*Open* Please telephone first
*Produce* Vegetables, mutton and lamb
*Directions* Map Ref TQ 833022

## Leigh on Sea

Safeway Food Stores Ltd
London Road
Leigh on Sea
Essex SS9 3NF

(Tel. 0702 713663)

## Loughton

Natural Foods Ltd
Days Farm
Lippitts Hill
High Beech
Loughton
Essex
(Tel. 01 502 2621 or 01 502 4106)
*Open* Please telephone first
*Produce* Vegetables, fruit, hen eggs, dairy produce (cow), meat, wholefoods

## Manningtree

Maurice Garnham
Pear Tree Mill
Church Road
Wrabness
Manningtree
Essex
(Tel. 0255 886210)
*Produce* Pork, flour and bran

## Romford

Wellgate Community Farm
Collier Row Road
Collier Row
Romford
Essex
(Tel. 01 599 0415)
*Open* Weekdays 9am–4pm; weekends 9am–12pm
*Produce* Vegetables, fruit, duck and hen eggs, rabbit, pork
*Directions* Opposite the Oaks Centre and between Sungate Nurseries and the Garden Centre

## Southend on Sea

Safeway Food Stores Ltd
Western Approaches
Off Eastwoodberry Lane
Eastwood
Southend on Sea
Essex SS2 6SH
(Tel. 0702 525651/525994)

# NORFOLK

## Burnham Market

Stubbings
Westgate Nurseries
Market Place
Burnham Market
Norfolk PE31 8HF
(Tel. 0328 738337)
*Open* Monday–Saturday
9am–5pm; early closing
Wednesday 1pm
*Produce* Vegetables, eggs (hen and
duck), dairy produce (goat and
cow), beef and pork, meat
products, wholefoods

Humble Pie Foods
Market Place
Burnham Market
Kings Lynn
Norfolk
(Tel. 0328 738581)
*Open* Tuesday–Saturday
9am–5pm; early closing
Wednesday
*Produce* Cheese

## Dereham

Dave Simmons
Loke Cottage
4 Scarning Fen
Dereham
Norfolk NR19 1LN

(Tel. 0362 5947)
*Open* Monday, Wednesday and
Saturday 10am–5pm, but please
telephone first
*Produce* Vegetables, strawberries

## Dickleburgh

Bob Flowerdew
Harvey Lodge
Harvey Lane
Dickleburgh
Norfolk IP21 4NL
(Tel. 0379 741216)
*Open* By appointment
*Produce* Vegetables, soft
fruit, eggs and table birds,
herbs, jams and preserves

## Diss

Natural Foodstore
Norfolk House
St Nicholas Street
Diss
Norfolk
(Tel. 0379 51832)
*Open* Monday–Saturday
9am–5.30pm; early closing
Tuesday 1pm
*Produce* Vegetables, apples, hen
eggs, wholefoods

## Gresham

Anne and Keith Hood
The Stables
Gresham
Norwich NR11 8AD
(Tel. 026 377 468)
*Open* Please telephone first
*Produce* Vegetables, goose eggs
(spring), dairy products (Jersey
cow), beef (winter), goslings at
Christmas, bread
*Directions* 3 miles south of
Sheringham (and 20 miles north

of Norwich), one and a half miles south of Pretty Corner on the Matlaske Road – down private drive leading to Gresham Hall

## Norwich

J. R. Kent
Church Barn Farm
Arminghall Lane
Norwich
*Open* Daylight hours (honesty box)
⊘ *Produce* Vegetables, blackcurrants, raspberries (PYO)

R. W. Maidstone
38 Hall Lane
Wacton
Norwich
Norfolk NR15 2UH
(Tel. 0508 31287)
*Open* Norwich Provision Market, Thursday 7.30am–12.30pm; Diss Friends Meeting House, Frenze Road, Friday 9.30am–11.45am; Long Stratton Village Hall, Ipswich Road, Friday 1.30pm–2.15pm
⊘ *Produce* Vegetables, poultry, beef, lamb, rabbits, butter

Mangreen Garden
William and Christopher Duffield
Mangreen
Swardeston
Norwich
Norfolk NR14 8DD
(Tel. 0508 70444)
*Open* Daily (honesty box), telephone orders accepted
⊘ *Produce* Vegetables, strawberries, melons

*Directions* 3 miles south of Norwich and half a mile west of A140 Ipswich Road

Rainbow Wholefoods Warehouse
124 St Mary's Works
Duke Street
Norwich
(Tel. 0603 630484)
*Open* Tuesday, Wednesday, Thursday, Friday 9.30am–5pm
*Produce* Wholefoods

Rainbow Wholefoods
16 Dove Street
Norwich
Norfolk
(Tel. 0603 625560)
*Open* Monday–Saturday 9.30–5pm
*Produce* Vegetables, eggs, goat's milk, yogurt (cow and sheep), wholefoods

Renaissance Ltd
4 St Benedicts
Norwich NR2 4AG
(Tel. 0603 625686)
*Open* Monday–Saturday 9am–5.30pm
*Produce* Vegetables, various citrus fruits, pears, apples, eggs (hen and occasionally goose/duck), yogurt (goat, cow and sheep), goat's milk, wholefoods

## Oxburgh

Mrs M. Wilson
Ferry Farm
Oxburgh
Kings Lynn
Norfolk PE33 9PT
(Tel. 036 621 287)
*Open* Sundays 2pm–6pm; also

Mildenhall Market Friday;
Thetford Market Sunday
 *Produce* Vegetables,
raspberries

### Stanhoe

M. J. and H. A. Hannay
Frogs Hall
Barwick
Stanhoe
Kings Lynn
Norfolk PE31 8PY
(Tel. 048523 534)
*Open* Daylight hours
*Produce* Vegetables,
strawberries, pork
*Directions* South of village of
Stanhoe on side of B1454

### Thetford

Jock Butler
Walnut Farm
Southburgh
Thetford
Norfolk IP25 7TE
(Tel. 0362 820218)
*Open* Please telephone first
*Produce* Eggs (duck and hen),
yogurt, cream and cream cheese
(Jersey cow), pork, bobby beef
*Directions* Three-quarters of a mile
north of Southburgh Church on
west side of the road (OS ref 999
055)

### Wood Dalling

Alan Chaple
Primrose Farm
Wood Dalling
Norwich
Norfolk NR11 6RN
(Tel. 026 387 254)
*Open* Daily

 *Produce* Vegetables

# SUFFOLK

### Beccles

The Hungate Health Store
4 Hungate
Beccles
Suffolk NR34 9TL
(Tel. 0502 715009)
*Open* Monday–Saturday
9am–5.30pm; early closing
Wednesday 1pm
*Produce* Summer vegetables, hen
eggs, cow's milk and yogurt,
wholefoods

### Bury St Edmunds

Caroline Holmes
Denham End Farm
Denham
Bury St Edmunds
Suffolk IP29 5EE
(Tel. 0284 810653)
*Open* Please telephone first
*Produce* Fresh herbs, tomatoes,
peppers, organic home-prepared
food for arranged courses and
groups

### Debenham

J. M. Chevallier Gould
The Cyder House
Aspall Hall
Debenham
Suffolk IP14 6PD
(Tel. 0728 860510)
*Open* Weekdays
9.30am–12.30pm,
1.30pm–3.30pm
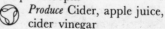 *Produce* Cider, apple juice,
cider vinegar

*Directions* 2 miles north of
Debenham on B1077

## Halesworth

Anthony Gaze
'Poplar Farm Organic
  Vegetables'
Poplar Farm
Silverleys Green
Cratfield
Halesworth
Suffolk IP19 0QJ
(Tel. 037 986 241)
*Open* Please telephone first
*Produce* Vegetables

## Ipswich

J. L. Thoroughgood
Bushy Ley Cottage
Offton Road
Elmsett
Ipswich
Suffolk IP7 6PQ
(Tel. 047 333 671)
*Open* Please telephone first
*Produce* Vegetables, hay,
  wheat, oats, beef

## Kersey

Sarah and Pete Partridge
Trickers Farm
Kersey
Nr Hadleigh
Ipswich
Suffolk
(Tel. 0473 827231)
*Open* Please telephone first
*Produce* Vegetables, hen eggs,
goat's milk and yogurt
*Directions* Half a mile along
Boxford Road from Kersey

## Saxmundham

Swallow Organics
High March Farm
Darsham
Saxmundham
Suffolk IP17 3RN
(Tel. 072 877 201)
*Open* Daily 8am–dusk
*Produce* Vegetables,
  herbs
*Directions* Between Darsham
Street and Westleton

## Shotley

West and Wayne
No. 1 Sytngham Cottages
Shotley
Nr Ipswich
Suffolk IP9 1PG
(Tel. 047 334 8870)
*Open* Daylight hours
*Produce* Soft fruit,
  vegetables

## Stowupland

W. G. and M. J. Cherry
Sweetapple Orchards
Stowupland
Stowmarket
Suffolk IP14 5DF
(Tel. 0449 674791)
*Open* August to end of January,
daily 9am–5pm; but please
telephone first
*Produce* Apples,
  pears

## Westleton

Kate and Desmond
Brick Kiln Farm
Westleton
Nr Saxmundham
Suffolk
(Tel. 072 873 600)

*Open* Please telephone first
*Produce* Vegetables
*Directions* 1 mile north of
Westleton on B1125

### Woodbridge

Loaves and Fishes
52 Thoroughfare
Woodbridge
Suffolk
(Tel. 03943 5650)
*Open* 8am–5.30pm; early closing
Wednesday
*Produce* Vegetables, apples,
strawberries, raspberries, hen
eggs, milk (Jersey cow and goat),
wholefoods

# THE NORTH WEST

## CHESHIRE

### Charlesworth

M. and P. Brown
33 Lee Vale Drive
Charlesworth
via Hyde
Cheshire SK14 6HD
(Tel. 04574 65278)
*Open* Please telephone first
*Produce* Vegetables, rhubarb,
blackcurrants, raspberries, hen
eggs, honey
*Directions* Off A626, going from
Marple Bridge towards Glossop,
first left after the George and
Dragon

### Chester

Safeway Food Stores Ltd
Mill Lane
Upton
Chester
Cheshire
(Tel. 0244 379373/379090)

### Hale

Safeway Food Stores Ltd
Ashley Road
Hale
Cheshire WA14 2LY
(Tel. 061 928 2409)

### Malpas

Mehr S. Fardoonji
Oakcroft Gardens
Cross o' th' Hill
Malpas
Cheshire SY14 8DH
(Tel. 0948 860213)
*Open* Please telephone first

*Produce* Vegetables,
strawberries, raspberries,
blackcurrants, some top fruit, hen
eggs, cheese, herb plants
*Directions* 1 mile towards Malpas
off the A41 at Nomansheath

## Neston

G. L. Nicholls
Ashfield Farm
Chester High Road
Neston
South Wirrall
Cheshire
(Tel. 051 336 4286)
*Open* Please telephone first
 *Produce* Vegetables

## Wallasey

Safeway Food Stores Ltd
44/52 Wallasey Road
Wallasey
Cheshire L45 4NW
(Tel. 051 638 2177)

## Wilmslow

Safeway Food Stores Ltd
Church Street
Wilmslow
Cheshire
(Tel. 0625 530879/530878)

# CUMBRIA

## Arnside

Lewthwaites
The Promenade
Arnside
Cumbria
(Tel. 0524 761279)
*Open* Monday–Friday 8am–5pm;
early closing Saturday 2pm

*Produce* Vegetables, hen eggs

## Little Salkeld

The Watermill
Little Salkeld
Penrith
Cumbria CA10 1NN
(Tel. 076881 523)
*Open* Monday–Friday
9.30am–12.30pm and
2.30pm–5.30pm
 *Produce* Eggs (duck
and hen), goat's
milk, yogurt and cheese, flour,
oat and cereal produce

## Penrith

Village Bakery Foodshop
Angel Lane
Penrith
Cumbria
(Tel. 0768 62377)
*Open* Monday, Tuesday,
Thursday, Friday 9am–5.15pm;
Wednesday 10am–1pm; closed
Sunday
*Produce* Vegetables, lemons,
apples, pears, hen eggs, dairy
produce (cow, sheep and goat),
beef, wholefoods

## Windermere

E. H. Booth and Co. Ltd.
The Station
Victoria Street
Windermere
Cumbria
(Tel. 09662 6114)
*Produce* Vegetables, apples,
oranges, grapefruit, avocados

# GREATER MANCHESTER

Harry Burnham
25 Fitton Avenue
Chorlton
Manchester 21
(Tel. 061 860 4663)
*Open* Please telephone first
*Produce* Vegetables, apples, pears,
oranges, lemons, grapefruit,
grapes, avocados, melons, eggs,
cheese

Safeway Food Stores Ltd
Wilbraham Road
Chorlton Cum Hardy
Manchester
(Tel. 061 860 5779)

Safeway Food Stores Ltd
Market Place
Market Street
Manchester M3 1RE
(Tel. 061 832 2608)

# LANCASHIRE

## Accrington

Green Seeds
9 Warner Street
Accrington
Lancs BB5 1NB
(Tel. 0254 383587)
*Open* Monday–Saturday
9.30am–5.30pm; early closing
Wednesday 1.30pm
*Produce* Vegetables, apples, pears,
oranges, lemons, grapefruit, hen
eggs, wholefoods

## Ashton-under-Lyne

Mossley Wholefoods
10 Stockport Road
Mossley
Ashton-under-Lyne
Lancs
(Tel. 045 75 5063)
*Open* Monday–Friday
9am–5.30pm; early closing
Tuesday 1pm; Saturday 4.30pm
*Produce* Vegetables, apples,
cheese, wholefoods

## Blackburn

Frank and Joan Roberts
4 Kendal Row
Belthorn
Blackburn
Lancs BB1 2PN
(Tel. 0254 52731)
*Open* Please telephone first
*Produce* Vegetables, herbs
*Directions* Take the Grane Road
to Haslingden from Blackburn.
Next to the Pack Horse Inn

Lovin Spoonfull
76 King William Street
Blackburn
(Tel. 0254 675505)
*Open* Monday–Saturday
9am–5.30pm
*Produce* Vegetables, apples,
lemons (oranges and grapefruit)
to order, eggs (duck and hen),
yogurt (cow, sheep and goat),
goat's milk and cheese,
wholefoods

## Blackpool

Glenn and Pam Wood
Infinity Wholefoods
4 Royal Oak Buildings
Waterloo Road
Blackpool
Lancs
(Tel. 0253 48626)

*Open* Monday to Wednesday
9am–5.30pm; Thursday to
Saturday 9am–6pm
*Produce* Vegetables, apples, eggs,
wholefoods

E. H. Booth and Co. Ltd
Highfield Road
Marton
Blackpool
Lancs
(Tel. 0253 64049)
*Produce* Vegetables, apples,
oranges, grapefruit, avocados

Safeway Food Stores Ltd
169 Victoria Road West
Thornton Cleveleys
Blackpool
Lancs SY5 3LB
(Tel. 0253 852684)

### Carnforth

S. and G. Fowler
Ferrocrete Farm
Arkholme
Carnforth
Lancs LA6 1AV
(Tel. 0468 21965)
*Open* Please telephone first
*Produce* Vegetables, damsons,
apples, hen eggs, dairy produce
(goat, cow, sheep), preserves
*Directions* On B6254 (exit 35 M6)
between Carnforth and Kirkby
Lonsdale

### Clitheroe

E. H. Booth and Co. Ltd
Station Road
Clitheroe
Lancs
(Tel. 0200 27325)

*Produce* Vegetables, apples,
oranges, grapefruit, avocados

### Formby

Safeway Food Stores Ltd
Formby Cloisters
Brows Lane
Formby
Lancs L37 3PX
(Tel. 07048 72360)

Cornucopia
167 Gardner Road
Formby
Merseyside L37 8DG (van
round)
(Tel. 07048 72643)
*Open* 9am–6pm
*Produce* Vegetables, hen eggs
(occasionally duck), goat's milk,
yogurt, wholefoods

### Lancaster

Single Step Co-op Ltd
78A Penny Street
Lancaster
Lancs LA1 1XN
(Tel. 0524 63021)
*Open* Monday–Saturday
9.30am–5pm; Friday to 5.30pm
*Produce* Vegetables and fruit (in
season), hen eggs, dairy produce
(goat and cow), wholefoods

### Preston

Amber Wholefood Co-operative
  Ltd
31 Cannon Street
Preston
Lancs
(Tel. 0772 53712)
*Open* Monday–Saturday
9.30am–5pm; early closing
Thursday 1.30pm

*Produce* Vegetables, apples,
oranges, hen eggs, cow's yogurt
and cheese, wholefoods

D. R. and A. P. Blair
Low Carr Nursery
Head Dyke Lane
Pilling
Nr Preston
Lancs
(Tel. 039130 471)
*Open* Please telephone first
(3 days' notice required). Bulk
orders only
*Produce* Vegetables
*Directions* On the A588, about 12
miles south of Lancaster

E. H. Booth and Co. Ltd
256/270 Sharoe Green Lane
Fulwood
Preston
Lancs
(Tel. 0200 716027)
*Produce* Vegetables, apples,
oranges, grapefruit, avocados

Keith Dickinson
Manor Farm
Shore Road
Hesketh Bank
Preston
Lancs
(Tel. 077 473 2530)
*Open* Please telephone first
*Produce* Vegetables,
rhubarb, plums, damsons,
apples, pears, eggs (hen, duck
and goose), herbs

Mr and Mrs J. Fletcher
Country Corner
13 Lytham Road
Fulwood

Preston
Lancs
(Tel. 0772 717040)
*Open* Tuesday–Friday
8am–5.30pm; Saturday to
3.30pm
*Produce* Vegetables, hen eggs,
dairy produce (cow)

### Southport

Safeway Food Stores Ltd
91 Lord Street
Southport
Lancs PR8 1RH
(Tel. 0704 30043)

Cornucopia
51 The Promenade
Southport
Lancs
(Tel. 0704 46623)
*Open* 9am–6pm
*Produce* Vegetables, hen eggs
(occasionally duck), goat's milk,
yogurt, wholefoods

## MERSEYSIDE

### Liverpool

Dancing Cat Trading Co-
operative
107 Lodge Lane
Liverpool L8 0QF
(Tel. 051 733 5205)
*Open* Monday–Saturday
9am–5.30pm
*Produce* Vegetables and fruit in
season, hen and duck eggs,
cheese, bread, wholefoods

**Wirral**

Coppers End
4 Hilbre Road
West Kirby
Wirral
Merseyside
(Tel. 051 625 1809)
*Open* Monday–Saturday
9am–5.30pm; early closing
Wednesday 1pm
*Produce* Vegetables, apples,
oranges, lemons, grapefruit,
avocados, kiwi, tangerines,
bananas, pears, Staffordshire
cheeses, pork, lamb, beef,
poultry, meat products,
wholefoods

# THE NORTH EAST

## CO. DURHAM

### Barnard Castle

Mrs R. H. Gray
Eggleston Hall
Eggleston
Barnard Castle
Co. Durham
(Tel. 0833 50378)
*Open* 9.30am–5pm
*Produce* Vegetables, soft fruit,
rhubarb

Partners Flower Shop
27 Horsemarket
Barnard Castle
Co. Durham
(Tel. 0833 38847)
*Open* Monday–Saturday
9.30am–5pm
*Produce* Vegetables and fruit

### Durham

Durham Community Co-op
85A New Elvet
Durham
(Tel. 0385 61183)
*Open* Monday–Friday
10am–5.30pm; Saturday to 5pm
*Produce* Vegetables, lemons,
oranges, apples, plums,
greengages

T. Carhart-Harris
Hedley Hill Health Services
Hedley Hill Villa
Cornsay Colliery
Durham DH7 9EX
(Tel. 0385 734376)

*Open* Only by special
arrangement through the clinic

# HUMBERSIDE

### Barrow upon Humber

Betty Whitwell
3 Thorngarth Lane
Barrow upon Humber
South Humberside DN19 7AW
(Tel. 0469 30721)
*Open* Please telephone first
*Produce* Vegetables, raspberries,
strawberries, hen eggs, cheese,
wholefoods

### Goxhill

Natural Garden Products
Soff Lane
South-end
Goxhill
South Humberside DN19 7NA
(Tel. 0469 30827)
*Open* Please telephone first
*Produce* Onions

Joan and Alan Gould
Woodrising
Thorn Lane
Goxhill
South Humberside
(Tel. 0469 30356)
*Open* Daylight hours
*Produce* Vegetables, Bramley
apples, goat's milk, yogurt,
cottage cheese, hard cheese,
poultry

### Grimsby

The Wholefood Co-op
7B East Street
Mary's Gate
Grimsby

South Humberside
*Open* Monday–Saturday
9am–5pm
*Produce* Vegetables, apples, other
fruit in season, hen eggs, goat's
milk, yogurt (goat and cow),
wholefoods

The Larder
39 Bethlehem Street
Grimsby
South Humberside DN31 1JQ
(Tel. 0472 361867)
*Open* 9am–5.30pm
*Produce* Vegetables, oranges,
plums, gooseberries, lemons,
apples, eggs, flour

### Hull

S. R. Crouch
'Daybreak'
Elstronwick
Nr Hull
North Humberside
(Tel. 0964 70209)
*Open* Please telephone first
*Produce* Most vegetables in
season, hen eggs

# NORTH YORKSHIRE

### Harrogate

Holmes Natural Farming Shop
146 Kings Road
Harrogate
(Tel. 0423 508760)
*Open* Monday–Friday
8.30am–5.30pm; Saturday to
5pm
*Produce* Vegetables,
blackcurrants, gooseberries,
raspberries, strawberries,
redcurrants, goat's milk and

yogurt, cow's yogurt, cream and cheese, lamb, pork, chicken, beef, wholefoods

## Hovingham

S. and D. G. Hodgson
Church House
Scackleton
Hovingham
York YO6 4NB
(Tel. 065 382 474)
*Open* Weekends noon–dusk; weekdays 6am–dusk
*Produce* Blackcurrants, raspberries, redcurrants, gooseberries, vegetables

## Pickering

M. and P. Sellers
Standfield Hall
Westgate Carr Road
Pickering
North Yorks
(Tel. 0751 72249)
*Open* Monday and Thursday afternoons, Saturday mornings
*Produce* Vegetables, rhubarb, gooseberries, hen eggs, beef (to order)
*Directions* Westgate Carr Road is on the west side of Pickering off A170. We are about a mile down the road, on the left

## Scarborough

Greatfruits
1a North Marine Road
Scarborough
North Yorks YO12 7EY
(Tel. 0723 374633)
*Open* Monday–Saturday 9am–5.30pm
*Produce* Vegetables, fruit, dairy

produce (cow and sheep), hen eggs, wholefoods

## Settle

D. and M. Hodgson
T. Lord and Sons
Cheapside
Settle
North Yorks
(Tel. 07292 3772)
*Open* Monday–Saturday 9am–5.30pm; early closing Wednesday 12.30pm
*Produce* Vegetables, lemons, oranges, apples and pears, rice

## Tollerton

G. P. Bucknall
Kyle Cottage
Tollerton
York YO6 2EQ
(Tel. 03473 8169)
*Open* By arrangement
*Produce* Vegetables, soft fruit

## Whitby

Mr and Mrs G. Heron
Bank House Farm
Glaisdale
Whitby
North Yorks
(Tel. 0947 87297)
*Open* Please telephone first
*Produce* Eggs (duck and hen), cockerels, duck, pork, bacon–all by arrangement to order only

## York

E. and E. G. Bullivant and Daughters
Vicarage Farm
Claxton
York YO6 7RY

(Tel. 090486 222)
*Open* Please telephone first
*Produce* Beef, pork
*Directions* Leave York on the A64.
After 7 miles turn right at
Newitts Warehouse at Claxton
Hall. Go down to Claxton over
crossroads to Bossall, first farm
on left, with 2 large silage towers

The Wholefood Trading
  Company
98 Micklegate
York YO1 1JX
(Tel. 0904 56804)
*Open* Monday and Tuesday
9am–5.30pm;
Wednesday–Saturday to 10pm
*Produce* Vegetables, fruit, dairy
produce, wholefoods

Gillygate Wholefood Bakery
Millers Yard
Gillygate
York YO3 7EB
(Tel. 0904 24045)
*Open* Monday–Saturday
9am–6pm
*Produce* Vegetables, dairy produce
(cow, goat and sheep), hen eggs,
wholefoods

Alligator
104 Fishergate
York YO1 4BB
(Tel. 0904 54525)
*Open* Monday–Friday
10am–6pm; Saturday 9am–6pm
*Produce* Vegetables, fruit, hen
eggs, wholefoods

R. Rickatson
Braemar
Wilberfoss
York
(Tel. 07595 8141)
*Open* By appointment only
  *Produce* Vegetables

*Directions* 6 miles east of York on
A1079 to Hull

# NORTHUMBERLAND

## Hexham

Down to Earth
Nether Warden
Hexham
Northumberland
(Tel. 0434 605111)
*Open* By arrangement only
  *Produce* Vegetables, apples,
  pears, strawberries,
raspberries

## Morpeth

Jill Harrison
Morrelhirst
Netherwitton
Morpeth
Northumberland
(Tel. 0669 20230)
*Open* Please telephone first
  *Produce* Goat's milk, yogurt,
  soft herb cheese,
coulommier cheese, herbs

Mr and Mrs A. J. Crerar
Grasmere House
56 Station Road
Stannington
Morpeth
Northumberland NE61 6NH
(Tel. 067 089 343)

*Open* March–October daily;
November–February, Thursday,
Friday, Saturday only

⊘ *Produce* Vegetables, herbs,
soft fruit

# SOUTH YORKSHIRE

## Doncaster

Mr and Mrs G. R. Bingham
The White House
Wroot Road
Finningley
Nr Doncaster
South Yorks DN9 3DS
(Tel. 0302 770077)
*Open* Please telephone first

⊘ *Produce* Vegetables,
honey

## Sheffield

Ridgeway Organic Farm
    Co-op Ltd
Kent House Farm
Main Road
Ridgeway
Sheffield 12
(Tel. 0742 474258)
*Open* Please telephone first

⊘ *Produce* Vegetables,
fruit
*Directions* Between Chesterfield
and Sheffield, 7 miles south-east
of Sheffield City Centre. 5 miles
from M1, public transport to
door

Heeley City Farm
Richards Road
Heeley
Sheffield S2 3DT
(Tel. 0742 580482)
*Open* Daily 9am–4pm

*Produce* Vegetables, goat's milk
and yogurt

Singin' Hinnies
344 Sharrovale Road
Sheffield S11 8ZP
(Tel. 0742 669147)
*Open* Monday–Wednesday
10am–7.30pm;
Thursday–Saturday to 9.30pm
*Produce* Vegetables, fruit, dairy
produce (goat), hen eggs,
wholefoods

Zed Wholefoods
3 Nether Edge Road
Nether Edge
Sheffield 7
(Tel. 0742 552153)
*Open* Monday–Friday 9am–8pm;
Saturday to 7pm
*Produce* Vegetables, fruit, hen
eggs, wholefoods

Abbey Wholefoods
12a Abbey Lane
Sheffield S8 0BL
(Tel. 0742 746490)
*Open* Monday–Friday
9am–5.30pm; Saturday to 5pm
*Produce* Vegetables, fruit, dairy
produce (goat), hen eggs,
wholefoods

# TYNE AND WEAR

## Newcastle upon Tyne

Only Natural
290 Chillingham Road
Heaton
Newcastle upon Tyne NE6 5LQ
(Tel. 091 265 0070)
*Produce* Vegetables, hen eggs,
wholefoods

City Farm Byker
Stepney Bank
Newcastle upon Tyne NE1 2PF
(Tel. 0632 323698)
*Open* Tuesday–Sunday
10am–4.30pm in winter; summer
to 7pm
*Produce* Vegetables, eggs (duck
and hen), goat's milk

Mandala Wholefoods
43 Manor House Road
Jesmond
Newcastle upon Tyne
(Tel. 091 281 0045)
*Open* Monday–Saturday
9.30am–6.00pm; Thursday to
7.30pm
*Produce* Vegetables, apples,
lemons, oranges, pears,
avocados, bananas, grapefruit,
grapes, kiwi fruit, etc., hen eggs,
yogurt (goat, cow and sheep),
goat's milk and cheese, rennet-
free cheese, wholefoods

Mrs Beryl-Anne Massey
Bowes Cottage
Birkheads
Sunniside
Newcastle upon Tyne NE16 5EL
(Tel. 0207 232863)
*Open* Please telephone first
&#x24D8; *Produce* Vegetables,
strawberries, rhubarb,
other soft fruit, herbs
*Directions* One and a half miles
south-west of Sunniside. Take
the Stanley Road out of
Sunniside, then first left fork,
over fell top to cross roads and
turn right

**Whitley Bay**

Yours Naturally
1 St Ronan's Road
Monkseaton
Whitley Bay
Tyne and Wear NE25 8AY
(Tel. 091 253 4060)
*Open* Monday–Saturday
9am–5.30pm; early closing
Wednesday
*Produce* Vegetables, apples,
oranges, bananas, lemons, hen
eggs, goat's milk, yogurt (cow,
sheep and goat), vegetarian
cheeses, wholefoods, herbs

# WEST YORKSHIRE

**Bradford**

Bradford City Farm
Illingworth Fields
Walker Drive
Bradford
West Yorks
(Tel. 0274 43500)
*Open* 9.30am–8pm in summer, to
6pm in winter daily
*Produce* Vegetables, eggs (duck
and hen)
*Directions* Travel out of city centre
via Thorton Road, turn right at
Girlington lights, up Whetley
Lane, Walker Drive is first on
left

Bradford Wholefoods Ltd
78 Morley Street
Bradford
West Yorks BD7 1AQ
*Open* Tuesday–Saturday
10am–5pm
*Produce* Vegetables, apples, pears,
soft fruit, oranges, lemons,

grapefruit, hen eggs, goat's milk yogurt and cheese, cow's milk yogurt, organic cheeses, vegetarian cheeses, butter, wholefoods

## Halifax

Susan Thomas
The Barn
Moorside
Old Lindley
Holywell Green
Halifax HX4 9DF
(Tel. 0422 76933)
*Open* Please telephone first
*Produce* Salad vegetables, hen eggs, lamb
*Directions* Exit 24, M62 travelling west, take Rochdale Road at roundabout for approximately one and a half miles. Turn right just after 'Wappy Spring' pub, then 600 yds turn right across footpath

I. and P. Osbourn
Bracken Farm
Priestly Green
Norwood Green
Halifax HX3 8RQ
(Tel. 0422 205578)
*Open* 10am–6pm
*Produce* Vegetables, raspberries, strawberries, gooseberries, blackcurrants

## Huddersfield

Susan Thomas
Stall No. 293
Huddersfield Open Market
*Open* Thursday 9am–4pm
*Produce* Vegetables, apples, oranges, rhubarb, gooseberries,

strawberries, raspberries in season, hen eggs, lamb, chicken

## Ilkley

Duncan W. and Barbara M. Pickard
Lane End Farm
Denton
Ilkley
West Yorks LS29 0HP
(Tel. 0943 609209)
*Open* Please telephone first
*Produce* Eggs (duck and hen), goat's milk, lamb and beef

## Leeds

Beano Wholefoods
36 New Briggate
Leeds LS1 6NU
(Tel. 0532 435737)
*Open* Monday–Saturday 9.30am–5.30pm
*Produce* Vegetables, lemons, oranges, apples, nectarines, pears, grapefruit, grapes, hen eggs, cheese, wholefoods

Meanwood Valley Urban City Farm
Sugarwell Road
Meanwood
Leeds 7
(Tel. 0532 629759)
*Open* Daily 8.15am–6pm
*Produce* Vegetables, gooseberries, blackcurrants, herbs

Safeway Food Stores Ltd
Bond Street
Leeds
West Yorks LS1 5BQ
(Tel. 0532 39377)

Safeway Food Stores Ltd
Arndale Centre
Otley Road
Headingly
Leeds
West Yorks LS6 2UE
(Tel. 0532 758238)

Safeway Food Stores Ltd
639 Roundhay Road
Oakwood
Leeds
West Yorks LS8 4BN
(Tel. 0532 401568/401733)

# WALES

## CLWYD

### Corwen

Simon's
4 Edyrnion Terrace
Corwen
Clwyd
(Tel. 0490 2297)
*Open* Monday–Saturday
9am–5.30pm
*Produce* Vegetables, fruit, eggs
(duck and hen), wholefoods

### Denbigh

C. J. Dear
Fron Fawr
Henllan
Denbigh
Clwyd
(Tel. 074 571 2882)
*Open* By arrangement only
*Produce* Vegetables,
strawberries,
blackcurrants, raspberries,
gooseberries

### Prestatyn

Beanies
226 High Street
Prestatyn
Clwyd
(Tel. 074 56 88774)
*Open* Monday–Saturday
9am–5.30pm
*Produce* Vegetables, dairy produce
(cow and goat), hen eggs,
wholefoods

## Ruthin

John and Maggie Brooker
Bryn Sguboriau
Llanelidan
Ruthin
Clwyd
(Tel. 0490 2497)
*Open* Daily
*Produce* Vegetables

# DYFED

## Aberystwyth

David Frost
Frost's Fresh Organic Produce
Tynyrhelyg Market Garden
Llanrhystyd
Dyfed SY23 5EE
(Tel. 097 46 364)
*Produce* Vegetables,
rhubarb, strawberries,
gooseberries, raspberries, black
and red currants, hen eggs,
goat's milk, herbs

Frost's Fruit and Flower Stalls
Market Hall
Great Darkgate Street
Aberystwyth
Dyfed SY23 1DW
(Tel. 0970 615980)
*Open* Monday–Saturday
9am–5pm
*Produce* Vegetables, fruit, eggs
(hen and duck), dairy produce
(Jersey and Guernsey cow),
goat's milk, sheep's cheese,
wholefoods, herbs, beansprouts

## Borth

G. and R. A. Rowlands
Brynllys
Borth

Dyfed SY24 5LZ
(Tel. 097 081 489)
*Open* Daylight hours, but please
telephone first
*Produce* Potatoes, carrots,
dairy produce (cow), lamb
and pork

## Cardigan

J. S. and V. A. Harding
Pentood Uchaf
Cardigan
Dyfed SA43 3NG
(Tel. 0239 612772)
*Open* Please telephone first
*Produce* Vegetables,
strawberries, raspberries,
blackcurrants, rhubarb, hen eggs,
dairy produce (cow), pork and
lamb, rye and bread wheat
*Directions* 1 mile from Cardigan
off the A487 Fishguard road

Neill Harris
Trewidwal Farm
Moylgrove
Cardigan
Dyfed SA43 3BY
(Tel. 0239 86211)
*Open* Daily 8am–8pm
*Produce* Vegetables

Glaneirw Housing Co-op
Blaenporth
Cardigan
Dyfed SA43 2HP
(Tel. 0239 810548)
*Open* Daily 9am–6pm
*Produce* Vegetables,
eggs
*Directions* North side of
Blaenporth village on the A487
Cardigan–Aberystwyth Road

## Carmarthen

John and Jenny White
Mount Pleasant
Pen y Bont
Trelech
Carmarthen
Dyfed
(Tel. 09948 315)
*Open* Daily, but please telephone first
*Produce* Celery, runner beans, goat's milk, yogurt and cheeses, pork

## Clynderwen

Hans Gunther Kern
Glanrhydwilym
Rhydwilym
Clynderwen
Dyfed SA66 7QH
(Tel. 09912 562)
*Open* Tuesday and Friday 8.30am–12 noon and 2pm–6pm; Saturday 8.30am–12 noon
🌏 *Produce* Vegetables, strawberries, blackcurrants, raspberries, gooseberries, rhubarb, duck eggs
*Directions* From Swansea take M4 /A48 to Carmarthen, then M40, turn right for Cardigan on to A478, Clynderwen, Llandisilio, then turn left for Rhydwilym

## Haverfordwest

Llangloffan Farmhouse
Llangloffan
Castle Morris
Haverfordwest
Dyfed
(Tel. 03485 241)
*Open* Monday–Saturday 10am–5pm (farm and to view cheesemaking)
*Produce* Cheese, cream and milk from Jersey cows. Mail order available

## Lampeter

Mulberry Bush Wholefoods
2 Bridge Street
Lampeter
Dyfed
(Tel. 0570 423317)
*Open* Monday–Saturday 9am–5.30pm; early closing Wednesday 1pm
*Produce* Vegetables, lemons, oranges, apples, pears, dairy produce (goat and sheep), hen eggs, wholefoods

## Llandeilo

D. and A. Campbell
Tyn Grug Esgerdawe
Llandeilo
Dyfed SA19 7SE
(Tel. 05585 400)
*Open* April–December, Tuesday–Saturday 10am–5pm
*Produce* Farmhouse cheese, pork
*Directions* 4 miles from Lampeter on A482

## Llandyssul

Chas and Anne Griffin
Bryn Saron Farm
Saron
Llandyssul
Dyfed SA44 5HB
(Tel. 0559 370405)
*Open* Please telephone first
🌏 *Produce* Vegetables, melons, strawberries, raspberries, blackcurrants, redcurrants,

gooseberries, eggs (duck and hen), garlic
*Directions* 13 miles north of Carmarthen on A484. Between Rhos and Saron is Bryn Saron school. Turn down the lane next to the school. Our farm lane is the second on the left

John Savage
Glynhynod Farm
Ffostrasol
Llandyssul
Dyfed
(Tel. 023975 528)
 *Produce* Hen eggs, farmhouse cheese and butter (cow), pork

### Llanon

Don and Karen Ross
Mesen Fach Farm
Bethania
Nr Llanon
Dyfed
(Tel. 097423 348)
*Produce* Ewe's milk yogurt and cheese, pork and lamb

### Whitland

J. Myers
Waungron
Cefn-y-pant
Whitland
Dyfed SA34 0TS
(Tel. 099 47 313)
*Open* By arrangement, please phone
*Produce* Cheese, pork, eggs
*Directions* OS Ref SN193 260

Penrhiw Farm Dairy
Cefn-y-pant
Llanboidy
Whitland
Dyfed
(Tel. 099 47 351)
*Produce* Yogurt, cream, butter, cottage cheese, vegetables, pork

# GLAMORGAN

### Cardiff

Cardiff City Farm
Off Sloper Road
Grangetown
South Glamorgan
(Tel. 0222 384360)
*Open* Daily 8am–5.30pm
*Produce* Vegetables, raspberries, blackcurrants, gooseberries, apples, eggs (duck and hen), goat's milk, pork, chickens, herbs
*Directions* Opposite Cardiff football ground

Wholefood Shop
1A Fitzroy Street
Cathays
Cardiff CF2 4BL
(Tel. 0222 395388)
*Open* Tuesday–Saturday 9am–6pm
*Produce* Vegetables, fruit, cow's yogurt, wholefoods

### Swansea

Ear to the Ground
68A Bryn-y-mor Road
Swansea
West Glamorgan
(Tel. 0792 463505) and in Swansea Market

*Open* 9am–6pm shop;
8.30am–5.30pm market
*Produce* Vegetables, apples, pears,
oranges, lemons, wholefoods

# GWENT

## Chepstow

Mrs U. M. Field
Medhope Organic Growers
'The Nurtons'
Tintern
Chepstow
Gwent
(Tel. 02918 797)
*Open* Please telephone first
    *Produce* Vegetables, soft and
    top fruit, hen eggs
*Directions* Drive is opposite the old
Tintern station just outside
village

## Newport

Mr J. J. Wood
'Seaview'
Caldicot Pill
Caldicot
Newport
Gwent
(Tel. 0291 421095)
*Open* Please telephone first
    *Produce* Vegetables, soft
    fruit

# GWYNEDD

## Llwyngwril

Nick and Margaret Smyth
Pentre Bach
Llwyngwril
Gwynedd LL37 2JU
(Tel. 0341 250294)
*Open* Daylight hours, please
telephone first

*Produce* Vegetables,
blackcurrants, rhubarb, apples,
pears, gooseberries, blackberries,
eggs (duck and hen), jams,
chutneys, cider apple vinegar
*Directions* Centre of village near
primary school

## Pwllheli

Janet and Peter Gomme
Pot Plants Nursery
Rhosfawr
Pwllheli
Gwynedd
(Tel. 076 688545)
*Open* Daylight hours
*Produce* Vegetables, soft fruit, eggs
(duck and hen)

# POWYS

## Glasbury-on-Wye

Mrs Sheila Leith
Wye View
Glasbury-on-Wye
Powys via Hereford
HR3 5NU
(Tel. 04974 354)
*Open* Please telephone first
*Produce* Vegetables, raspberries,
currants, gooseberries,
tayberries, and other berries,
rhubarb, apples (including old
varieties), sweet chestnuts, fruit
juice
*Directions* Leave A438, Hereford
to Brecon road at Glasbury, by
turning up lane, almost opposite
the bridge, in a southeasterly
direction. 200 yds on, after going
under old railway bridge, turn
right at telephone kiosk, and Wye
View is on the left

## Llandrindod Wells

Van's Fruit and Veg Shop *and*
Van's Good Food Shop
Laburnum House
Middleton Street
Llandrindod Wells
Powys
(Tel. 0597 4681 and 3074)
*Open* Monday–Saturday
9am–5pm; early closing
Wednesday 1pm
*Produce* Vegetables, oranges,
lemons, apples, pears, hen eggs,
wholefoods

## Llanfyllin

Pam and Hugh Coleman
   (Greengrocer)
Tan-y-Vorlan
Llanfyllin
Powys SY22 5LY
(Tel. 069 184 514)
*Open* Thursday and Friday
8am–5pm; Saturday to 1pm
*Produce* Vegetables, fruit, hen eggs

## Machynlleth

Abergarfan Organic Growers
Abergarfan Isaf
Pantperthog
Machynlleth
Powys SY20 9RA
(Tel. 0654 3222)
*Open* Monday–Saturday
9am–dusk
   *Produce* Vegetables, soft
   fruit
*Directions* On A487, 2 miles north
of Machynlleth

## Welshpool

Morris
Little Wern
Pool Quay
Welshpool
Powys SY21 9LQ
(Tel. 097 885 555)
*Open* Gate sales
   *Produce* Vegetables, honey,
   eggs, fruit
*Directions* On Welshpool–
Oswestry road, turn left at Pool
Quay, signed 'Wern'. The
property is the first house on the
left after the canal bridge

# SCOTLAND

## CENTRAL

### Stirling

I. and A. Lambie
Tigh Voulin
Thornhill
Stirling
(Tel. 0786 85367)
*Open* July–September, please
telephone first
*Produce* Vegetables,
raspberries and
strawberries, herbs
*Directions* Last cottage on left at
end of Doig Street

## DUMFRIES AND GALLOWAY

### Dumfries

Camphill Village Trust
Loch Arthur Village Community
Beeswing
Dumfries DG2 8JQ
(Tel. 038 776 249/224)
*Open* By arrangement
*Produce* Vegetables,
eggs
*Directions* At church in Beeswing,
turn left on New Abbey Road.
Take first drive on right to
Lochend Farm

### Moniaive

Tim and Fabienne Rapsey
Woodhead Cottage
Craigdarroch Gardens
Moniaive
Thornhill
Dumfries DG3 4JB
(Tel. 084 82 406)

*Open* Thursday, Saturday,
Monday am
*Produce* Vegetables

*Directions* 3 miles west of
Moniaive on the Ayr road

## FIFE

### Auchtermuchty

Reediehill Farm (Fletcher)
Reediehill Farm
Auchtermuchty
Cupar
Fife KY14 7HS
(Tel. 0337 28369)
*Open* Sunday–Friday 9am–5pm;
closed Saturday. Other times
please telephone first
*Produce* Hen eggs, venison, geese
at Christmas, cow cheese, meat
products
*Directions* Auchtermuchty is on
the A91. In the middle of the
town turn onto the B983
(signposted Newburgh and
Perth). Continue half a mile
through Auchtermuchty until you
see a prominent white gable end
in a fork in the road. A 'venison'
signpost directs you to fork left
here. The farm is just under 2
miles up this minor road, on the
left-hand side

### Falkland

Bruce Bennett
Pillars of Hercules
Falkland
Cupar
Fife
(Tel. 0337 57749)
*Open* Please telephone first

*Produce* Vegetables, hen
eggs
*Directions* 1 mile outside Falkland
towards Strathmiglo

Lomond Butchers
High Street
Freuchie
Fife
(Tel. 0337 57330)
*Open* Monday–Friday
8am–5.30pm; Thursday and
Saturday to 12.30pm
*Produce* Vegetables, apples, pears,
oranges, grapefruit, lemons,
plums, grapes, bananas, hen
eggs, cheese, Christmas turkeys,
pork, lamb and other poultry

### Glenrothes

Balbirnie Community Farm
Balbirnie Park
Glenrothes
Fife KY7 6NR
(Tel. 0592 752558)
*Open* Daily 9am–5pm
*Produce* Vegetables, hen and duck
eggs
*Directions* Off A92, follow quarry
road round to Balbirnie Mains

### Kirkcaldy

Safeway Food Stores Ltd
8/20 High Street
Kirkcaldy
Fife KY1 1LV
(Tel. 0592 268328/9)

### St Andrews

T. P. N. Erskine
Cambo House
Kingsbarns
Nr St Andrews
Fife KY16 8QD

(Tel. 0333 50313)
*Open* 10am–6pm
 *Produce* Cabbages

*Directions* Between St Andrews
and Crail

# GLASGOW

Safeway Food Stores Ltd
241 Stonelaw Road
Burnside
Rutherglen
Glasgow G73 3RJ
(Tel. 041 647 5306)

Safeway Food Stores Ltd
2 Sylvania Way
Clydebank
Glasgow G81 2TL
(Tel. 041 952 3231)

Safeway Food Stores Ltd
Edinburgh House
East Kilbride
Glasgow G74 1JL
(Tel. 035 52 23169)

Safeway Food Stores Ltd
728 Anniesland Road
Knightswood
Glasgow G18 6LW
(Tel. 041 959 4330)

Safeway Food Stores Ltd
384/390 Clarkston Road
Muirend
Glasgow G44 3JL
(Tel. 041 637 9275)

Safeway Food Stores Ltd
2130 Paisley Road West
Glasgow G52 3SQ
(Tel. 041 882 6593)

Safeway Food Stores Ltd
136 Kilmarnock Road
Shawlands Cross
Glasgow G41 3PG
(Tel. 041 632 4390)

Safeway Food Stores Ltd
High Common Road
St Leonards Neighbourhood
  Centre
East Kilbride
Glasgow G74 2AG
(Tel. 035 52 33407)

# GRAMPIAN

## Aberdeen

Ambrosia Wholefoods Ltd
160 King Street
Aberdeen
(Tel. 0224 639096)
*Open* 9.30am–5.30pm; early
closing Wednesday 1pm; late
evening Thursday 7pm
*Produce* Vegetables,
oranges, apples, pears,
grapes, peaches, strawberries,
gooseberries, rhubarb,
raspberries, blackcurrants,
redcurrants, nectarines,
tangerines, hen eggs, goat's
cheese and milk, sheep's cheese
and yogurt, cow's cheese,
wholefoods

## Ellon

A. E. Hayman
3 Cairnleith Croft
Ythanbank
Ellon
Aberdeenshire AB4 0UB
(Tel. 03587 298)
*Open* Please telephone first

*Produce* Vegetables,
raspberries, hen eggs,
small quantities of pork, lamb
and poultry
*Directions* From Ellon take B9005
to Ythanbank. Pass through the
village and take first right turn to
Schivas. Take first tarmac road
on right signposted Cairnleith
Crofts. Continue up hill and at
T-junction turn right.
3 Cairnleith Croft is first dwelling
on track

## Mosstowie

Fieldfare (Organic Growers)
Burnside Farm
Mosstowie
by Elgin
Morayshire IV30 3UW
(Tel. 034 385 237)
*Open* Please telephone first
*Produce* Vegetables

## Turriff

J. and P. Bennett
Blakeshouse
Crudie
Turriff
Aberdeenshire
(Tel. 08885 276)
*Open* Please telephone first
*Produce* Vegetables,
beef

# HIGHLAND REGION

## Glenfinnan

John G. Whyte
Torr Beitheach
Glenfinnan
Inverness-shire PH37 4LT
(Tel. 0397 83 206)

*Open* July–October, but please telephone first
*Produce* Vegetables, apples, small quantities of various berries

## Invergordon

A. R. Hutchison
Meiklejohns Croft
Lamington
Nr Invergordon
Ross-shire IV18 0PF
(Tel. 086 284 2358)
*Open* 9am–6pm
*Produce* Goat and sheep cheese, ewe's milk, yogurt, vegetables
*Directions* 1 mile off the A9 at Kildary on the back road between Tain and Alness (OS NH751775)

# LOTHIAN

## Dunbar

'The Diggers'
Belton Gardens
Dunbar
East Lothian
(Tel. 0368 62101)
*Open* Please telephone first
*Produce* Vegetables, figs, grapes, soft fruit
*Directions* Follow B6370 Gifford Road one and a half miles from West Barns

## Edinburgh

Gorgie City Farm
51 Gorgie Road
Gorgie/Dalry
Edinburgh EH11 2LA
(Tel. 031 337 4202)
*Open* Daily 9am–5pm

*Produce* Vegetables, eggs (duck and hen), pork occasionally

Real Foods
8 Brougham Street
Tollcross
Edinburgh EH3 9JH
(Tel. 031 228 1651)
*Open* Monday–Saturday 9am–6pm; Wednesday to 5.30pm
*Produce* Wholefoods, wine

Real Foods
37 Broughton Street
Edinburgh EH1 3JU
(Tel. 031 557 1911)
*Produce* Monday–Saturday 9am–6pm; Wednesday to 5.30pm
*Produce* Wholefoods, wine

The Edinburgh Organic Shop
132 Lauriston Place
Tollcross
Edinburgh EH3 9HX
(Tel. 031 228 3405)
*Open* Tuesday–Saturday 10am–5.30pm; closed Monday
*Produce* Vegetables, apples, grapefruit, grapes, lemons, peaches, pears, plums, oranges, strawberries, raspberries, gooseberries and blackcurrants, tangerines, hen eggs, cow's milk cheeses, wholefoods

Eastwind Ltd
Unit 1/10 St Mary's Workshop
Henderson Street
Leith
Edinburgh EH6 6DD
(Tel. 031 553 0832)
*Open* Please telephone first

*Produce* Alfalfa sprouts

Safeway Food Stores Ltd
33–39 Cameron Toll Shopping
  Centre
6 Lady Road
Edinburgh
(Tel. 031 664 6190/6822)

Safeway Food Stores Ltd
36 Crammond Road South
Davidson's Main
Edinburgh EH4 6AA
(Tel. 031 336 4234)

Safeway Food Stores Ltd
Maybury Drive
East Craigs
Edinburgh EH12 8UG
(Tel. 031 339 2072)

Safeway Food Stores Ltd
Falcon Avenue
Morningside Road
Edinburgh
(Tel. 031 447 9955/8878)

Safeway Food Stores Ltd
Piersfield Terrace
Portobello Road
Edinburgh EH8 7BQ
(Tel. 031 661 7372/7387)

**Livingston**

Safeway Food Stores Ltd
Carmondean Centre
Deans
Livingston
West Lothian EH54 4PT
(Tel. 0589 33224)

# ORKNEY

C. N. Dow
Ladyhaven
Burray
Orkney
(Tel. 085673 316)
*Open* Daily, until 9pm
*Produce* Vegetables, raspberries
*Directions* Turn sharp right at
Burray school. Continue to
greenhouse half a mile on

# STRATHCLYDE

### Airdrie

Safeway Food Stores Ltd
Graham Street
Airdrie
Lanarkshire ML6 6LB
(Tel. 02364 55085)

### Argyle

R. and I. Reid
Achnacarnan
Tarbert
Argyll PA29 6YF
(Tel. 08802 440)
*Open* Please telephone first
*Produce* Vegetables, blackcurrants
and raspberries, hen eggs, goat's
milk and yogurt, wholefoods

### Ayr

Safeway Food Stores Ltd
31 Beresford Terrace
Ayr
Strathclyde KA7 2EV
(Tel. 0292 61651/67951)

## Hamilton

Safeway Food Stores Ltd
Regent Way
Duke Street
Hamilton
Strathclyde M13 7DZ
(Tel. 06982 281660)

## Prestwick

Safeway Food Stores Ltd
135/147 Ayr Road
Prestwick
Ayrshire KA9 1TW
(Tel. 0292 70941)

## Wishaw

Safeway Food Stores Ltd
76 Kirk Road
Wishaw
Strathclyde ML2 7BS
(Tel. 06983 74424)

# TAYSIDE

## Aberfeldy

John and Maggie Fraser
Living Earth
Edradynate
Strathtay
by Aberfeldy
Perthshire
(Tel. 08874 301)
*Open* Please telephone first,
preferably between 8am and
9am
*Produce* Vegetables,
peaches, apples, grapes
*Directions* 4 miles from Aberfeldy,
2 miles from Strathtay village on
the north side of the river Tay.
Follow the estate road

## Broughty Ferry

Safeway Food Stores Ltd
Brook Street
Broughty Ferry
Dundee
Tayside DD5 1DS
(Tel. 0382 74890)

## Dundee

Safeway Food Stores Ltd
Strathmarine Road
Dundee
Tayside DD3 7SE
(Tel. 0382 810932)

## Pitlochry

Hugh and Cynthia McArthur
Drumnagowan
Glen Fincastle
Pitlochry
Perthshire PH16 5RJ
(Tel. 0796 3175)
*Open* Please telephone first
*Produce* Vegetables, strawberries,
blackcurrants, eggs (hen, duck,
goose and guinea fowl), goat's
milk and cheese, rabbit, jam
*Directions* 3 miles north of
Pitlochry along A9, turn left over
Garry Bridge, keep left 3 miles,
down steep hill, then one and a
half miles up no-through road

# IRELAND

## Dublin

Superquin Superstores at the
   following branches:
Sutton
Black Rock
Blanchardtown
All sell organic fruit and
   vegetables

Marcus Fresh
Nut Grove Shopping Centre
Dublin 14
*Produce* Vegetables, fruit

Here Today
South Anne Street
Dublin 2
*Produce* Vegetables, fruit

Tony Quin Health Centre
66 Eccles Street
Dublin 7
*Produce* Vegetables, fruit

Tony Quin Health Centre
2 Winnfield Road
Rathmines
Dublin 6
*Produce* Vegetables, fruit

## Dundalk

Marcus Fresh
Dundalk
Co. Louth
*Produce* Vegetables, fruit

Tony Quin Health Centre
18 Jocelyn Street
Dundalk
Co. Louth
*Produce* Vegetables, fruit

## Manorhamilton

The Co-op Shop
Main Street
Manorhamilton
Co. Leitrim
*Open* Monday to Saturday
9.30am–6pm; closed Wednesday
*Produce* Vegetables,
blackcurrants and
strawberries in season, eggs,
goat's milk to order, herbs

## Navan

Marcus Fresh
Navan Shopping Centre
Navan
Co. Neath
*Produce* Vegetables, fruit

## Rossinver

Rod Alston and Dolores Keegan
Eden Plants
Eden
Rossinver
Co. Leitrim
*Open* Daylight hours
*Produce* Vegetables, herb
plants

## Sligo

Tir na nog
Gratton Street
Sligo
(Tel. 071 62752)
*Open* Monday to Saturday
9.30am–6pm
*Produce* Vegetables, a little
fruit, eggs, wholefoods

# CHANNEL ISLANDS

**Guernsey**

David Fletcher
Gramercy
Les Landes
Vale
Guernsey
Channel Islands
(Tel. 0481 44635)
 *Produce* Vegetables

# 10   A GUIDE TO WHOLESALERS

The country is now covered by firms that sell whole and natural foods wholesale, supplying retail shops in their own localities. For the most part only a small proportion of the lines they stock is described as organically grown. The first part of this section covers the principal firms that I know of that make this distinction in their catalogues. This section also includes millers of organically grown grains.

The second part covers companies which have sprung up during the last few years to develop the market for fresh organic produce. Many of them also stock a good range of organic dried foods such as cereals and pulses. Some sell dairy produce but hardly any of them supply organically produced meat.

Section 3 covers distributors of what is often sold as 'additive-free' but what might best be described as naturally reared meat. Most suppliers would not meet the strict standards laid down to qualify as organically produced, usually because of the limitations regarding feedstuffs (see Appendix 3). Nevertheless since such produce offers a distinct improvement on meat from intensively raised livestock the addresses are included here.

If you are unable to find a shop or supplier of organic produce in your locality in this Guide contact your nearest wholesaler who will be able to give you more up-to-date information.

## 1 Wholesalers Supplying Limited Quantities of Organic Food and Millers of Organically Grown Grain

### South West

Quantock Foods
Queenswood Farm
Broadlands Lane
Bridgwater
Somerset TA5 2AR
(Tel. 0278 423440)
*Distribution* South West,
Southern England, South
Wales

Nature's Store
Unit E,
Motorway Distribution Centre
Avonmouth Way
Avonmouth
Bristol BS11 9YA
(Tel. 0272 828211)
*Distribution* South West,
Southern England, South
Wales and Midlands

Nova Wholefoods
Unit 1
Barton Hill Industrial Estate
Bristol
*Distribution* South West, South
Wales, London

The Granary (Truro) Ltd
Newham Road
Truro
Cornwall TR1 2ST
(Tel. 0872 74343)
*Distribution* South West

Harvest
Unit 2a
Bath Riverside Business Park
Riverside Road
Bath BA2 3DW
(Tel. 0225 336474)
*Distribution* 60 mile radius Bath

### Southern England

Clive Edwards and Company
Burlton
Shillingstone
Nr Blandford Forum
Dorset DT11 0SP
(Tel. 0258 860641)
Distributors of organically
produced wine

Doves Farm Flour
Ham
Marlborough
Wiltshire
(Tel. 0488 4374)
Millers under the Doves Farm
label

Rushall Farms
The Manor
Upavon
Pewsey
Wilts
(Tel. 0980 630264)
Millers

## South East

Brewhurst
Alfonal House
Abbot Close
Oyster Lane
Byfleet
Surrey
(Tel. 09323 54211)
*Distribution* All of Britain and
Northern Ireland

Infinity Foods Co-operative
67B Norway Street
Portslade
Brighton BN4 1AE
(Tel. 0273 424060)
*Distribution* London and the
South East

Loseley Park Farms
Nr Guildford
Surrey GU3 1HM
(Tel. 0483 71881)
*Distribution* South East, London
and the Home Counties,
Midlands

## London and the Home Counties

Farm Shop
No 1 Neal's Yard
Covent Garden
London WC2
(Tel. 01 836 1066)
*Distribution* Delivery service in
London plus mail order
throughout the UK

Community Foods Ltd
Unit 1
Brunswick Industrial Park
Brunswick Park Road
New Southgate
London N11 1JL
(Tel. 01 368 9211)
*Distribution* Throughout
England

Wholesome Trucking
Unit 9
Higgs Industrial Estate
2 Herne Hill Road
London SE24 0AU
(Tel. 01 733 2614/737 2658)
*Distribution* London and the
Home Counties, East Anglia,
South East, West Midlands

Harmony Distributors Ltd
Unit D
Western Trading Estate
Park Royal Road
London NW10 7LU
(Tel. 01 961 5544)
*Distribution* Throughout
mainland UK

Whole Earth
Unit D
Western Trading Estate
Trading Estate Road
London NW10 7LY
(Tel. 01 961 5544)
*Distribution* Cash and carry

## West Midlands

Drop in the Ocean
(Wholesalers)
Unit Y1
Binley Industrial Estate
Herald Way
Brandon Road
Coventry
(Tel. 0203 449566)
*Distribution* West Midlands

Survival Foods Ltd
Unit 2
Cobnash Road
Kingsland
Nr Leominster
Herefordshire HR6 9RW
(Tel. 056 881 344)
*Distribution* West Midlands,
Wales

Sam Mayall and Son
Lea Hall
Harmer Hill
Shrewsbury
Shropshire SY4 3DY
(Tel. 0939 290342)
Millers under the Pimhill label

Caradoc Ltd
Broome
Stourbridge
West Midlands DY9 0HD
(Tel. 0562 700394)
National distributors of Holle
babyfoods, biodynamically
grown herbs, sugarbeet syrup
and powder

## East Midlands

Goodness Foods
London Road
Daventry
Northants NN11 4SA
(Tel. 0327 706611)
*Distribution* Nationwide

Daily Bread Co-operative
The Old Laundry
Bedford Road
Northampton NN4 0AD
(Tel. 0604 21531)
*Distribution* Cash and carry

## East Anglia

Organic Farmers and Growers
(OFG Ltd)
Abacus House
Station Yard
Needham Market
Ipswich
Suffolk 1P6 8AT
(Tel. 0449 720838)
*Distribution* Organic growers'
marketing co-operative
specializing in cereals. Products
available nationally. Also runs
an import-export business
(Organic Farmers and Growers
(Imports and Exports) Ltd),
products of which are for
wholesale distribution

Bramble Wholefoods
1 The Mazes
East Street
Braintree
Essex CM7 6JT
(Tel. 0376 42337)
*Distribution* East Anglia

Life and Health Foods
Chase Road
Northern Way
Bury St Edmunds
Suffolk IP32 6NT
(Tel. 0284 66265)
*Distribution* England and Wales

Hofels Pure Foods
Stowmarket Road
Woolpit
Suffolk
(Tel. 0359 40592)
Millers

## North West

The Watermill
Little Salkeld
Penrith
Cumbria CA10 1NN
(Tel. 076 881 523)
Millers

## North East

Suma Foods
Unit AX1
Dean Clough Industrial Park
Halifax HX3 5AN
(Tel. 0422 45513)
*Distribution* East Midlands to the
Scottish borders

Hider Food Imports Ltd
Wiltshire Road
Hull HU4 6PA
(Tel. 0482 561137)
*Distribution* Midlands to the
Scottish border, North Wales

## Wales

Jedwells Foods
Unit 13
W.D.A. Factories
Corwen
Clwyd LL21 9LD
(Tel. 0490 2024)
*Distribution* Throughout the UK

Good Food Distributors
The Goods Yard
Builth Wells
Powys
(Tel. 0982 553598/9)
*Distribution* Wales

## Scotland

Booker McNab Whole World
22 Inglis Green Road
Edinburgh EH14 2HZ
(Tel. 031 443 5219)
*Distribution* Most of Scotland

Green City Wholefoods
23 Fleming Street
Glasgow G31 1PH
(Tel. 041 554 7633)
*Distribution* All of Scotland
including Orkney and Shetland

Real Foods
Ashley Place
Edinburgh EH6 5PX
(Tel. 031 554 4321)
*Distribution* Entire United
Kingdom and Eire. Mail order
service

Hebridean Shellfish Growers
(Lewis and Harris) Ltd
1 Quidinish
Isle of Harris PA89 3JQ
(Tel. 0859 83 311)
*Distributors* of high quality
plankton-fed mussels off the
Hebridean coast

## Ireland

Lifeforce Foods
4 Halston Street
Dublin 7
(Tel. 0001 730117)
*Distribution* Ireland

## 2 Wholesalers Primarily Supplying Fresh Organic Produce

### South West

South West Organic Growers
Lesperrow
St Michael Penkivel
Truro
Cornwall
(Tel. 0872 52 508)
*Distribution* Cornwall

W. J. Blake
Flaxdrayton Farm
South Petherton
Somerset TA13 5LR
(Tel. 0460 40855)
*Distribution* South West

Somerset Organic Producers
  Ltd
Fernham
Buckland Hill
Buckland St Mary
Chard
Somerset TA20 3JF
(Tel. 046 034 425)
A West Country marketing co-operative for organic growers

### Southern England

Tony Smith (The Organic
Man)
The Willows
Mockbeggar Lane
Ibsley
Ringwood
Hants
(Tel. 042 54 2116)
*Distribution* Bournemouth,
Southampton, Portsmouth and
parts of Hampshire and Dorset

### South East

Broadwater Produce Ltd
Southdownview Road
Broadwater Trading Estate
Worthing
West Sussex
(Tel. 0903 204274/34091)
*Distribution* Surrey and Sussex

### London and the Home Counties

Odin UK
Stands B32/33
New Covent Garden
London SW8
(Tel. 01 622 3099)
*Distribution* Throughout
England

Naturefreight
63 Tremadoc Road
London SW4 7NA
(Tel. 01 622 1210)
*Distribution* London and Home
Counties, South East

### West Midlands

Clean Foods
Unit 5
New Enterprise Workshop
4 Mount Street
Nechells
Birmingham 7
(Tel. 021 327 0386)
*Distribution* Midlands

## East Midlands

Bloomsgorse Natural Foods
Bloomsgorse Cottage
Deerdale
Bilsthorpe
Newark
Notts
(Tel. 0623 870792)
*Distribution* East Midlands,
South Yorkshire

## North West

Trans Pennine Organic
  Vegetable Wholesalers
White Crow Industrial Estate
South Road
Lancaster LA1 4XQ
(Tel. 0524 381038)
*Distribution* Northern England


L.P.A. Organic Ltd
Unit 1
Tattenhall Road
Tattenhall
Chester CH3 9BD
(Tel. 0829 71061)
*Distribution* West Midlands,
North West, East Midlands,
North Wales


Harry Burnham
25 Fitton Avenue
Charlton
Manchester 21
(Tel. 061 860 4663)
*Distribution* Greater Manchester


Merseyside Organic
  Wholefoods
107 Lodge Lane
Liverpool
(Tel. 051 733 5205)
*Distribution* Merseyside

Blairs Organic Growers
Low Carr Nursery
Head Dyke Lane
Pilling
Nr Preston PR3 6JS
(Tel. 039 130 471)
Large-scale grower of salad
crops under Blairs label –
distributed widely

## North East

Yorkshire Organics
184 Wrose Road
Wrose
Bradford
West Yorks
(Tel. 0274 591882)
*Distribution* Nationally

## Wales

Organic Farm Foods (Wales)
  Ltd
Unit 25
Lampeter Industrial Estate
Lampeter
Dyfed
(Tel. 0570 423099/423130)
*Distribution* Wales and the
Borders

## Scotland

Organic Farm Foods (Scotland)
  Ltd
Unit 8, Block 4
Whiteside Industrial Estate
Bathgate
Edinburgh EH48 2RX
(Tel. 0506 632911)
*Distribution* Throughout
Scotland

**Ireland**

E. McManus
The Fruit Market
Dublin 7

Donnolly and Sons
North King Street
Dublin 7

## 3 Distributors Supplying Naturally Reared Meat and Meat Products

Richard J. Guy
The Real Meat Company
East Hill Farm
Hentesbury, Wilts
(Tel. 0985 40436)

F. A. and J. Jones and Son
Red House Farm Butchers Shop
Spalford Lane
North Scarle
Lincoln LN6 9HB
(Tel. 052277 224)

Hockeys Naturally
Newtown Farm
South Gorley
Fordingbridge
Hants SP6 2PW
(Tel. 0425 52542)

## 4 Supermarkets

Although organic foods may be found in a range of multiple stores only Safeway has introduced fresh organic produce on any scale into its stores. For further details contact the head office at Safeway Food Stores Ltd, Beddow Way, Aylesford, Maidstone, Kent ME20 7AT (Tel. 0622 72000).

## Appendix 1  ORGANIC FARMING – A DEFINITION

The Standards document of the International Federation of Organic Agriculture Movements (IFOAM, 1981) gives the following description:

1 To work as much as possible within a closed system, and to draw upon local resources.

2 To maintain the long-term fertility of soils.

3 To avoid all forms of pollution that may result from agricultural techniques.

4 To produce foodstuffs of high nutritional quality and sufficient quantity.

5 To reduce the use of fossil energy in agricultural practice to a minimum.

6 To give livestock conditions of life that conform to their physiological needs and to humanitarian principles.

7 To make it possible for agricultural producers to earn a living through their work and develop their potentialities as human beings.

To which can be added the following:

1 To use and develop appropriate technology based on an understanding of biological systems.

2 To use decentralized systems for processing, distributing and marketing of products.

3 To create a system which is aesthetically pleasing to both those within and outside the system.

4   To maintain and preserve wildlife and their habitats.

Although it misses out some of the important considerations of organic farmers, the United States Department of Agriculture has provided a handy definition of organic agriculture:

> Organic farming is a production system which avoids or largely excludes the use of synthetically compounded fertilizers, pesticides, growth regulators and livestock feed additives. To the maximum extent feasible, organic farming systems rely on crop rotations, crop residues, animal manures, legumes, green manures, off-farm organic wastes, mechanical cultivation, mineral-bearing rocks, and aspects of biological pest control to maintain soil productivity and tilth, to supply plant nutrients and to control insects, weeds and other pests.

## Appendix 2  ORGANIZATIONS

The list of organizations which follows is by no means comprehensive but it does reflect the larger and more active groups within the organic movement. Many of them are registered charities, some are membership organizations and all of them would welcome support, either financial or otherwise.

## The Henry Doubleday Research Association (HDRA)

The Henry Doubleday Research Association is Britain's largest organization concerned with organic gardening. Its main purpose is to discover improved methods of growing fruit and vegetables, without using artificial fertilizers and pesticides, which are appropriate to gardeners and other small-scale growers.

It receives no direct state support and relies for its income on the subscriptions and donations of its 10,000 or so members.

The most obvious benefit of joining the Association is the quarterly newsletter which every member receives. It is designed to keep everyone in touch with the latest developments in organic gardening research around the world, as applied to their own back garden. It is packed full of useful gardening tips including a beginners' section. The Association also publishes a range of books and booklets which are available at a 25 per cent discount to members. Since many of the fertilizers and safe pesticides that are recommended, especially the biological control insects for whitefly and red spider mite, are difficult to obtain, it also runs a mail order service.

Every new convert to organic gardening has a host of questions they want answered and many of the answers can be found in our literature. However, if a specific problem requires a specialized answer members of the Association can draw upon the free advice service.

The Association is also concerned at the rapid loss of old vegetable varieties as a result of plant breeding legislation and has campaigned for several years on this issue. It runs a Vegetable Seed Library for the benefit of its members. Seeds of old or otherwise unobtainable varieties are available free of charge and in this way are kept in cultivation.

In 1985 the Association moved to new premises in the Midlands, where on 5 July 1986 it opened to the public Ryton Gardens, The National Centre for Organic Gardening. This 22-acre national showpiece for organic gardening methods is open all year round. HDRA members have free access as often as they like.

The present cost of joining is just £10 per year, £6 concessionary membership which includes OAPs, students, children, unwaged or disabled. Family membership costs £12, Life Membership £150 and Group membership £12.

Further details from HDRA, National Centre for Organic Gardening, Ryton-on-Dunsmore, Coventry CV8 3LG, Tel. 0203–303517 (2 lines).

## The Soil Association

There is something old and new about the organic way of farming and gardening. It is based upon methods that have been practised successfully for hundreds, if not thousands, of years; creating a fertile soil by returning animal manures and crop wastes to the land. The organic approach builds upon this basis using up-to-date knowledge and methods to preserve and pass on to following generations a sustainable and healthy agricultural environment.

The Soil Association was founded some forty years ago by people who foresaw the detrimental effects of a chemical-based agriculture, and its members have been working ever since for a widespread return to more sensible, sound and forward-looking methods. Today, the message is finally getting through and the Association has a tremendous opportunity to make rapid progress. With the crisis on our farmland and in our food becoming more acute by the day, the job of educating the public – and government organizations – on the safety and economic good sense of the organic way is increasingly vital and urgent.

The Soil Association runs a Symbol scheme which guarantees the quality of organic food grown to rigorous standards. The Symbol is awarded to farmers, growers and processors who conform to these standards. Regular inspections monitor crop protection and animal welfare. Strict procedures and tight control mean that the consumer can have absolute confidence that the Symbol is the guarantee of genuine organic produce.

To develop its work as a registered charitable organization the Soil Association needs support. Please write to: The Soil Association, 86 Colston Street, Bristol BS1 5BB (Tel. 0272 290661).

## The Organic Growers Association

The Organic Growers Association is the national organization for all commercial growers interested in organic horticulture in the United Kingdom.

A registered charity, it was formed in 1980 by a group of organic growers in response to the obvious need for an organization to advise and represent other organic growers and to provide a forum for debate, technical development and research within the horticultural industry.

Since its formation OGA's membership has increased steadily and there are now members throughout the country with an increasing emphasis on regional groups.

In conjunction with its sister group, British Organic Farmers, OGA produces a quarterly journal, *New Farmer and Grower*, which is the only publication in the country specifically for organic producers and aims to provide readers with news, comment and information, including detailed technical articles on an extensive range of crops and cultivation methods.

An extensive range of farm walks throughout the summer provides members with the opportunity to meet and to learn from other growers' experience and these walks are widely considered by members to be the most valuable way to gain practical knowledge and expertise at first hand.

OGA is actively involved with MAFF, university and polytechnic research, environmental groups and county and district councils, both sponsoring and assisting with a variety of long- and short-term projects. It also co-operates with organizations like the Ministry of Agriculture, the Agricultural Training Board and *The Grower* magazine to provide speakers for conferences and workshops.

The first national conference was held at the Royal Agricultural College, Cirencester in 1980 and has now become a regular event, every two years.

Though, as a registered charity, OGA has no commercial interests, it aims to promote professional marketing through the packaging available from its subsidiary trading company, OGA Packaging. A range of packaging both for producers holding the Soil Association Symbol and for retailers is available.

For further details, please send a large s.a.e. to OGA, 86 Colston Street, Bristol BS1 5BB.

## British Organic Farmers

British Organic Farmers was formed in 1983 as the producer association for Britain's growing organic farming community.

It is due to become a charity in 1986 and is run by a committee of organic farmers. Membership is open to anyone with a serious interest in sustainable farming systems.

BOF works closely with its sister organization, the Organic Growers Association, and aims to support and help existing organic farmers, to assist those wanting to convert to an organic system and to work actively to promote research and development in organic agriculture.

In addition to the journal, *New Farmer and Grower*, produced jointly with the OGA, BOF provides a regular newsletter for members and stages a series of farm walks, technical seminars and conferences.

A computerized information service enables a rapid supply of information and contacts to be made between members.

The computer provides comprehensive and up-to-date data on organic farming in the UK.

BOF has been active in developing new markets and marketing structures for organic produce and has helped in the establishment of producer co-operatives to supply vegetables and animal products throughout the country.

It works closely with agricultural organizations such as the Ministry of Agriculture and research institutions to plan new strategies for organic agriculture based on solid research and development work.

BOF also maintains close links with international organizations through IFOAM, the International Federation of Organic Agriculture Movements.

British Organic Farmers is firmly committed to the Soil Association Symbol scheme for the marketing of organic produce and works closely with the association in the constant monitoring and refinement of the British Organic Standards.

For further details send a large s.a.e. to British Organic Farmers, 86 Colston Street, Bristol BS1 5BB.

## Elm Farm Research Centre

Elm Farm Research Centre was incorporated as a registered educational charity (Progressive Farming Trust Ltd) in August 1980. Its Council of Management and advisers are drawn from several professions; they include Professor Dr Hartmut Vogtmann, holder of the Chair of Alternative Agriculture at the University of Kassel, West Germany, and Dr Adam Onken of the Inter-Disciplinary Research Group on Appropriate Technology at Kassel.

The Trust operates from Elm Farm, a 232-acre farm near Newbury, where most of its activities are based. Previously an intensive dairy enterprise run on conventional lines, Elm Farm is in the process of conversion to a total biological system, with an emphasis on developing techniques to meet the economic constraints of British agriculture. It is a mixed farm, with a dairy, cereals, a small beef unit and the fattening of store lambs as its enterprises.

Operating alongside the farm is the J. A. Pye Research Laboratory. The research is of an applied nature, as it is clear that in many areas of biological husbandry – composting, manure management, weed control and green manures especially – mainland Europe is somewhat further developed than this country. The intention is to take some of these developments and adapt them to British conditions.

One of the main services provided by the Research Laboratory is a Soil Analysis and Advisory Service for organic producers.

On a wider front, Elm Farm Research Centre has sponsored several meetings of farmers, growers and agricultural advisers from within and outside Britain.

The Centre maintains close contacts with scientists at university and Ministry level. Through the International Federation of Organic Agriculture Movements (IFOAM), EFRC is associated with a number of research institutions in Europe and the United States.

The final aspect of EFRC's work is on the production of publications. As a result of its first conference a Report on the Research Needs of Biological Agriculture in Great Britain was published in 1981. EFRC also produces a series of Practical Handbooks for farmers and growers.

Further information may be obtained from Elm Farm Research Centre, Hamstead Marshall, Nr Newbury, Berks RG15 0HR (Tel. 0488 58298).

## Bio-Dynamic Agricultural Association

We promote a system of agriculture which aims for each holding to be as ecologically self-contained as possible. Ideally, each holding should become an organism in itself with a harmonious balance of livestock, pasture, arable land, hedgerows, ponds, orchards, woodland, wildlife and human beings. With regard to gardening, we also try to create this balance as far as it is possible.

Bio-Dynamics works with the formative forces behind nature, both earthly (sound organic husbandry) and cosmic (which includes the influence of the sun, planets and stars). We endeavour to achieve a dynamic balance between these forces and work with the picture of the earth as a living organism in a living universe.

This impulse was founded by Rudolf Steiner in 1924, who gave indications of how these forces could be enhanced. These include the Bio-Dynamic preparations which are made from entirely natural products, and are used in homoeopathic quantities. They enhance the vitality of the soil and plant and aid the formation of an active humus in compost and manure heaps. Our aim is to help heal the earth and to produce a truly nutritive food for humanity today.

The Association has over 600 members, nine local groups, publishes a regular magazine (*Star and Furrow*) twice yearly, members' newsletters, supplies books and products (including the preparations) and organizes conferences and workshops on biodynamic themes. We also administer the Demeter quality symbol which is an internationally recognized symbol of organic quality.

The address of the Bio-Dynamic Agricultural Association is: Woodman Lane, Clent, Stourbridge, West Midlands DY9 9PX (Tel. 0562 884933). Literature about the Association will be sent on request.

## The International Institute of Biological Husbandry Limited

The main aim of the Institute is to try to put a scientific base into organic farming, to eliminate much of the 'muck and magic', and to initiate research that will increase yields without detracting from the quality of the crop.

The Institute's approach to biological farming is totally scientific, meaning that all recommendations and research are backed by accurate knowledge and reasoning up to that time, and that we do not recommend courses of action because we feel 'they are right'.

We have organized so far two very successful Conferences at Wye College, one in 1980 and one in 1984. These Conferences are totally scientific, and the book produced as a result of the 1980 one is probably the first scientific book on biological husbandry.

Another job of the Institute is to monitor the Conservation grade for W. Jordan (Cereals) Ltd. This grade allows the use of certain chemicals, and it is in this respect that the knowledge of the scientists co-operating with the Institute really comes into its own. The present ruling is that any agrochemical used do no harm to the biology of the soil, and must not be in the harvested crop, thus affecting the consumer of that crop.

The potential in the future for the Institute is immense and once funding is successfully found we can really start to play our part. Certainly as far as overseas is concerned we receive constant letters from all over the world requesting help in various ways to improve the yields of biological husbandry. This we are anxious to do as soon as possible, and this is what we are working towards in every way possible.

Up to now all contributions by scientists and others to the Institute have been voluntary and unpaid, but an immediate aim is to raise sufficient funds to employ a full-time administrator. A subsequent intention is to employ a research assistant. Then the Institute will be able to begin playing its role in life, namely research to improve biological agriculture, education to teach students how to farm biologically and the production of various publications to spread accurate knowledge on all aspects of biological husbandry. International Institute of Biological Husbandry (IIBH), Abacus House, Station Yard, Needham Market, Ipswich IP6 8AT (Tel. 0449 720838).

## The Farm and Food Society

Founded in 1966, membership throughout the British Isles, in the EEC, Hong Kong, USA and Australia. Aims to create a social climate which will enable farming to combine the best traditional organic methods with wise use of technology; a non-violent system in harmony with the environment and with humane treatment of animals. Is lobbying the Government to provide research and advice facilities for organic farming; working for a ban on the export of animals for slaughter, for improved methods of keeping farm animals, and protection of consumers against dangers from pesticides, etc. Is represented on the British Organic Standards Committee and the Farm Animal Welfare Co-ordinating Executive; affiliated to the International Federation of Organic Agricultural Movements and the National Council of Women (with representatives on special committees dealing with Environment, Health,

Consumer Affairs, Scientific Development, and Animal Welfare). Produces a lively and informative Newsletter, Annual Report, and occasional papers on specific subjects (currently available: 'The Long Way Ahead: New Concepts of Agriculture', 75p; 'The Role of Animals in a Biological Farming System', 35p; 'Responsible Husbandry as a Basic Educational Principle', 25p). The AGM always includes a speaker on one of the Society's special interests – livestock, organic farming or nutrition – and a general forum in which members take part. Present Patrons include the Rev. the Lord Soper, Professor Peter Singer, Professor E. N. Willmer, Dr R. W. D. Turner and Professor Henryk Skolimowski. Hon. Scientific Adviser: Professor Harry A. Walters, FIBiol., FIMLS, FRSH, FIFST. All work is voluntary. Minimum subscription: £4 p.a. 4 Willifield Way, London NW11 7XT.

# British Organic Standards Committee

The co-ordinating committee which draws up the Standards which form the basis of all symbol schemes operating in Britain. It meets regularly to review the Standards, to incorporate amendments and additions. Its current chairman is Lawrence Woodward of Elm Farm Research Centre and its honorary secretary is Mrs Joanne Bower of the Farm and Food Society. Delegates from each of the following organizations are represented on the Committee:

> Bio-Dynamic Agricultural Association
> Henry Doubleday Research Association
> Soil Association
> International Institute of Biological Husbandry
> British Organic Farmers
> International Federation of Organic Agricultural
>    Movements
> Organic Farmers and Growers Ltd
> Organic Growers Association
> Federation of Organic Food Manufacturers
> Wholefood Trust

# WWOOF (Working Weekends on Organic Farms)

Formed in 1971, WWOOF is an exchange scheme which enables members to stay and learn through work experience on a wide variety of organic farms and smallholdings throughout the UK. WWOOF has several aims:

* To get first-hand experience of organic farming and gardening.
* To get into the countryside
* To help the organic movement, which is often labour-intensive and does not rely on artificial fertilizers for fertility or persistent poisons for pest control.
* To make contact with other people in the organic movement and to provide access to organic education.

Details of WWOOF farms and smallholdings needing weekend help are listed in the bi-monthly newsletter *WWOOF News*. Members can then book for the weekends they wish to go on and if a place is available will receive full details including travel information. (Lifts can be given from the local station if needed.) Members generally travel Friday evening and return home Sunday evening, and provide their own work clothes and sleeping bag. Although members must be at least sixteen years old, some farms are happy to accept children with parents.

WWOOF is an ideal 'gateway' to country living, and has enabled many people to take up a rural career. The current subscription is £5 a year. For brochure please send s.a.e. to: WWOOF, 19 Bradford Road, Lewes, Sussex BN7 1RB.

# National Federation of City Farms and Community Gardens

Our cities have become productive – yielding meats and manure, dairy produce and vegetables.

These are the products of City Farms and Community Gardens – independent and innovative charities. Sixty or so of them are members of the National Federation of City Farms and Community Gardens, which is a co-ordinating body and advisory agency that exists to assist and support them.

Local people take over and manage derelict and underused land in the inner city and on the urban fringe. They raise livestock and grow crops organically for themselves and for sale to the public.

Different schemes specialize in different enterprises: perhaps meat for a freezer club, or herbs and pot-plants. Most can offer a range of vegetables, free-range eggs and goat's milk. The majority have surplus farmyard manure available for the organic gardener.

These projects welcome volunteers from the neighbourhood – to undertake practical work like raising fruit or feeding poultry – or to become involved in the farm or garden's management committee and help it develop.

Anyone who is interested in buying produce, or becoming involved, should contact the nearest project directly. They exist in most major cities. The National Federation of City Farms and Community Gardens, 66 Fraser Street, Bristol BS3 4LY (Tel. 0272 660663) will provide addresses and can supply other details to those wishing to set up their own projects (please enclose s.a.e.). A range of specialist information for the city gardener and small-scale livestock producer is available, together with periodicals including the quarterly *City Farmer*.

## Appendix 3  BRITISH ORGANIC STANDARDS COMMITTEE PRODUCTION STANDARDS FOR ORGANIC PRODUCE

## Introduction

Organic (biological) agriculture seeks to produce food of optimum quality and quantity. The principles and methods employed aim to co-exist with and not dominate natural systems; to be not only sustainable, but also regenerative.

The development of biological cycles involving micro-organisms, soil fauna, plants and animals is the basis of organic agriculture. Therefore, sound rotations, the extensive and rational use of manure and vegetable wastes, the use of appropriate cultivation techniques, the avoidance of fertilizers in the form of soluble mineral salts, and the prohibition of agrochemical pesticides form the basic characteristics of organic agriculture.

The standards are under constant review and the Committee reserves the right to amend them from time to time.

## Husbandry standards

*A  Manures and composted manures.* Manure from all types of livestock carried on the farm should be utilized, preferably composted with straw and/or other crop residues. It is a principle of biological husbandry that stock should be maintained under extensive conditions (*see* Livestock Husbandry Standards) and every effort should be made to obtain manure or animal by-products from these sources. All bought-in manures must be approved by the Inspectorate before use. It is recognized that a great deal of potential organic matter is available from intensive production, including straw from conventional agriculture, but manures resulting from factory-farming methods may be used only if absolutely necessary and there is no alternative; and providing the level of toxic residues and heavy metals are within the permitted range. In some cases the Inspectorate may insist on the composting of such manures before use. Permission to use such materials in no way implies approval by the organic movement of the methods used to produce them.

Aeration of slurry is strongly recommended. Untreated animal slurry should only be used on grassland, green manure crops or stubble. Care should be taken to avoid excessive dressings harmful to worm populations. Raw slurry must not be used on green crops intended for human consumption.

Spent mushroom compost and some municipal composts may be used with the approval of the Inspectorate.

Sewage sludge may be used not more than one year in three after a soil analysis on grass or forage crops, only with the approval of the Inspectorate.

If plants are to be sold to third parties as 'organically raised' then proprietary composts containing chemical fertilizers must not be used. However, for the time being, given that there are no proven alternatives commercially available, it is permitted to use such proprietary seed, potting and blocking composts for raising plants to be grown to fruition in the soil. Similarly, it is permitted to buy in conventionally raised plants whether pulled or in blocks, trays, etc., though organically raised plants must be used wherever possible.

*B   Animal by-products.* Such products should not form the basis of the manurial programme but may be used as adjuncts.

Shoddy from the woollen industry often contains persistent toxic residues caused by sheep dipping. Further research into this problem is required. Therefore, the use of shoddy is not allowed at this time.

Dried blood is a highly available source of nitrogen; it can be used but with care and up to a maximum of three cwts (36 units N) per acre. Other traditional organic by-products and wastes are allowed. The Inspectorate will maintain a list of approved materials.

*C   Vegetable by-products.* It is likely that vegetable by-products such as spent hops, market vegetable wastes, apple residues, coffee grounds, banana stalks, straw from conventional agriculture, etc., contain residues of agrochemical treatments. Their use is allowed with the Inspectorate's approval.

Sawdust, woodshavings and bark can be used only if they are derived from timber not chemically treated.

The Inspectorate should be consulted before any other type of off-farm vegetable waste is used.

*D   Mineral fertilizers.* The following fertilizers are allowed: basic slag; limestone, gypsum (calcium sulphate), ground chalk, ground phosphate rock (though Senegal phosphates are not allowed); magnesian limestone (dolomite); felspar; Adularian shale (rock potash).

Other rocks and dusts which do have value as fertilizers can be used after consultation with the Inspectorate.

All other mineral fertilizers including urea are not allowed.

*E   Seaweed products.* The use of fresh seaweed, ground calcareous seaweeds, seaweed meal and pure seaweed foliar feeds is allowed.

*F   Insect control.* The following products are permitted: pure pyrethrum; derris (dangerous to fish and should not be used near watercourses); nicotine (has high mammalian toxicity and should be used with extreme caution); garlic, herbal and homoeopathic sprays and preparations; quassia.

*G   Biological pest control.* The following organisms are permitted: Encarsia formosa, Phytosieulus persimilis; Bacillus thuringiensis; Trichoderma viride; Cephalosporium lecanii.

It is recognized that this is an area of rapid change. Acceptable organisms may be developed in the near future and the Inspectorate should be consulted about the use of any not included in the above list.

*H   Fungus control.* Use of the following fungicides on plants is permitted; potassium permanganate; sodium silicate (water glass); herbal and homoeopathic sprays and preparations.

Dispersable sulphur and copper fungicides are allowed. The BOSC recognizes the need for urgent research to find alternatives to these latter substances. They will be replaced as soon as possible. Only steam soil sterilization is permitted.

*I   Herbicides*. No herbicides are permitted under any circumstances.

*J   Sundries*. Growth inhibitors or a combination of growth regulators and inhibitors such as may be used on standing corn, are forbidden. Likewise, sprout inhibitors for potatoes are not permissible.

Every effort should be made to avoid dressed seed. Mercurial seed dressings are forbidden. Any new products on the market not covered by the above must be approved by the Inspectorate before use. If a breakdown in the system occurs necessitating the use of any prohibited materials the Inspectorate must be notified and the field or fields in question will revert to being considered as in conversion. The Inspectorate will deal with each case on its merits.

## Livestock husbandry

The general conduct of animal husbandry should be governed largely by ethical considerations, having regard to behavioural patterns evolved over millions of years and the basic needs of animals. The European Convention on Farm Animals requires that they should be kept according to their physiological and ethological needs. This would rule out cages, tethering and penning except for short periods, unsuitable feeding, growth promoters or other interference with the normal growth pattern. Such treatment can be as economically rewarding and sometimes more so than modern restrictive practices.

*A   Housing*. Housing must allow free movement to stock and a sleeping area with adequate bedding must be provided.

In addition, it is recommended that buildings allow the maximum amount of fresh air and daylight, and that there should be regular access to pasture for all stock in fair weather.

The permanent housing of breeding stock is prohibited.

*B   Management practices*. Debeaking and the fitting of spectacles to poultry; growth hormone injections; vaccinations to remove natural growth controls are all prohibited.

De-tailing and the teeth-cutting of pigs are prohibited except for veterinary reasons due to accident or disease.

It is strongly recommended that castration of pigs for pork or bacon should not be practised.

*C Feeding*
* Grazing must be on herbage grown to the BOSC's general husbandry standards.
* Feeding stuffs: Every effort should be made to provide feeding stuffs produced according to the BOSC's general husbandry standards. Where this is impossible a maximum of 20 per cent dry matter of the daily intake may be of non-organic origin.

Foods supplemented with growth promoters (including copper for pigs), antibiotics and hormones are prohibited.

* Mineral additives: Rock salt; calcified seaweed; seaweed powder; steamed bone flour are allowed.

Mineral additives fed to animals due to a deficiency in the soil are allowed only on a short-term basis in consultation with the Inspectorate.

The use of any other mineral additive without consultation with the Inspectorate is prohibited.

* Added vitamins: Every effort should be made to use only products containing natural vitamins, e.g. cod liver oil, yeast.
* Others: Urea is prohibited. Every effort should be made to avoid the use of synthetic amino acids, antioxidants, emulsifiers, chemical colourants that influence the colour of egg yolks. Feed containing animal manure is prohibited. Coccidiostats and anti-blackhead drugs are allowed in the early stages of poultry rearing for the time being, but the BOSC recognizes that further research on this subject is necessary.

*D Disease treatment.* In veterinary medicine, the use of herbal and homoeopathic remedies is strongly recommended. However, it is recognized that much research still needs to be done in this area. Until acceptable alternatives are developed, the following are permitted in case of emergency: antibiotics and other drugs; anthelmintics for fluke, lung and gutworm infestation; livestock vaccines. Use must be declared to the Inspectorate.

Routine use of other drugs and antibiotics is not allowed, including inter-mammary application of antibiotics for dairy cows. The use of organophosphorous compounds for warble disqualifies from the use of the Symbol for meat and milk products for a period to be decided at the discretion of the Inspectorate. This applies also to the use of organochlorine compounds for sheep dip.

## Final Product Standards

*A   Meat.* Must be from animals and poultry reared according to the BOSC's general and livestock husbandry standards.

*B   Liquid milk and cream.* Must be from animals kept according to the BOSC's general and livestock husbandry standards.

*C   Butter.* The cream must be from milk produced in accordance with the BOSC's general and livestock husbandry standards.

Sea salt must be used.

Chemical colourants or additives are not permitted. Aluminium containers and utensils for any milk products are not recommended.

*D   Cheese.* Must be made from milk produced in accordance with the BOSC's general and livestock husbandry standards.

Sea salt must be used. Only herbs grown to the Board's general husbandry standards, natural spices and aromatic plants may be used.

Colourants and chemical additives are prohibited.

Equipment must not be greased with liquid paraffin.

*E   Plain yogurt.* Milk produced according to the BOSC's general and livestock husbandry standards must be used.

All additives other than bacterial starter culture are prohibited.

*F   Fruit yogurt.* Fresh or preserved fruit can be used, but it must have been grown according to the BOSC's general husbandry standards.

Colourants, antioxidants, preservatives and artificial flavourings are prohibited.

*G  Eggs.* Must be from hens kept in accordance with the BOSC's general and livestock husbandry standards.

*H  Vegetables and fruit.* Must be grown according to the BOSC's general husbandry standards. Post-harvest chemical treatment is prohibited.

*I  Fruit juices.* Must be made from fresh fruit grown according to the BOSC's general husbandry standards.

Colourants, sulphur dioxide, antioxidants, preservatives and artificial flavourings are prohibited.

*J  Cider.* Fresh apples grown according to the BOSC's general husbandry standards must be used.

Colourants, dried or pulped apples treated with sulphur dioxide, antioxidants, preservatives, artificial flavourings are prohibited.

*K  Cider vinegar.* Fresh apples grown according to the BOSC's general husbandry standards must be used. Fermentation must be by natural fermentation processes.

Colourants, dried or pulped apples treated with sulphur dioxide, antioxidants, preservatives, artificial flavourings, unnaturally produced or added acetic acid are prohibited.

*L  Jams.* Fresh fruit grown according to the BOSC's general husbandry standards must be used.

Natural beet syrup and unrefined sugars are preferred.

It is recommended that non-stick or aluminium cooking ware is avoided; colourants, antioxidants, preservatives, artificial flavourings are prohibited.

*M  Cereals and cereal products.* Whole grain, grain flakes and flour must be from cereals grown according to the BOSC's general husbandry standards. Chemical treatments for storage are prohibited.

Bread must be made from flour grown according to the above standards, yeast, natural leaven, sea or rock salt, biosalt, vegetable oil (cold pressed), honey or approved molasses, milk powder/soya milk replacer should be used.

217

Artificial leavening processes, mineral oils and preservatives are prohibited. It is recommended that non-stick or aluminium cooking ware is avoided. Care should be taken in selection of tin-greasing oil.

## Conclusion

The British Organic Standards Committee is aware that this Standards Document has shortcomings. However, the knowledge and techniques of organic growing are rapidly being improved and developed: consequently we will ensure that our standards are regularly amended to keep pace with this development. Detailed guidelines by which these standards will operate are being drawn up and will be available on request.

# Appendix 4 REFERENCES

1 *Environmental Protection and Agriculture*. CPRE evidence to the European Parliament's Committee on the Environment, Public Health and Consumer Protection. August 1985. 4 Hobart Place, London SW1W 0HY.

2 *A Second Look*. Countryside Commission (CCP168), 1984.

3 *Objectives and Strategy for Nature Conservation in Great Britain* by Dr Derek Ratcliffe, Chief Scientist, Nature Conservancy Council, 1983.

4 Shoard, M. 1980. *The Theft of the Countryside*. Temple Smith.

5 Bunyan, P. J., Stanley, P. I. 1983. 'The environmental cost of pesticide usage in the United Kingdom. *Agric. Ecosystems Environ.*, 9: 187–209.

6 British Agrochemical Association (1985). Annual Report and Handbook 1984–85.

7 Bull, D. 1982. *A Growing Problem – Pesticides and the Third World Poor*. Oxfam.

8 Carson, R. 1962. *Silent Spring*. Penguin.

9 Pimental, D. *et al.*, 1978. Benefits and costs of pesticide use in US food production. *Bioscience* 28(12): 772–84.

10 Debach, P. 1974. *Biological Control by Natural Enemies*. Cambridge University Press.

11 *Beneficial Insects and Mites*. HMSO HGD1 (formerly Bulletin 20), 1978.

12 *Farmers Weekly*, 25 November 1983, p. 49.

13    Myers, J. H. 1985. Effect of physiological condition of the host plant on the ovipositional choice of the cabbage white butterfly. *Jnl. An. Ecol.*, 54, 193–204.

14    *Pesticides out of Control.* Soil Association, March 1984.

15    Hodges, R. D. 1985. *Agriculture, Nitrates and Health.* Soil Association, September 1985.

16    Cooke, G. W. 1979. Some priorities for British soil science. *Jnl. Soil Science*, 30, 187–213.

17    Oakes, D. B. *et al.* 1981. The effects of farming practices on groundwater quality in the U.K. *Science of the Total Environment*, 21, 17–30.

18    The Royal Society. 1983. *The Nitrogen Cycle of the United Kingdom.*

19    Farmers face charges. *Farmers Weekly*, 3 January 1984.

20    *Agriculture and Pollution.* 1983. Pollution Paper No. 21, HMSO.

21    Hodges, R. D. 1978. *Who Needs Inorganic Fertilizers Anyway? The Case for Biological Agriculture.* International Institute of Biological Agriculture.

22    Vogtmann, H. 1986. *Research on Organic Farming in Europe.* Proc. Conf. Organic Farming – the Natural Alternative, R.A.S.E., Stoneleigh, Warwicks, UK.

23    Hemsley, M. C. 1982. *Straw for the Future.* CPRE.

24    Needham, P. 1985. The soils of England and Wales – is there cause for concern? *Jnl. R.A.S.E.*, 146, 82–99.

25    Long, E. 1983. Don't wash away profit. *Farmers Weekly*, 25 November, pp. 54–8.

26    Ellis, E. A. 1985. A country diary: Norfolk, *Guardian*, 30 December.

27    Brown, L. R. and Wolf, E. C. 1984. *Soil Erosion: Quiet Crisis in the World Economy.* Worldwatch Paper 60. Worldwatch Inst., 1776 Massachusetts Ave., N.W., Washington D.C. 20036, USA.

28    Rosenberry, P., Knutson, R., Harmon, L. 1980. Predicting

effects of soil depletion from erosion. *Jnl. Soil Water Cons.*, May/June.

29 Miller, M. F. 1936. Cropping systems in erosion control. Missouri Experimental Station, Bulletin 366, reprinted in National Agricultural Lands Study, *Soil Degradation. Effects on Agricultural Productivity* (Washington, D.C.: 1980).

30 Harrison Reed, A. 1979. Accelerated erosion of arable soils in the UK by rainfall and run-off. *Outlook on Agriculture*, 10, 41–8.

31 Fischer, Lloyd K. 1982. Discussion comments, in Halcrow, H. G. *et al.*, eds. *Soil Conservation Policies, Institutions and Incentives* (Ankeny, Iowa: Soil Cons. Soc. America).

32 Soil scientists axed after grant is cut. *Guardian*, 6 November 1985.

33 European Communities Working Document 1985–86. Ref. Document A 2–154/85. Report drawn up on behalf of the Committee on the Environment, Public Health and Consumer Protection on the genetic diversity of cultivated plants and trees.

34 *Vegetable Sanctuaries.* 1982. Henry Doubleday Research Association.

35 Mooney, P. R. 1979. *Seeds of the Earth. A Private or Public Resource?* Int. Coalition. Dev. Action.

36 Harrison, R. 1964. *Animal Machines.* Stuart.

37 Multi-million £ illegal traffic in farm drugs. *Farmers Weekly*, 23 September 1983.

38 McCarrison, R. quoted in Balfour, Lady E. B. 1975. *The Living Soil and the Haughley Experiment.*

39 Crawford, M. A., quoted in Mount, J. L. 1979. *The Food and Health of Western Man.*

40 *Pesticide Residues and Food. The Case for Real Control.* 1986. Pete Snell and Kirsty Nicol. Published by the London Food Commission, PO Box 291, London N5 1DH.

41 Report of the Working Party on Pesticide Residues (1982–85). MAFF Food Surveillance Paper No. 16, HMSO 1985.

42    Egginton, J. 1980. *Bitter Harvest*. Secker and Warburg.

43    Laseter, J. L. *et al.* 1983. Chlorinated hydrocarbon pesticides in environmentally sensitive patients. *Clinical Ecology*, Vol. II, No. 1.

44    Monro, J. 1984. What agribusiness does to you. *Soil Association Quarterly Review*, September.

45    Melville, A., Johnson, C. 1986. *Persistent Fat and How to Lose It*. Century.

46    *Guardian*, 9 July 1986.

47    Jollans, L. 1984. *Agriculture and Human Health*. Centre for Agricultural Strategy, University of Reading, Early Gate, Reading RG6 2AT.

48    Blair, A., White, D. W. 1985. Leukaemia cell types and agricultural practices in Nebraska. *Archives of Env. Health*. July/Aug. 1985. Vol. 40, No. 4.

49    Weir, D., Schapiro, M. 1981. *Circle of Poison – Pesticides and People in a Hungry World*. Institute for Food and Development Policy, San Francisco, USA.

50    Vogtmann, H. 1985. The nitrate story – no end in sight. *Nutrition and Health*, No. 4, Vol. 3.

51    Schuphan, W. Qual. Plant. 1974 – Pl. Fds. Hum. Nutr. Vol. 23(4), pp. 333–58.

52    Howard, Sir A. 1945. *Farming and Gardening for Health and Disease*. Faber and Faber.

53    Petterson, B. D. 1978. A comparison between conventional and biodynamic farming systems as indicated by yields and quality. *Proc. 1st. Int. Res. Conf.* IFOAM Verlag Wirz Aarau, pp. 87–94.

54    Samaras, I. 1977. Nachernteverhatten unterschiedlich gedungter Gemusearten mit besonderer Berucksichtigung physiologischer und mikrobiologischer Parameter.

55    Aubert, C. 1975. Die Muttermilch ein erschreckender Stand der Toxiditat. *Leb. Erd.* 6/7, 8–13.

56    *Guardian*. 13 June 1985.

57    *Guardian*. 9 July 1986.

58  *Guardian*. 16 May 1984.

59  *Observer*. 15 June 1986.

60  Body, R. 1984. *Farming in the Clouds*, and 1982. *Agriculture: The Triumph and the Shame*. Both published by Temple Smith.

61  Phillips, M. C., Whitehouse, J. M. 1985. Report on Organic Farming Methods, West Germany and Holland, 2–11 June 1985. MAFF Project No. 12 in the Agriculture Service Overseas Study Tour Programme, 1985/86.

62  Norton Taylor, R. 1982. *Whose Land Is It Anyway?* Turnstone Press.

63  Down on the automated farm. *New Scientist*, 21 November 1985. pp. 56–60.

64  *Farmers Weekly*. 16 December 1983. p. 37.

# INDEX